A SH
HISTORY OF
IRAQ

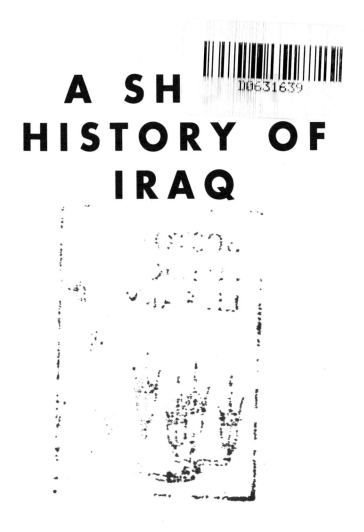

A SHORT HISTORY OF IRAQ
FROM 636 TO THE PRESENT

Thabit A. J. Abdullah

London • New York • Toronto • Sydney • Tokyo • Singapore
Hong Kong • Cape Town • Madrid • Paris • Amsterdam • Munich • Milan

PEARSON EDUCATION LIMITED

Head Office:
Edinburgh Gate
Harlow CM20 2JE
Tel: +44 (0)1279 623623
Fax: +44 (0)1279 431059
Website: www.pearsoned.co.uk

First edition published in Great Britain in 2003

© Pearson Education Limited 2003

ISBN 0 582 50579 8

British Library Cataloguing in Publication Data
A CIP catalogue record for this book can be obtained from the British Library

Library of Congress Cataloging in Publication Data
A CIP catalog record for this book can be obtained from the Library of Congress

10 9 8 7 6 5 4 3 2 1

Set by Fakenham Photosetting Limited, Fakenham, Norfolk
Printed and bound in Malaysia

The Publishers' policy is to use paper manufactured from sustainable forests.

iv

To my father, Dr Abdul-Jabbar Abdullah
A scientist, poet and Iraqi patriot.

And to the woman who made him what he was,
my mother, Kismet al-Fayadh.

CONTENTS

ACKNOWLEDGMENTS

This book has taken far longer than I had anticipated. This is partly due to the fact that historians often underestimate the difficulty of writing a general summary meant for readers not familiar with the topic. But it is also due to the enormous changes which Iraq witnessed at the time of writing. The first draft was completed in August 2002, just as the crisis with the United States was heating up. The second draft was done in Damascus, Syria, as the crisis escalated toward armed conflict. Having been born and raised in Baghdad, scenes of the city in flames, stories from refugees of the horrors they witnessed, and the lack of news concerning relatives and friends have been overwhelming. As these lines are being written, American and British troops seem on the verge of completing their conquest of Iraq. This event will certainly prove to be a major turning point in the country's history requiring an additional chapter to the present work in the future.

I would like to thank the many fine people who assisted me in the writing and publication of this work. Dina Khoury, a friend and one of the best historians of Iraq, initially recommended me to the editor. Gordon Martel, who asked me to write this work, made several helpful suggestions to the first draft, as did Haitham Abdullah who also did an excellent job editing the text. Alex Whyte edited the final draft. Heather McCallum, Bree Ellis and Melanie Carter of Pearson Education, ran the complicated administrative and editorial work smoothly and efficiently. In Damascus, the Institut Francais d'Etudes Arabes de Damas provided me with first rate research facilities. Edouard Metenier, who made suggestions to the third and fourth chapters, and Vanessa van Renterghem, who made suggestions to parts of chapter one, are both destined to become excellent historians of Iraq. Most importantly, my heartfelt thanks to my wife Samera for her support, and our two children Yasmine and Rami who are still too young to understand but will one day grow up to be proud of their Iraqi heritage.

The publisher is grateful to the following for permission to reproduce copyright material:

Tables 5.1 and 5.2 from *The Old Social Classes and Revolutionary Movements of Iraq: A Study of Iraq's Old Candid and Commercial Classes and of its Communists, Ba'thists and Free Officers*, Copyright © 1978 by Princeton University Press, reprinted by permission of Princeton University Press (Batatu H. and Batatu J. 1978).

In some instances we have been unable to trace the owners of copyright material, and we would appreciate any information that would enable us to do so.

CHRONOLOGY OF MAIN EVENTS

836–892	Capital temporarily moved north from Baghdad to Samarra.
868–883	Rebellion of the Zanj slaves.
c. 900	Population of Baghdad reaches around 1.5 million.
935	Hamadanid Arabs seize Mosul and establish an autonomous dynasty. The establishment of the new post of Amir al-'Umara signaling the decline of the caliph's powers.
941	Twelfth Shi'i imam, Muhammad ibn al-Hasan, known as the Mahdi, goes into miraculous occultation.
945–1055	Shi'i Buwayhid Persians control the Amir al-'Umara post and rule much of Iraq.
961–1150	Mazyadid Arabs control much of southern Iraq from their capital of Hilla.
1010–1097	'Uqaylid Arabs control most of northern Iraq including Mosul.
1055–1160	Seljuk Turks occupy Iraq and restore Sunni rule.
1180–1225	Reign of the Caliph al-Nasir.
1258	Mongol armies under Hulago sack Baghdad and bring the Abbasid Caliphate to an end.
1295	Conversion of the Mongol ruler Ghazan to Islam.
c. 1335–1410	Iraq under weak rule of Jalayrid Mongols.
1347	Bubonic plague decimates the population and economy.
1401	Timur Lang sacks Baghdad.
1410–1469	Iraq under Turkoman Qara Qoyunlu rule.

1436	The beginning of the Musha'sha' movement in the south.
1469–1508	Iraq under Turkoman Aq Qoyunlu rule.
1508	Baghdad taken by Safavids of Persia.
1514	Battle of Chaldiran. Parts of northern Iraq fall under Ottoman rule.
1534	Sultan Sulayman the Magnificent conquers the rest of Iraq for the Ottoman Empire.
1623	Shah 'Abbas returns Baghdad to Safavid rule but fails to take the rest of Iraq.
1625–1668	The Afrasiyab dynasty in Basra.
1638	After a grueling siege Sultan Murad IV enters Baghdad and Iraq remains under Ottoman rule for nearly three centuries.
1639	The Treaty of Zuhab, also known as the Treaty of Qasr-i Shirin, between the Ottomans and Safavids.
1723	The English East India Company establishes a permanent trading house in Basra.
1732–1743	The wars of Nadir Shah.
1750–1831	Mamluk governors of Baghdad and Basra move Iraq toward greater autonomy from Istanbul.
1776–1779	Persian occupation of Basra.
1802	Wahhabis sack Karbala.
1831	Plague and flood pave the way for the Ottoman re-conquest of Baghdad and the establishment of direct rule.
1847	The Treaty of Erzerum delineates the Ottoman Iraqi border with Iran.

1869	The opening of the Suez Canal strengthens Basra's direct maritime trade with Europe.
1869–1872	Midhat Pasha's governorship of Baghdad inaugurates far-reaching reforms.
1899	Britain declares a protectorate over Kuwait.
1903	Ottoman government grants a German company a concession to build the Berlin-to-Baghdad rail line.
1906	Constitutional Revolution in Iran.
1908	Young Turk Revolution in Istanbul. Discovery of oil in Iran.
1914–1918	World War I. The Ottoman Empire joins Germany and Austria against Britain, France and Russia.
1914	British forces land in Basra.
1916	Sykes–Picot Agreement signed in which Britain and France agreed to divide the Ottoman Middle East after the war.
1917	General Maude enters Baghdad.
1920	League of Nations establishes a British mandate over Iraq. Rebellion in southern Iraq against the British.
1921	Faysal ibn al-Husayn enthroned as the first king of Iraq.
1927	Discovery of oil near Kirkuk.
1930	Anglo–Iraqi Treaty guarantees continued British dominance.
1932	Formal independence of Iraq under the monarchy.
1934	Formation of the Iraqi Communist Party.

1936	First military coup signals the direct interference of the army in politics.
1939–1945	World War II.
1941	The anti-British Rashid 'Ali Movement in Baghdad triggers attacks against the Jewish population.
1948	Broad uprising against British hegemony. Iraq contributes a token force in the first Arab–Israeli war.
1952	Nasir's revolution in Egypt.
1955	The Baghdad Pact is formed.
1958	A revolution led by General Qasim's Free Officers overthrows the monarchy and establishes a republic.
1963	Elements of the military allied with the Ba'th Party overthrow Qasim's government.
1967	Symbolic presence for the Iraqi army in the June Arab–Israeli war.
1968	Ba'th Party seize sole control of government. Formation of the Da'wa Party.
1970	Agreement to establish autonomy in Kurdistan.
1972	Nationalization of the oil industry.
1973	October Arab–Israeli war.
1974	Formation of the Ba'thist-led National Progressive Front which includes the Iraqi Communist Party.
1974–1975	War in Kurdistan.
Feb. 1979	Revolution in Iran.
Jul. 1979	Saddam Husayn becomes president of Iraq.

1980–1988	The Iran–Iraq War.
1990	Invasion and annexation of Kuwait. The United Nations imposes strict sanctions on Iraq.
1991	American-led coalition evicts Iraqi troops from Kuwait and occupies parts of Iraq. Spontaneous uprising against Saddam's rule is crushed.
1992	Under allied protection, elections are held for an autonomous Kurdish parliament.
1997	Oil for Food Program comes into effect.
1998	UN arms inspectors forced to leave the country.
Mar. 2002	Iraq restores relations with Saudi Arabia.
Sept. 2002	Suicide bombings of the World Trade Center and Pentagon in the United States.
Nov. 2002	In response to repeated accusations by the United States and Britain, the United Nations calls on Iraq to re-admit international inspectors and fully disarm its chemical, biological and nuclear weapons.
Mar. 2003	After failing to win the backing of the United Nations for military action, the United States and Britain invade Iraq with the stated objective of ending Saddam's dictatorship.
Apr. 2003	U.S. forces enter Baghdad. Iraq under American and British military occupation.

Map 1: Modern Iraq

Map 2: Iraq and the modern Middle East

INTRODUCTION

This book presents a concise survey of the main events and important transformations that occurred in Iraq from the Arab conquest of the seventh century to the dictatorship of Saddam Husayn with greater emphasis on the modern period. Its primary focus is the struggle of the country's diverse peoples to coexist in an unstable region. While the Tigris and Euphrates rivers formed a strong basis for social unity, the country's central location and potential wealth have attracted numerous invasions and migrations which constantly upset the communal balance. It is also situated between the Persian and Mediterranean culture zones, both of which have had a profound influence on Iraqi society and constantly caused the country to shift its orientation between east and west.

The term "Iraq" has referred to different areas at different times. During most of the period covered by this book, "Arab Iraq" was understood to include the lands between the Tigris and the Euphrates rivers from around the region of Tikrit in the north down to the Persian Gulf in the south. To simplify matters in this work, the term "Iraq" will cover all the lands of the modern Iraqi state, which was born in 1921. The Arab conquest of this land is taken as the starting point because it introduced two of the most important defining features of Iraqi society today. The first was the Arabic language, which later became the foundation of an Arab national identity. Though it eventually became dominant, the Arabic language did not completely eliminate all linguistic or ethnic identities like Kurdish, Assyrian and Turkoman. The second was the Islamic religion, which also came to dominate Iraqi society without eradicating religious diversity. Islam, in fact, introduced a new level of diversity in the form of its two rival Sunni and Shi'i branches.

Chapter One examines how Iraq emerged from the fall of the Persian Empire to re-establish its position as the center of a new prosperous empire. Up to the mid-tenth century, Iraq's governing group came from predominantly Arab or Arabized elements. From about 950 to the early twentieth century, however, groups originating from the east (Persians, Turks and Mongols) formed the dominant ruling classes. While the period of Iraqi prosperity began to wane much earlier, the Mongol invasion of 1258, examined in Chapter Two, can be taken as an important event marking the decline of Iraq. Henceforth, Iraq assumed the unfamiliar position of a poor provincial backwater oriented to the east rather than to the Mediterranean. Chapters Three and Four deal with the period of Ottoman rule from 1534 to 1918. During the long rule of the Ottoman Turks, relative stability returned to the country as it was reoriented toward Anatolia and the Mediterranean world. In the nineteenth century (Chapter Four) Iraq began to emerge from its provincial isolation as a result of the centralizing efforts of the Ottoman state and its economic integration into the expanding European economy. With the end of World War I, Iraq found itself under British control. Under British aegis (Chapter Five) a new Arab ruling group assumed control of the country and began to build the modern independent state of Iraq. The development of state institutions and nation-building proved to be a turbulent process taking the country from monarchy to republic (Chapter Six), which, after two decades of intense political struggles, made way for the dictatorship of Saddam Husayn (Chapter Seven). Throughout these centuries of political and social change, Iraq's numerous communities have constantly had to find ways to redefine their relationships toward each other in a difficult and painful search for national harmony.

chapter one

FROM THE ARAB CONQUEST TO THE FALL OF BAGHDAD, 636–1258

When the first Arab Muslim army approached the west bank of the Euphrates river in 633 AD, the land known today as Iraq contained a highly heterogeneous population. The majority spoke various Aramaic dialects and worked on lands usually controlled by the *dahaqin*, a Persian aristocratic and administrative class. The desert regions to the west of the Euphrates were dominated by Arab tribes, both nomadic and settled, while the Kurds, whose language is related to Farsi, inhabited the northwest along the foothills of the Zagros Mountains. In different parts of the country there were pockets of Greeks, Indians, Africans, and even some groups who continued to speak late Babylonian dialects. By the seventh century, probably most of the population had converted to Nestorian Christianity with a few Jacobite communities in the north. Jewish communities were found throughout the country and Mazdakite Zoroastrianism was dominant among the Persian soldiers and administrators. There were also significant numbers of Mandaean and Manichean gnostics, various pagan groups and a smattering of Indian religious traditions. With few exceptions, notably at the end of Persian rule, an atmosphere of peaceful coexistence under generally tolerant government prevailed. The establishment of Arab Muslim rule promoted greater social cohesiveness in Iraq through the introduction of a single dominant religion and language, and through the centralizing efforts of the new state.

The last years of Sasanid rule

In 224 AD, the Sasanid Persians conquered the land of Iraq which soon became the wealthiest and most populated part of their far-flung empire. Ctesiphon, the capital city, was located on the Tigris river just south of modern Baghdad, on the northen edge of the rich agricultural plain of south-central Iraq known to the Arabs as the *Sawad*, "black land". A sophisticated network of irrigation canals, requiring constant maintenance by the state, had made the *Sawad* the breadbasket and chief revenue source of the empire. The Sasanids were the implacable foes of the Byzantine Empire and between 602 and 628 the conflict between these two regional superpowers grew particularly destructive.

Under Shah Khusraw II the Sasanids launched a massive invasion of Byzantine territories capturing Syria, Egypt and, in 615, threatened the capital city of Constantinople. The tide would turn, however, when Emperor Heraclius drove the invading armies all the way back across the Euphrates and deep into Iraq. Heraclius even managed, in 627/8 to sack the royal palaces on the outskirts of Ctesiphon itself before securing a heavy tribute as the price of withdrawing. This offensive and counter-offensive left a huge trail of devastation. After the killing, looting and burning of cities and crops, came the ruin of irrigation canals, flooding, plague and political instability. By 632, a degree of order was restored by Shah Yazdagerd III and it seemed likely, with time, that the country could rebuild some of its former prosperity. Ironically, this was the same year that the Prophet Muhammad, the founder of Islam, died in distant Medina leaving behind a movement which would finally ring the death-knell of the exhausted Sasanid Empire.

In addition to the obvious weaknesses caused by the war with Byzantium, the Arab conquest of Iraq was made easier by the Sasanids' policy toward their Arab vassals. Most of the pre-Islamic Arabs belonged to tribes of various sizes, whose cohesion was based on notions of kinship through a common ancestor and the encouragement of endogamous marriage. While homogeneous in appearance, tribes were in fact quite open to the inclusion of outsiders who eventually attained full status as fellow tribesmen. Though each tribe recognized a single leader, a paramount *shaykh*, they also contained several subgroups which were not always amiable to each other. The scarcity of grazing land in the desert gave rise to endemic tribal conflicts and a war-like culture.

For centuries the Lakhmid Arabs, based at Hira on the edge of the Arabian desert, had been recognized as an autonomous kingdom subservient to Ctesiphon. In return for cash subsidies and weapons the Lakhmids protected the empire's desert boundaries from unruly Arab tribes and acted as proxies in the conflict with Byzantium and its allies. In 580, the Lakhmid king Nu'man III converted to Nestorian Christianity, further integrating his tribal kingdom to the predominant community of Sasanid Iraq. This successful relationship was pushed to breaking point in 602 when, as part of their overall more aggressive posture, the Sasanids incorporated Lakhmid territories ending the autonomy of the vassal kingdom. Not surprisingly, this increased the bitterness and hostility of the Arabs, as exemplified by the battle of Dhu Qar in 611, where a coalition of Arab tribes defeated a Sasanid force. More importantly, the incorporation of Lakhmid territories eliminated the buffer zone that separated the empire from the desert tribes.

The first Muslim army, under the seasoned commander Khalid ibn al-Walid, met little resistance when bringing the Arab tribes east of the Euphrates within Medina's orbit. According to most chronicles, both Hira and 'Ubulla to the south were temporarily occupied by early 634 (the dates of the Iraq campaign are not known with certainty). Such an advance would not have been possible without the assistance of local sympathizers such as al-Muthana ibn Haritha al- Shaybani, one of the illustrious shaykhs of the powerful Banu Bakr tribes, and a convert to Islam. The appeal to Arab kinship and the promise of booty and paradise also played important roles in winning over many, though by no means all, of the tribes of Iraq against the Sasanids. At Medina the new leader of the Muslim community, the Caliph 'Umar ibn al-Khattab, was eager to channel the boiling energies of the desert tribes toward external conquest. For the next three years Arab Muslims fought several skirmishes with the Sasanids and their still considerable Arab allies. Despite being soundly defeated at the Battle of the Bridge in 634, the Muslims were able to fall back on the desert which continued to provide a safe haven when needed. Within a few years a new army was raised under the command of Sa'd ibn Abi Waqqas. In 636, bolstered by news of Muslim victories in Syria, the audacious Sa'd led his army in a decisive victory over a substantially larger Sasanid force.[1] The Battle of Qadisiyya, fought near Hira, lasted a grueling three days during which the backbone of the main Sasanid army was broken and its most capable commander, Rustam, was killed. Iraq now lay open to Muslim conquest. Sa'd's forces immediately moved on to sack Ctesiphon and, in 641, Mosul and the whole Jazira region was taken by a force under the command of 'Utba ibn Farqad.

Iraq under the early caliphate

The early Arab narratives of these events are full of references to the utter amazement that the desert tribesmen felt upon their entry into the glittering Sasanid capital. Few had seen such architectural wonders as the massive royal palace known as *Iwan Kisra* or the riches it contained. Camphor, thought to be salt, was used in the making of bread. Many did not understand the value of gold and readily exchanged it for the less valuable silver. In one story (which may have been fictitious) a tribesman sold a Persian noblewoman he had captured for the low price of 1000 silver *dirhams* because he could not imagine a higher number. While the unpolished Arabs were clearly not accustomed to the cultured environment of Sasanid Iraq, they hardly felt intimidated. Even before Islam was to give the Arabs a new sense of pride as the bearers of the "true" religion, the desert tribesman usually looked upon the settled peoples of Iraq with contempt for being weak and servile. They were seen as lacking any sense of honor, readily submitting to a strict social hierarchy and absolutist rule. This sense of superiority served to protect the identity of the conquerors who would soon adopt much of the culture of the vanquished Sasanids.

To make sure that this wealth would not sap the Arabs of their martial spirit, the Caliph 'Umar ordered that garrison towns, known as *amsar*, be set up to house the occupying troops and their families. The sites

---

[1] There is some disagreement over the date of this battle with some historians arguing that it took place in 637 and others in 638.

were chosen on the edge of the desert to guarantee security and regular communication with Medina. In this manner Kufa and Basra were established as the two major administrative centers in Iraq with Mosul as a smaller military settlement (jund) in the north. Within these garrison towns the warriors, with their distinctive Arabic language and Muslim religion, were a majority living aloof from the rest of the country's inhabitants. The idea was that isolation would protect their sense of identity and enhance their solidarity as a separate military caste ready to strike out if the need arose. 'Umar further strengthened this bond by sending a number of Qur'anic reciters[2] and instructions on tightening religious practices. To an extent, this arrangement also suited the local inhabitants since the Arab Muslims were initially prevented from owning land outside the amsar, appropriating existing religious sites, or generally interfering in local affairs. Within the amsar, the tribal nature of the army left its imprint on the structure of the city with each tribe usually residing in separate quarters. In Kufa, for example, the town was divided into 15 sections each allocated to one of the main tribes. The early success of the conquests triggered a large wave of migration from Arabia. Hoping to find wealth and glory through the ongoing conquest of Iran, these migrants poured into the amsar swelling the ranks of the warriors and causing tensions to rise. The non-Arabs of the surrounding suburbs, attracted by the amsar's markets, also contributed to their growth.

Administratively, 'Umar retained the basic Sasanid system along with most of the officers who manned its bureaucracy. Most of Iraq, from Tikrit to just north of Basra, was administered from Kufa. Basra's governor was responsible for large areas in southern Iran. Mosul was originally under the jurisdiction of Kufa but during the caliphate of 'Uthman ibn 'Affan (r. 644–56) it was included within the

---

[2] During the early Islamic period a number of pious men, known as Qur'anic reciters, memorized large portions of the Qur'an (God's revelations to the Prophet Muhammad) and were valued as authorities on Islamic belief and practice.

governorship of Jazira. State lands were seized and converted to *fay'*, the common property of the Muslim community under the trusteeship of the caliph. In Iraq, these lands were considerably greater than those seized in Egypt or Syria because the latter's local notables had secured favorable terms of surrender whereas the Sasanids continued to resist the Islamic conquest. Nevertheless, most of the Persian landowners soon adapted themselves to Muslim rule, successfully protecting their properties by converting to the religion of the new ruling elite. Normally, one-fifth of all moveable properties won as booty was sent to the caliph's central treasury, with the remainder being distributed to the warriors. Non-moveable properties, chiefly land, were taxed. Abu Musa al-Ash'ari, the governor of Basra, is credited with conducting the first cadastral survey after the conquest in 637, establishing a land tax based roughly on productivity. In general, Arab Muslims were exempt from all the important taxes. Non-Muslims had to pay a poll tax known as the *jizya* as well as various kinds of taxes, including the land tax, known collectively as the *kharaj*. The total tax burden was higher than it was under the Sasanids though that would change later with the gradual conversion of the population to Islam. During the following decades the *jizya* came to be defined as a special poll tax on certain protected non-Muslim groups (*dhimmis*). *Dhimmis* were defined as those who believed in a single god, had a revealed scripture, and accepted Muslim rule. In the case of Iraq, this included the Christians, Jews, Mandaeans and, at times, the Zoroastrians. This notion of protected religious communities was also derived from earlier Sasanid policy.

Early Islamic administration emphasized the Arab identity of the rulers. It was a state governed by a military aristocracy composed of Arab tribal warriors bound together by Islam. Islam, however, contained a universalist outlook and conversion, though actively discouraged at times, was possible. In keeping with tribal customs early converts were forced to attach themselves to a particular tribe as "clients" (*Mawali*). Despite their conversion these non-Arab Mawali suffered numerous discriminations. They continued to pay the *kharaj* tax, resided in separate quarters, worshiped in separate mosques, and were not allowed to marry Arab women. Those who volunteered for the army were only enrolled in the infantry and did not receive the normal pensions. While this issue was still in its infancy, the broader question of how to create a functioning centralized rule for the now vast Islamic Empire posed a much greater threat to stability. The tribal warriors who formed the backbone of the empire's army were still repulsed by the idea of a centralized state that would impose discipline and limit their freedom. 'Umar's strong and able leadership kept the situation in check but his assassination in 644 at the hands of his Persian Christian slave soon brought the matter to a head.

Tensions and civil war

'Umar's successor, 'Uthman ibn 'Affan, was a highly contentious figure. Though generally regarded as pious and loyal to the Prophet Muhammad, he was also weak and, more disturbingly, a member of the Banu Umayya clan whose leaders had been the Muslims' worst enemies at Mecca. The appointment of his kinsmen to various important posts raised accusations of nepotism. In Iraq, he could not have chosen a worse appointment for the governorship of Kufa. This was 'Uthman's half brother al-Walid ibn 'Uqba who once spat at Muhammad and had a reputation for corruption and public drunkenness leading to repeated complaints to the caliph. 'Uthman also allowed the merchants of Mecca and Medina to purchase land in Iraq, a practice strictly curtailed by 'Umar. This angered the amsar tribesmen who were not allowed the same right. In the meantime, the conquests in the east which were directed from Kufa and Basra, came to a halt in eastern Persia resulting in a marked fall of booty revenues. At Kufa, Basra and, to a lesser extent, Mosul, large numbers of migrants, who had been attracted by prospects of conquests and booty, loitered around with nowhere to channel their irrepressible energies. While Basra's able governor, ibn 'Amir, was astute enough to control the rising resentment, at Kufa riots broke out at the slightest provocation. For example, when 'Uthman standardized the various texts of the Qur'an into one officially sanctioned copy (a crucial step in state centralization), several of the Qur'anic reciters at Kufa, including the highly respected ibn Mas'ud, refused to accept it. Kufan insubordination was further demonstrated when tribal leaders, against the wishes of 'Uthman, chose Abu Musa al-Ash'ari as governor.

In 656, 'Uthman was killed by a group of malcontents from the amsar of Egypt. By then, however, the divisions within the Muslim ruling elite had reached a point where the simple removal of the caliph could not resolve the problems. The choice of 'Ali ibn Abi Talib, the cousin and son-in-law of Muhammad, was immediately challenged by Muhammad's favorite wife, 'A'isha, and two of the prophet's closest companions, Talha and Zubayr. Accusing 'Ali of failing to punish 'Uthman's assassins, they went to Basra where they raised the banner of revolt. 'Ali, hot on their heals, sought support from the warriors of Kufa where he was highly regarded as a valiant, pious soldier and a champion of their rights. The ensuing battle, known as the Battle of the Camel because 'A'isha urged her troops on while riding a camel, marked the beginning of the first *Fitna* or inter-Muslim war. After emerging victorious, 'Ali had to turn to another center of opposition to his rule forming in Damascus under the leadership of its popular governor and 'Uthman's relative, Mu'awiya ibn Abi Sufyan. The two met in 657 in the Battle of Siffin. While the accounts are hopelessly contradictory it appears that 'Ali was on the verge of victory when the wily Mu'awiya ordered his troops to raise copies of the Qur'an indicating a demand for arbitration. The pious but naive 'Ali accepted the demand and called off the attack. Mu'awiya's move had an immediate demoralizing impact on 'Ali's forces. A section of 'Ali's army denounced the negotiations claiming that "arbitration belongs to God alone" to which 'Ali replied that this was a "word of truth whose intent is unjust". The rebellion of the Kharijis, "seceders", as they came to be known, forced 'Ali to defeat them at Nahrawan in 659. In the meantime, the arbitration did not go well for 'Ali. It seems likely that the arbiters recommended that both 'Ali and Mu'awiya renounce their claim to the caliphate even though the latter had not yet claimed it. In 661, a man by the name of ibn Muljam, a Khariji sympathizer, murdered 'Ali in Kufa while he was preparing for his next confrontation with Mu'awiya. Once the news reached Damascus, Mu'awiya was declared caliph. He quickly proceeded to secure his leadership by successfully threatening, then offering a huge income to Hasan, 'Ali's son, in return for his acquiescence. The caliphate of Damascus lasted from 661 to 750, during which it remained in the hands of the Banu Umayya and is therefor called the Umayyad Caliphate.

The first Fitna highlighted a number of crucial developments taking place in Iraq and the Islamic lands as a whole. The fact that the belligerents chose Basra, Kufa and Damascus as their bases rather than Mecca or Medina, indicates that the old centers of Middle Eastern civilization were reasserting their dominance. In many ways, the Battle of Siffin was the latest event in an ancient and continuing struggle between Syria and Iraq over mastery of the region. 'Ali's forces, backed by the wealth of Iraq, faced Mu'awiya's disciplined Syrian army organized along Byzantine lines. There is no doubt that the main reason for the divisiveness of 'Ali's forces reflected the fractious nature of tribal armies in general. Nevertheless, the influences of Iraq's highly varied ethnic and religious population should not be completely discounted. While the Mawali accounted for only a fraction of 'Ali's army, elements of their pre-Islamic beliefs and practices played a crucial role in giving ideological clarity to the arguments of the contending groups thereby sharpening the lines of division. The Kharijis, for example, would survive as an opposition movement defined by strict puritanism and political egalitarianism. They argued that any man, "even if he were a slave", can become caliph if he is "the best of men" in religion and leadership. 'Ali's supporters, known as the Shi'is, also developed into an opposition party of elements who feared the controlling power of an Arab aristocracy. They came to emphasize the importance of 'Ali's (and his descendants') blood ties with the Prophet Muhammad as the source of legitimate claim to the caliphate. After his death, 'Ali was portrayed as having been almost superhuman in his nobility, piety, wisdom and compassion for the poor and dispossessed. Later he was considered to have been divinely inspired, free of sin and error, and, among some of the extremist Shi'is (*ghulat*), he was regarded as God incarnate. The clearest example of local influences on opposition groups was in the development of messianic beliefs, an importation from Judaism and Christianity. In 685, a Shi'i by the name of al-Mukhtar ibn Abi 'Ubayd led a rebellion against Damascus in the name of Muhammad ibn al-Hanafiyya, a son of 'Ali. The rebellion, which started in Kufa and spread to the countryside, attracting widespread support from the Mawali, was finally crushed in 687 when both al-Mukhtar and ibn al-Hanafiyya were killed. Their followers, however, believed that ibn al-Hanafiyya was the *Mahdi*, "the rightly guided", who did not die but had been miraculously concealed by God and would return at some unknown time to fill the world with justice. The idea of the Mahdi would later permeate the beliefs of most of the emerging Muslim sects. As for the majority of Muslim leaders and pious thinkers, they argued that the most important lesson of the first Fitna was the need for unity. As distasteful as Mu'awiya was for many, the fact that he eventually succeeded in bringing about the unification of the Muslims, overrode all other considerations and made him worthy of support. This group formed the foundation for the later development of the majority Sunni branch of Islam.

The troublesome province of the Umayyads

Mu'awiya's reign, from 661 to 680, brought unity and consolidation of Muslim territories which soon enabled the conquests to resume across North Africa, Anatolia, and into Central Asia. His main concern was the unity of the ruling elite which he strove to solidify by emphasizing its Arab identity. He also named his son, Yazid, as his successor thereby establishing the principle of hereditary rule. In Iraq, despite the benefits which the eastern conquests brought, Mu'awiya's rule was not popular because it was based on Syrian military power. Resentment against Syrian rule was made worse by the fact that Iraq was the most populous and one of the wealthiest lands of the caliphate. Most of the old Persian landowning classes, while technically Mawali and liable to pay extra taxes, were able to avoid taxation through their control of the administrative and fiscal apparatus. Non-Muslims and lower-class Mawali, whose numbers continued to grow, tended to bear the brunt of the tax burden. Arab discrimination against the Mawali made them particularly prone to support the opposition. Their resentment was expressed through the great proliferation of Shi'i and Khariji groups. Hujr ibn Adi, the governor of Kufa and a Shi'i sympathizer, for example, was strongly supported by the Mawali when he refused to recognize Mu'awiya's authority leading to his later execution. His replacement, al-Mughira ibn Shu'ba was instructed to govern with an iron hand. Mu'awiya, however, is best known for his Machiavellian ability to balance the carrot and the stick in securing his authority. In this regard, his treatment of the bastard Ziyad ibn Abih, "the son of his father", is most instructive. Early on Ziyad had expressed Shi'i sympathies. Recognizing his abilities, Mu'awiya declared that Ziyad was his illegitimate half-brother and assigned him the governorship of Basra. Grateful for this gesture, Ziyad proved to be a loyal and able governor, successfully and ruthlessly keeping sedition in check. He was rewarded with an appointment to Kufa and authorized to pacify and govern Iraq as a whole, which he did through the development of a Sasanid-type secret police force.

Unruly Iraq needed little excuse to rise in rebellion when news arrived of the death of Mu'awiya in 680. 'Ali's second son, Husayn, the Prophet's only surviving grandson, quickly became the new champion of the Shi'i cause. Responding to letters from Kufan notables urging him to lead them against the new Caliph Yazid, he left Medina with his family members and a small party of supporters only to be intercepted by an Umayyad army not far from Kufa in a plain known as Karbala. The new governor of Kufa, 'Ubaydullah, the son of Ziyad, had used the best of his father's skills in destroying the rebels prior to

Husayn's arrival. Those who were not killed were terrified into submission by the sight of hundreds crucified along the main streets of
Kufa. Husayn had little chance when, on the tenth day of the Muslim
month of Muharram, known as 'Ashura, he along with most of his
band were massacred. This was a defining moment for the embryonic
Shi'i movement where Husayn proved to be far more potent as a
martyr and his death continues to be commemorated with ritual
lamentations and passion plays. The "Prince of Martyrs" became the
symbol of all that was pure, just and heroic, and his suffering and death
were seen as a means of redemption for the Shi'is. The main branch of
Shi'ism would later argue that the descendants of 'Ali through his marriage with Fatima, the daughter of the Prophet, alone can provide the
divinely-inspired *Imams* to lead the community. Each would be identified by his predecessor and obedience to this Imam was obligatory for
all believers. Since one of Husayn's sons, who was too ill to take part
in the battle, survived, the line of 'Ali and Fatima was not broken and
continued to provide the Shi'is with Imams well into the tenth century.

At the time, however, Husayn's rebellion did not represent a major
threat. A far more dangerous opponent was 'Abdullah ibn al-Zubayr,
whose father was killed by 'Ali at the Battle of the Camel. His rebellion in Mecca gained much ground after the death of Yazid in 683. At
that time, ibn al-Zubayr was declared caliph in opposition to the
Umayyad caliph in Damascus. Between 683 and 692, the Islamic lands
plunged into division and civil war where tribal loyalties once again
played a crucial role in determining the nature of alliances. Iraq,
during this turbulent time, recognized the authority of ibn al-Zubayr
where his brother Mus'ab governed from Kufa. Nevertheless, his hold
on power was quite tentative since Shi'is and Kharijis took advantage
of the chaos to push their own claims. At one point, there were four
or five different claimants to the caliphate. Umayyad authority was
not re-established until the Caliph 'Abdul-Malik ibn Marwan
(r. 685–705) defeated ibn al-Zubayr at Mecca and reconquered Iraq.

'Abdul-Malik's governor for Iraq was one of the most fascinating figures in Iraqi history. Charged with crushing the Shi'i and Khariji threat, the indomitable al-Hajjaj ibn Yusuf, known for his eloquence and severity, wasted no time in laying down the rules before the "people of Iraq" whom he referred to as a "people of discord and dissembling and evil character". In 694, he appeared unexpectedly in disguise at the main mosque of Kufa where a large rebellious crowd had gathered. Mounting the pulpit, he removed his disguise and, in words still taught to Iraqi children at schools, addressed the assembled in the following manner:

> By God, I shall make evil bear its own burden; I shall shoe it with its own sandal and recompense it with its own like. I see heads before me that are ripe and ready for plucking, and I am the one to pluck them, and I see blood glistening between the turbans and the beards. ... The Commander of the Faithful [the Umayyad caliph] emptied his quiver and bit his arrows and found me the bitterest and hardest of them all. Therefore he aimed me at you. For a long time you have been swift to sedition; you have lain in the lairs of error and have made a rule of transgression. By God, I shall strip you like bark, I shall truss you like a bundle of twigs, I shall beat you like stray camels. ... By God, what I promise, I fulfill; what I propose, I accomplish; what I measure, I cut off ...[3]

Al-Hajjaj's family was of modest means. He gave up his position as school master in Ta'if to eventually become one of 'Abdul-Malik's (and his son al-Walid's) most loyal and dependable lieutenants. Before his appointment to Iraq he had successfully dealt with mutinous troops in Damascus, led the Umayyad army in its victory over ibn al-Zubayr, which included the bombardment of the Ka'ba, and ruthlessly pacified Yemen and Hijaz. In Iraq, he first restored discipline among the caliph's troops by severely punishing insubordination. He then sent his

---

[3] Quoted in Bernard Lewis (ed.), *Islam: From the Prophet Muhammad to the Capture of Constantinople*, vol. 1, pp. 23–24.

army from one region to the other wiping out Khariji rebels. The greatest danger he faced, however, came in 697 when the cream of his Iraqi forces, known as the "Peacock Army", commanded by 'Abdul-Rahman ibn al-Ash'ath, rebelled. At its heart, ibn al-Ash'ath's rebellion was directed against Syrian rule over Iraq and gained widespread support throughout the province. After seizing Kufa and most of Basra, al-Hajjaj was able to secure victory in 701 only after large Syrian reinforcements.

But al-Hajjaj is not simply remembered for his pacification of unruly Iraq. Once peace was achieved he turned his considerable energies to development. In this regard he established a new provincial capital, Wasit, in 702, located between Kufa and Basra. This was to serve as a secure garrison for his loyal Syrian troops who were now clearly an occupying force. He directed several agricultural projects notably the draining of marshes and the construction of canals in the Sawad. When large numbers of Mawali peasants left the land to migrate to the amsar, al-Hajjaj forced them back and made sure that they were liable to pay the kharaj tax. As part of 'Abdul-Malik's efforts to Arabize the administration, al-Hajjaj established a mint which struck coins bearing Arabic Islamic inscriptions. He was also instrumental in approving the use of new vowel points for the Arabic script and producing a single reading of the Qur'an. Before his death Iraq was already becoming a center for learning. At Kufa and Basra Islamic theology and jurisprudence was developed under such figures as al-Hasan al-Basri (d. 728). Probably of Mandaean or Manichean origin, al-Basri brought gnostic influences and emphasized the centrality of reason. A critic of tyranny, he nevertheless called for Muslim unity and obedience to the Umayyad Caliph. In general, al-Hajjaj's meticulous administration and success in mercilessly dealing with corruption and bribery, did bring about overall prosperity. Nevertheless, his severity, though often exaggerated in the sources, has earned him an unpleasant place in the collective memory of Iraqis. He died in 714 and was buried near Wasit in an unmarked grave to protect it from his many enemies.

The 'Abbasid revolution

Though the Umayyads succeeded in suppressing all revolts, Iraq continued to be their most dangerous province with Shi'i and Khariji threats lingering throughout the period. In addition to the resentment against Syrian rule, Iraq contained one of the largest concentrations of Mawali. As their numbers continued to rise with conversions, the inherent contradiction between Islam's universalistic appeal and the rule of an Arab military caste became untenable. The Umayyads were also unable to solve the problem of tribal divisions which actually grew worse through an official policy of favoritism. The persistence of the tribes brought with it an inherent rejection of centralized rule. The great conquests of the Umayyads kept some of these tensions in check by bringing in booty and channeling the energies of the tribes away from the central lands. Iraqis participated eagerly in these conquests, playing important roles in the subjugation of Sind and Central Asia. But once these conquests had reached their limits by the middle of the eighth century, the crisis grew. Thousands of warriors (both Arab and Mawali) roamed the amsar with nothing to do. Hatred of the Umayyads became so intense that attempts at serious reforms failed to reverse the rebellious mood.

The group that would provide the leadership for this revolutionary ferment was based around the 'Abbasid family. The 'Abbasids, who claimed descent from one of the Prophet's uncles, appealed to the Shi'is by arguing that the caliphate must rest with the Prophet's family. They also appealed to the Kharijis and the Mawali by attacking the Umayyads' lack of piety and promising equality for all Muslims. The center of their movement was eastern Persia, but they also had many supporters in Kufa. In 747, their agent Abu Muslim (himself a member of the Mawali), succeeded in raising a large army that headed toward Iraq. The army's black banners, hoisted as a symbol of rebellion and mourning, were henceforth associated with the 'Abbasids. The decisive battle took place in 750, near the Great Zab river in northern Iraq where the Umayyad army was routed. Even before this final battle, the head of the 'Abbasid household, Abu al-'Abbas, had been declared the first caliph of the new dynasty in Kufa. In victory, the 'Abbasids were anything but chivalrous. Every member of the Ummayad family, young and old, was hunted down and put to the sword. Those who resisted, like the governor of Wasit, were promised amnesty and then treacherously killed. Once Syria and Egypt were secured, the 'Abbasids turned against their erstwhile allies, the Shi'is and Kharijis.

The 'Abbasid takeover was a true revolutionary event in the sense that it brought about a thorough social transformation. The center of the empire was moved from Syria to Iraq where it remained for over 200 years. The Mawali were finally recognized as the equals of Arab Muslims and a detailed system of Islamic law, which did not distinguish between members of the same faith, was developed. Most importantly, the nature of the empire changed from one geared for expansion to one organized for internal development. This brought with it a concomitant change in the nature of the ruling class from one dominated by Arab warriors to a more cosmopolitan group of officials, merchants, landlords and religious jurists. The outlook and culture of this class did not emphasize the stern tribal values of warriors, but the more refined, milder values of urbanites.

The splendor of Baghdad

The 'Abbasid period is still considered the golden age of Iraq. As the new center of a far-flung empire, Iraq grew even more wealthy through trade and the inflow of taxes from the provinces. Its own resources, notably the Sawad region, became more productive with a further development of the irrigation canal networks. By 900, Iraq's population had climbed to over 20 million people, slightly less than it is today. In government, the caliph's image took on the characteristics of a great imperial ruler surrounded by the finest Persian tradition of pomp and ceremony. The "Shadow of God Upon the Earth", as he was now called, also became more distant from his subjects, protected by an intimidating bureaucracy. Persian advisers and ministers were instrumental in a series of reforms that rationalized administration and standardized taxation. The new office of *wazir* (chief minister), second only to the caliph, was usually occupied by a Persian. Shi'is, Christians and Jews were often given important posts as ministers or advisers. The height of the 'Abbasid Caliphate was reached during the reigns of the fabled Harun al-Rashid (786–809) and his two sons al-Amin and al-Ma'mun (809–833).

Arguably, the crowning achievement of the 'Abbasids was the establishment of the new capital city of Baghdad in 762. Built upon the site of a village by that name, it was nevertheless a wholly new construction.[4] The site was chosen by the Caliph Abu Ja'far al-Mansur (r. 754–775) who personally supervised its construction. Situated in central Iraq at the point where the two rivers almost meet, it had easy access to communications, by boats or caravans, a fertile hinterland, and a defensible position. Officially known as *Madinat al-Salam* (City of Peace), it was designed as a round city on the west bank of the Tigris reserved for the caliph's residence, barracks for his elite guards and various government offices. Outside a huge metropolis of markets, mosques and residential quarters spanned both sides of the river. The Round City had two major avenues connecting four opposite gates. At the center was the great cathedral mosque used for religious and civic occasions. The main palace, known as *Bab al-Dhahab* (the Golden Gate), accentuated the separation and near other-worldly stature of the caliph. At the top of its large green dome, some 48 meters high, stood the fabled statue of a mounted knight said to miraculously point in the direction of an approaching enemy.

Baghdad quickly eclipsed all other cities in Iraq reducing Kufa, Basra and Wasit to mere satellites. In 800, its population was around 500,000, reaching 1.5 million a century later, making it one of the largest cities in the world outside China. The city's population was

---

[4] The name is likely of Persian origin meaning "The Gift of God".

highly cosmopolitan, reflecting all the ethnic, religious and linguistic groups of the empire. Different communities tended to live in separate quarters and manage their own internal affairs with little intervention from the state. A center of government and trade with a sophisticated banking system, Baghdad also boasted a large manufacturing sector. Most industries, like sword-making, leather, textiles and copper ware, were small family-run affairs. Others, especially the glass and paper industries, required factories employing hundreds of workers. Visitors marveled at the city's baths, hospitals, public libraries, literary salons and zoo. Nor was the city free of places of vice such as bars and brothels, usually situated near the river.

The major cities of Iraq, especially Baghdad, became leading lights of learning and art under the patronage of the 'Abbasids and the powerful wealthy classes. Early on, the caliphs had reached an informal agreement with the religious scholars (the 'ulama) of Islam granting them considerable freedom in formulating and interpreting the law in return for their recognition of the legitimacy of 'Abbasid rule. After a long, contentious process of debate and discussion, four schools of Islamic law (the shari'a) emerged within the mainstream Sunni branch. The founders of three of these schools, Abu Hanifa (d. 767), Muhammad al-Shafi'i (d. 820) and Ahmad ibn Hanbal (d. 855), lived and taught in Baghdad at some time. The fourth, Malik ibn Anas (d. 795), lived in Medina. While different caliphs favored different schools, eventually all four were granted legitimacy. The shari'a became the fundamental law governing the behavior of all Muslim societies regardless of whether they fell under the direct political control of Baghdad or not. With the development of the shari'a, the judge (qadi) also rose in importance. The Shi'i branch developed its own school of jurisprudence, though it was not usually given official recognition by the caliphs. After initially supporting the 'Abbasid takeover, the Shi'is were suppressed and slipped back into their familiar role of opposition. At times, their theologians were tolerated, allowing such eminent scholars as Ja'far al-Sadiq (d. 765) of Medina to teach. He elaborated the Shi'i idea of the divinely-inspired, infallible *Imam*, a descendant of 'Ali and Fatima, whose role was to correctly interpret the word of God. Ja'far al-Sadiq, the sixth Imam of the main Shi'i branch, was brought to Baghdad just before his death. His descendants continued to live and teach there.

The 'Abbasids strongly encouraged the translation of works dealing with all manner of scientific, philosophical or literary subjects from Aramaic, Greek, Persian and Sanskrit. Most of these translations were carried out at the House of Wisdom, *Bayt al-Hikma*, established in 830. This academic research center was equipped with a library and usually administered by Christian scholars such as Yuhanna ibn Masawayh (d. 857). Especially popular were works of Greek philosophy which influenced all aspects of Islamic thought and science. Far from being mere passive translators, the scholars of *Bayt al-Hikma* contributed their own commentaries followed by original works. Soon, a vibrant indigenous scholarly community was producing important contributions to philosophy, mathematics, science and medicine. In literature and the arts, great works of history appeared, poets, such as Abu Nuwas of Basra, established new genres reflecting the taste of his opulent patrons, while others, such as the belletrist al-Jahiz, also of Basra, wrote piercing satirical works in which they criticized the evils of the age. Mosul produced famous musicians while painting, sculpture and architecture all witnessed refreshing innovation. At Basra, which had become one of the greatest ports of the Indian Ocean, Arabic grammar was standardized and one of the most influential intellectual movements, the rationalist Mu'tazila school, was developed. Christian, Jewish, gnostic as well as Shi'i and Sunni Muslim scholars and artists contributed to this magnificent page of Iraqi history. Little wonder that the contemporary al-Ya'qubi refered to Iraq as "the center of this world, the navel of the earth", and to Baghdad as "the greatest city, which has no peer in the east or the west of the world".[5]

---

[5] Quoted in Bernard Lewis, *Islam: From the Prophet Muhammad to the Capture of Constantinople*, vol. 2, p. 69.

The Caliphate in crisis

Even at the height of this power, certain problems were evident. Upon his death, Harun al-Rashid divided the caliphate between his two sons, al-Amin and al-Ma'mun. The relationship between the two brothers quickly grew hostile and a destructive civil war broke out during which al-Ma'mun, who ruled over Persia, besieged Baghdad for over a year. After his victory, the caliphate was reunited and progress resumed but the incident was an early warning of things to come. At the heart of the empire's future problems was its huge size stretching from North Africa all the way to Central Asia. With time, the governors of the outlying provinces, supported by the local elites, loosened their ties to Baghdad. While the symbolic importance of the caliph as the head of the entire Sunni Muslim community never waned, politically and financially the provinces began to assert their independence under various petty dynasties. One after the other provinces in North Africa, Egypt, Syria, Persia and Central Asia, ceased to send their tax revenues to the capital. By 900, the caliph's control rarely extended beyond Iraq.

Concomitant with regional separatism was a growing internal crisis apparent in the number of both urban and rural uprisings. The wealth of Iraq tended to be concentrated in the hands of an elite which grew more arrogant and exploitive. Among the early revolts to test the stability of the caliphate, was the uprising of the Zutt, an impoverished rural community of Indian origin. Between 820 and 835, they wreaked havoc throughout the south before finally being brought to heel. In 868, the south was again the scene of a massive revolt, this time of African slaves. As part of their efforts at establishing plantation-like agriculture in the Sawad, the 'Abbasids imported thousands of slaves from East Africa. The *Zanj*, as these slaves were known, worked under extremely harsh conditions to clear the soil of salination. Under the leadership of one 'Ali ibn Muhammad, who claimed to be a messianic savior, the Zanj rebels eventually controlled much of the south. From their fortress capital of Mukhtara, located in the marshes of the south, they terrorized the cities, sacking Basra and Wasit, collected tolls and taxes, and even threatened the outskirts of Baghdad. After numerous failures the caliphal forces were finally able to destroy Mukhtara and crush the rebellion in 883. Most of these movements had both egalitarian and Shi'i pretensions. The clearest in this regard was the so-called Qarmatian movement. Based originally in Kufa, the leaders of this radical Shi'i sect claimed esoteric knowledge of the Qur'an and spread a message of strict economic egalitarianism and rebellion against the rich. During their formative period, they played some role in the Zanj rebellion, but by 899 they had grown so strong, especially among the poor peasants and desert nomads, that they were able to create an independent state along the eastern shore of Arabia. From there, they launched raids into Iraq and Syria culminating in the sack of Basra in 923. Once again, the caliph had to divert valuable resources to restore order.

The break-up of the empire and the growing rural unrest led to a decline in trade and revenues. This was sharply felt in the cities where shortages and unemployment gave rise to bread riots and outbreaks of violence. A number of moral reformers attempted to address the growing crisis through religious reform. The mystic al-Hallaj, for example, was a pantheist who emphasized the nearness of God and the spiritual equality of all humans. His famous declaration, "I am the Truth" (i.e. God), in 922, caused such outrage within orthodox Islamic circles that he was put to death on orders of the caliph. At the other end of the ideological spectrum, followers of Ahmad ibn Hanbal, founder of a strict orthodox school of Islamic jurisprudence, repeatedly went into the streets beating up men deemed to have lax morals or smashing bars and other places of vice. Such conditions had a negative impact on the treatment of non-Muslims. While overall, monotheists like the Christians and Jews enjoyed considerable rights, there were periods of persecution represented by such acts as special dress codes and forcible conversions. To check the decline in law and order, the 'Abbasids resorted to greater reliance on the military, especially mercenary and slave forces. The Turks, a rugged steppe people from Central Asia, were one of the favored groups brought in ever-increasing numbers to bolster the army. With time, Turkish military commanders exerted greater control over the caliph and the succession process. In 836, in an effort to escape the troubles in Baghdad and to reduce the influence of the Turkish soldiers, the Caliph al-Mu'tasim moved his court to Samarra, just to the north of Baghdad. Massive investments went into the establishment of the new capital. A huge mosque, with a distinctive spiral minaret still evident today, was the city's greatest building. Nevertheless, Baghdad retained its centrality and the caliph was forced to return there in 892. Samarra was mostly abandoned and reduced to a small town.

In addition to the rise in military expenditures and decline of trade, Iraq also suffered from a drop in agricultural production. The exhaustion of the land from centuries of intensive cultivation was one cause, but certainly the rising disturbances in the countryside and the neglect of irrigation works also played a role. In 935, for example, the important Nahrawan canal was breeched to stop the movements of a rebellious army. Large tracts of fertile fields were flooded causing long-term damage to productivity. Since tax revenues were falling, the caliphs resorted more and more to tax farming or the so-called *iqta'* grants in order to pay their military commanders. The *iqta'* was an old practice by which the ruler grants the right to collect and keep most of the revenue of a particular estate. It was temporary, non-hereditary and did not include a system of mutual obligations. The *iqta'* encouraged further fragmentation and severe exploitation of the peasantry. By 935, Mosul and its fertile hinterland (especially the Jazira region) had become virtually independent under the Hamdanid dynasty. Its founder, Nasir al-Dawla, was a great *iqta'* holder. Other petty dynasties included the Baridis in Basra and several Kurdish chiefdoms in the north. During this time of crisis, society witnessed a change in the nature of the elite from classes of merchants, landowners and officials, to the domination of military commanders. In 935, this process was given formal recognition when the Caliph al-Radi handed over effective powers of the state to a military commander by the name of ibn Ra'iq with the new title of *Amir al-'Umara* (Prince of Princes). By then, the caliph's authority rarely extended beyond the gates of his palace, though he retained a formidable image as the religious leader of Sunnis throughout the Islamic world. In 945, the chief of a Persian clan, the Buwayhids, secured the position of Amir al-'Umara and established a powerful dynasty which continued to rule most of Iraq for the next century.

Shi'i rule under the Buwayhids

The Buwayhids originated from the region south of the Caspian Sea. They offered their services as mercenaries and proved to be highly successful fighters thanks to their strong sense of solidarity and loyalty to their chiefs. The height of their power came under the rule of 'Adud al-Dawla who initiated administrative reforms, cleared irrigation canals, and gave lavish support to the arts. He launched several campaigns to check the growing power of the tribes. In 977, he took Mosul and generally reunited Iraq. Soon after his death in 983, however, central power declined.

On the whole, the Buwayhid period was one of political turbulence and economic decline, but also of great cultural and scientific productivity. Though they nominally controlled most of Iraq and western Persia, regional fragmentation continued to plague the country and Sunni-Shi'i animosity often broke out into dangerous urban riots. The sectarian conflict was at times fueled by the Caliph-Amir al-'Umara's struggle for leverage. They were rough, uneducated, and professed Shi'i Islam. The fact that a Shi'i Amir al-'Umara could rule Iraq was even more demonstrative of the weakness of the caliph. As the foremost protector of Sunni Islam, it was ironic, not to mention humiliating, for him to accept the rule of a heretic. But, the fact that the Buwayhids never attempted to completely do away with the caliph was testimony to the religious respect still accorded to the 'Abbasid family. To give further official recognition of his exalted position, the name of the Amir al-'Umara was announced after that of the caliph during the public Friday prayers, and his name was printed, alongside that of the caliph, on all coins. Iraq, during this time, came under increasing pressure from the rival Fatimid Caliphate of Egypt. The Fatimids were also Shi'is but of the opposing Isma'ili branch. Under Buwayhid patronage, and that of several petty princes, mainstream Shi'ism reached full maturity. Most Shi'is in Iraq and Iran continued to give their allegiance to a descendant of 'Ali and Fatima but in the late ninth century, the twelfth Imam, Muhammad ibn al-Hasan, disappeared without designating an heir. Shi'is believed that he had gone into miraculous occultation in 941, and would return in the future as the Mahdi, the savior who would rid the world of injustice. Henceforth, mainstream Shi'is were called Twelvers or Imamis to distinguish them from other Shi'i sects, including the Isma'ilis of Egypt. The Buwayhids also encouraged Shi'i festivals and the public lamentations, known as 'Ashura, in which the faithful recall the deeds of the Imams and mourn their death, especially that of Husayn. Shrines and mausolea were erected on the tombs of the Imams and their trusted followers, with the foremost being those at Najaf and Karbala. Shi'i scholars received lavish rewards and Shi'i schools multiplied.

For Sunnis, watching these developments with awe, the most objectionable Shi'i practice was the visitation of shrines in which the faithful ask for the Imam's blessing. To the strict Hanbalis, this was tantamount to idol worship, the most terrible crime in Islam. In 971, Hanbali militants led a mob to the venerated Husayn shrine in Karbala and set fire to it, leading to several days of violent clashes in Baghdad. Neighborhoods were more tightly segregated along sectarian or communal lines and the individual relied more on a sense of neighborhood solidarity for his protection rather than the ineffectual state authority. Such conditions, coupled with the continuing decline of the economy, gave rise to the phenomenon of neighborhood gangs known as the 'ayyarun, or vagabonds. They proliferated especially in the eleventh century where, between 1030 and 1033, Baghdad was almost ruled by one of these gangs under the notorious leader Burjumi. Mostly, however, the *'ayyarun* were small gangs with elaborate initiation rites. While they were certainly involved in criminal activities such as theft and extortion, they also adopted a chivalrous code of protecting the honor of women, defending their neighborhoods, and helping the poor. Some swore to only target the rich and the police. By the end of their reign, the Buwayhids had made urban decline worse through their incessant family squabbles. In the countryside the *iqta'* became more widespread, leading to reduced revenues for the state. During the reign of Jalal al-Dawla (1025–1044), the state had grown so poor that he was forced to release most of his servants and sell his horses. As the state weakened, irrigation systems were neglected and floods started to afflict Baghdad with alarming regularity. Floods normally brought epidemics in their wake leading to a steady fall in Iraq's population. Meanwhile, trade began to shift away from Basra and the Persian Gulf to the more secure area of the Red Sea and Egypt. Yet in the midst of this increasingly unstable situation, Baghdad remained an intellectually vibrant center. In many ways the fragmentation provided more freedom for scholars and artists to pick and choose their patrons. While overall construction slowed down considerably, one of the most notable achievements of this age was the building of the 'Adudi hospital in 982. It had 60 full-time physicians, separate specialized wards including an insane asylum, and places where students could learn under the guide of a master. Students came to this hospital from all over the Islamic world and beyond since a certificate from one of the 'Adudi physicians was a mark of great prestige.

While irrigation suffered, the mostly rain-fed fields of the Jazira region provided Mosul with a solid agricultural base. For most of the tenth century, the Hamadanids continued to rule Mosul as the nominal dependents of the Buwayhids. The Hamadanids were Shi'is of Arab Beduin origin whose main rivals were the Marwanid Kurds of neighboring Diyar Bakr. At their peak, they made use of Kurdish and Turkish soldiers as well as their Arab tribal forces to extend their rule all the way to Aleppo. By the late tenth century, the north gradually came under the domination of the Arab 'Uqaylids of the Banu Ka'b tribe. Like the Hamadanids, the 'Uqaylids were Shi'is, but they never relinquished their nomadic lifestyle, nor did they resort to standing armies of Turks even after controlling Mosul. By 1010, they ruled over a vast territory from Mosul to Kufa around Baghdad. The eleventh century witnessed the growing migration of Turkish tribes into northern Iraq and Anatolia. In 1040, the 'Uqaylids formed a large coalition of Arab tribes which defeated the Turks and ensured the continuing Arab domination of the Jazira. In the south, another Shi'i tribe from the desert, the Asad under the leadership of the Mazyad family, established a flourishing state with Hilla as its capital. The rise of Hilla in 1101, was mostly at the expense of Kufa, the old capital of Iraq under the early caliphs. The Mazyadids (961–1150), who also ruled over Najaf and Karbala, were especially famous for their patronage of learning. During their reign, Hilla became the leading center of Shi'i scholarship and contributed to the expansion of Shi'ism throughout Iraq, particularly among the Arab tribes. These Arab tribal leaders of Mosul and Hilla are remembered fondly in modern Iraq for their nobility, chivalry and generous patronage. While still nominally under the paramountcy of Baghdad, they often acted against the wishes of the Buwayhids and tried to gain greater independence by playing the caliph against the Amir al-'Umara, or one Buwayhid leader against another.

The Seljuks and the return of Sunni dominance

As waves of Turkish migrants continued to arrive, settling mainly in the regions of northern Persia and Anatolia, a number of principalities developed. During the mid-eleventh century, the tribe of Seljuk Turks succeeded in dominating most of Persia and, in 1055, their leader Tughril Bey[6] seized Baghdad. Being Sunni, the caliph was initially

---

[6] The Turkish title of "Bey", is roughly equivalent to the Arabic Shaykh, or the Kurdish Agha, all meaning a tribal chief

delighted, believing that this champion would soon restore 'Abbasid authority. It did not take long for him to realize that the Seljuk leader had no intention of relinquishing power. Tughril Bey did not even bother to meet the caliph after defeating the Buwayhids. Instead, he went north taking Mosul in 1057, but keeping a member of the 'Uqaylid family as governor. After reducing most of Iraq, the caliph granted him the titles of "Sultan" and "King of the East and West". During the Seljuk period, the caliph and sultan came to represent a clearer separation in functions between religious and secular leadership respectively. Seljuk sultans almost always sought to enhance their legitimacy as the protectors of Sunni Islam through marital arrangements with the caliph's family. As with the Amir al-'Umara, the sultan's name appeared with the caliph's on all coins and his name was mentioned after that of the caliph during Friday prayers.

Initially, the return of Sunni power to Baghdad did not lead to a major anti-Shi'i backlash and Shi'is continued to occupy high government posts. Sunnis and Iraq's Twelver Shi'is had a common cause in fighting against the increasingly aggressive Isma'ili state of Egypt under the Fatimids. Now in control of Syria, the Fatimids succeeded in winning over a number of provincial leaders fearful of the power of the new Seljuk state. With direct Fatimid support, a leader by the name of al-Basasiri succeeded in forming a broad coalition of Shi'i forces, including the 'Uqaylids and Mazyadids. As an ex-member of an elite Buwayhid force of slave soldiers, al-Basasiri was able to rally enough support to take Baghdad in the name of the Fatimid caliph in 1058. After forcing the 'Abbasid caliph into exile, al-Basasiri moved south to include Wasit and Basra. Iraq's political subjugation to Cairo hardly lasted one year. Soon after al-Basasiri's victory, Fatimid aid ceased and his shaky coalition of Arab tribes, who in any case were mostly Twelver Shi'is, broke apart. When the Seljuks returned to Baghdad in 1060, they met only light resistance. With the downfall of al-Basasiri's movement and the reinstatement of the 'Abbasid caliph under Seljuk tutelage, Shi'is faced widespread reprisals. The leading Shi'i notables, including their most eminent religious scholars, fled to Najaf which was fast becoming the new center of Shi'i leadership. The scourge of sectarian violence even spread outside the Sunni-Shi'i conflict to include major clashes between rival Sunni factions of Shafi'is and Hanbalis. Within this atmosphere, non-Muslims, especially the Christians and Jews of Baghdad, faced increasing persecution. In 1091, some Christian communities were forced to convert to Islam, while the segregation of Jews became more pronounced.

Under the Seljuks, Baghdad lost something of its luster. Most of the sultans normally chose Persian cities, such as Isfahan, as capitals of an empire which included Persia, Iraq and much of Anatolia. Throughout the second half of the eleventh century, Seljuk power remained relatively strong. But the centrifugal forces affecting the entire Muslim world were still strongly felt in the form of various opposition movements based in the provinces. To help to stabilize their rule, the Seljuks turned to one of the greatest political minds of the Islamic Middle Ages, the Persian wazir known as Nizam al-Mulk (d. 1092). Nizam al-Mulk sought to reform the administration to establish greater centralization of power in the hands of the Sultan. One of his main concerns was the lack of ideological unity within the ruling circle and the state bureaucracy, with the Sunni-Shi'i division being the most obvious example. To cure this problem, he established a number of colleges known as *madrasas*, whose primary goal was the promotion of Sunni Islam particularly within the bureaucracy. The curriculum emphasized Sunni theology and jurisprudence, (especially those of the more flexible Hanafi and Shafi'i schools), as a direct counter to Shi'i ideas. In Iraq, three madrasas were built with the Nizamiyya of Baghdad (opened in 1067) being the most prestigious. Nizam al-Mulk also attempted to establish greater control over the numerous *iqta'* grants that had become virtual private estates. *Iqta's* were reclaimed by the state and redistributed to Turkish commanders and beys. To make sure that the sultan did not need to rely too much on the *iqta'*-holders, the system of slave soldiers, known as *mamluks*, was expanded. As the personal property of the sultan the mamluks acted as a sort of elite praetorian guard.

The Seljuks were quite successful in eventually bringing a degree of order over Iraq and the unruly neighborhoods of Baghdad. In 1096, they overthrew the 'Uqaylids of Mosul and replaced them with their own governors. The Mazyadids retained their hold over Hilla by paying tribute and carefully avoiding problems with the sultan. They even managed to expand their territory to include Wasit, Basra and even as far north as Tikrit. But in 1108, fearful of their growing power, the Seljuks destroyed their army and occupied Hilla. Under the Seljuks' most capable sultans, Alp-Arslan (1063–1073) and Malik Shah (1073–1092), the country prospered with trade and agriculture regaining some of their old vitality. As a result of the conflict with Egypt, however, Iraq under the Buwayhids and Seljuks lost part of its commercial and cultural contacts with the Mediterranean region and was oriented more toward Persia and the east. By the early twelfth century, Seljuk power began to wane. In 1127, the Seljuk governor of Mosul, 'Imad al-Din Zangi, founded an independent dynasty that produced one of the most celebrated figures in Islamic history: Salah al-Din ibn Ayyub. Though the European Crusades never reached as far as Iraq, the Zangid state was actively engaged in this struggle. First under 'Imad al-Din, then his son Nur al-Din, the Zangids managed to score a series of victories against the hitherto unassailable European invaders. The greatest prize, Jerusalem, was taken by Salah al-Din in 1187, after the epic battle of Hittin. Born in Tikrit in 1138 of Arab-Kurdish parents, he entered the service of the Zangids and was sent to aid the crumbling Fatimid state in Egypt. In 1171, Salah al-Din overthrew the last Fatimid caliph and established his own dynasty in Cairo which re-acknowledged the symbolic authority of the Sunni caliph of Baghdad. Under the Ayyubids, Egypt was no less ambitious with Salah al-Din himself twice laying siege to Mosul in an unsuccessful attempt to reunite the Islamic heartland. As early as 1120, the Seljuk realm was suffering from division and incessant in-fighting. Taking advantage of

Seljuk inability to control a new wave of 'ayyarun activity in Baghdad, the 'Abbasid caliph began to attract support for an effort to regain his political authority. In 1135, the Caliph al-Mustarshid raised an army which failed to dislodge the Seljuk governor.

During the Buwayhid and Seljuk periods, shari'a-minded Islam, which emphasized the importance of the law and normally received official sanction from the state, was challenged by a popular turn toward mysticism. The weakening of the state and the declining stature of the caliph certainly contributed to this tendency. Mystical or *sufi* Islam, had its origins in the very dawn of the religion. Clearly influenced by Christian monasticism and eastern religions, it stressed the emotional link between a loving, merciful God and the individual believer. This link could be discovered through a difficult process of intuitive search usually involving meditation or, more commonly, public liturgical sessions in which a number of mystics repeated certain phrases eventually reaching a trance. Large sufi orders or brotherhoods bound tightly by a hierarchy of master–disciple relationships, sprung up throughout the Islamic world. One of the most influential of these orders was the Qadiriyya founded in Baghdad by the disciples of 'Abdul-Qadir al-Gaylani (d. 1146). Stressing the need to respect the shari'a while exploring the mystical way, the Qadiriyya order spread throughout the Islamic world and played an important role in maintaining religious unity at a time of political fragmentation. Other orders tended to downplay the importance of the shari'a in favor of faith. Members of the Rifa'iyya order, founded by disciples of Ahmad al-Rifa'i (d. 1183), in Basra, were known to perform superhuman acts such as the swallowing of swords or walking barefoot on embers. Their closeness to God, they claimed, protected them from all harm. As mystical Islam expanded, the sufi lodge came to compete with the mosque and the sufi master with the 'ulama. On one level, mysticism represented a popular challenge against an increasingly oppressive elite. On another level, many members of the elite, including the Seljuk sultans themselves, embraced aspects of sufism and patronized sufi leaders and orders.

The ʿAbbasid resurgence

The failed attempt by al-Mustarshid to regain political authority was resumed under his successor. Between 1136 and 1160, the Caliph al-Muqtafi succeeded in gaining complete independence from Seljuk authority by raising an army which also brought Hilla, Wasit, Kufa and Tikrit under his control. Nevertheless, the caliph's new found power was constantly threatened by religious divisions and the proliferation of urban gangs. Supplanting the ʿayyarun were new gangs called the futuwwa. Roughly translated as "young manliness", these neighborhood groups of young "toughs" were a cross between the modern youth clubs and mafiosi gangs. Their most distinguishing feature, which separated them from the ʿayyarun, was the influence of sufism. In addition to their neighborhood solidarity, sufi Islam contributed to a stronger bond which, at times, transcended the neighborhood or even the city. Many of the futuwwa groups were wholly innocuous focusing on sports or providing assistance for the poor and needy, others were known more for their criminal activities. Like the ʿayyarun, they had initiation ceremonies, now laced with sufi influence, and some wore uniforms which identified their group. Widely popular among the lower classes, the futuwwas acted to limit state authority and even threatened its stability by spearheading urban riots.

In 1180, one of the most energetic and broad-minded caliphs ascended the throne of the ʿAbbasids. This was the Caliph al-Nasir who was to do more than any other to rejuvenate ʿAbbasid rule. Though ultimately his reforms were too late, they still stand as a remarkable example of turning adversity into advantage. He set out to tirelessly correspond with all Muslim rulers urging them to close ranks and rally behind the caliphate. Offering his services as mediator between the numerous antagonistic princes, he successfully enhanced his stature, and with it, his influence. He made the most of his religious station by studying and becoming an authority in all four schools of Sunni jurisprudence. At the same time he demonstrated special respect for the Prophet's family by visiting Shiʿi shrines and spending generously on their maintenance. In an additional gesture toward Sunni-Shi'i peace, he appointed a Shi'i as his wazir. But certainly the most innovative policies were reserved for the *futuwwas*. Rather than suppressing them, as his predecessors had tried, he met their leaders and even sought their assistance. Then, to the amazement of many of his aides, he announced that he would himself become a member of a *futuwwa* group. This act did much to curb the criminal tendencies of the *futuwwas*. Proud that the caliph was now one of their own, the *futuwwa* members came to identify more with the broader interests of the state. Al-Nasir worked on uniting the *futuwwas* and turning them away from crime and mysticism. And by the end of his life in 1225, the *futuwwas* had become one of the foundations of the resurgent 'Abbasid state. With the establishment of order, Baghdad witnessed a limited economic revival and new construction activity. The famous Mustansiriyya college, which still stands today, was completed at this time.

Not all of al-Nasir's schemes worked. To make sure that the Seljuk threat would not return, he formed a dangerous alliance with the ambitious Khwarizm Shahs of eastern Persia. In 1194, after the last Seljuk sultan was killed, the Khwarizm Shah demanded that al-Nasir recognize his authority in Iraq. After refusing to comply, a huge army moved in the direction of Baghdad and would surely have taken the city were it not for the intervention of nature. While crossing the mountains from Persia in 1217, a blizzard completely destroyed the army before it had entered Iraq. The *futuwwa*-based state also proved too limited to project the caliph's authority outside the city. With the countryside slipping out of control once again, the old story of declining revenues and food shortages affected the delicately balanced urban peace. Sectarianism and inter-quarter conflicts intertwined with floods and outbreaks of plague. In 1255 and 1256, even the caliph's troops participated in pillaging. As Baghdad teetered on the brink of chaos, another far more dangerous storm was forming in the steppes of Central Asia. Fate, which had smiled on Baghdad in 1217, was about to abandon the city of the caliphs to one of its greatest catastrophes at the hands of the approaching Mongols.

The Arab conquest of Iraq in 636 introduced a new foundation for social harmony through the Arabic language and the Islamic religion that was gradually adopted by the majority of the inhabitants. While old religious and linguistic communities persisted, and new divisions such as the Sunni-Shi'i schism developed, a degree of harmony under the notion of autonomous communities was established. By the late Umayyad period, the threat of a destructive social conflict had emerged with the problem of tribal competition and the discrimination against the Mawali. In 750, the 'Abbasid revolution introduced a new vision for social harmony founded on a powerful absolutist central government in Iraq, the equality of all Muslims, and a greater commitment to internal development. The new cosmopolitan cities of Iraq, especially Baghdad, became the centers of wealth and the phenomenal flowering of culture. This balance began to unravel by the tenth century when regional separation, class conflict, the introduction of new peoples from Central Asia, and overall economic decline gave way to rising sectarian violence. During the Buwayhid and Seljuk periods, some attempts were made to address these problems, but no different vision appeared to set the country on a new course and central authority grew weaker. The country's internal weakness left it vulnerable to repeated invasions which would destroy much of the wealth and deepen communal divisions.

chapter two

IRAQ UNDER MONGOL AND TURKOMAN RULE, 1258–1534

In retrospect, it seems the height of folly that the ʿAbbasid rulers of Iraq had even considered resisting the Mongol conquest. By the end of the thirteenth century, the great force unleashed from the steppes of Central Asia had swept across the entire Asian continent laying waste to multitudes of empires and kingdoms, including those in China, Persia, Russia and east Europe. In 1206, Chingiz Khan, the founder of what was to become the largest land empire in history, successfully unified the main nomadic Turkic and Mongol tribes east of the Altai Mountains under his command.[1] To maintain this unity he set out on a life-long career of conquest that was continued by his descendants after his death in 1227. In addition to their individual ruggedness and valor, collective solidarity, and rapid mobility, Mongol success was also a result of widescale brutality and terror. The destruction and massacres that accompanied their advance spread fear and hastened the submission of new territories. Cities were given the choice between surrender and payment of tribute or a general massacre of the male population with the women and children carried off into slavery. Chingiz Khan's first foray into Muslim territory, for example, was highlighted by a terrible massacre at Merv, one of the major cities of eastern Persia. Contemporary sources say that even dogs and cats were slaughtered after the extermination of the entire population. Similar fates befell the cities of Balkh, Herat and Nishapur which, in Mongol minds, did not represent anything of value to their nomadic, pastoral lifestyle. What made matters even worse was that the Mongols were shamanists who were not awed by the religious symbols of Islam. The Mongol conquest inaugurated a tumultuous period of tribal ascendency and recurring foreign invasions which sorely tested the relations between Iraq's many communities.

---

[1] The Turko-Mongol armies were sometimes called "Tatar" in reference to one of the main tribes under Chingiz Khan's confederation.

The fall of Baghdad

After a series of internal struggles culminating in 1251, Mongke, Chingiz Khan's grandson, assumed general command of Mongol forces. In 1253, he dispatched his brother, Hulago, at the head of a large army of around 70,000 men to conquer the Islamic lands of the Middle East. While still in Persia attending to the remaining Isma'ili strongholds, Hulago sent word to the 'Abbasid Caliph al-Musta'sim demanding his submission. Al-Musta'sim stood his ground threatening the Mongols with the wrath of the entire Muslim world should any harm befall him. This empty threat did not deter Hulago who entered Iraq in 1257 and by 11 January 1258 had completely besieged Baghdad. It became clear that the city could not hold out for long against the Mongols' superior Chinese artillery. The caliph, after repeatedly proposing negotiations to no effect, made a desperate eleventh-hour attempt to avoid disaster by approaching Hulago in person, accompanied by Baghdad's leading notables. On the 10th of February, the Commander of the Faithful, the 37th 'Abbasid caliph, the successor to the Prophet Muhammad, stood trembling before an unimpressed pagan khan begging him to spare the population in return for surrender. It was, however, too late. In one story it is related that the caliph was locked up with all his gold and left to starve to death. However his execution might have been, soon thereafter the Mongols entered the city. There are a number of descriptions, some based on eyewitness accounts, of the massacre and destruction that continued unabated for over a week. Ibn al-Athir's is among the best known:

> For several years I put off reporting this event. I found it terrifying and felt revulsion at recounting it and therefore hesitated again and again. Who would find it easy to describe the ruin of Islam and the Muslims? ... O would that my mother had never borne me, that I had died before and that I were forgotten! ... The report comprises the story of a ... tremendous disaster such as had never happened before and which struck all the world, though the Muslims above all. If anyone were to say that at no time since the creation of man by the great God had the world experienced

anything like it, he would be telling the truth. ... It may well be that the world from now until its end ... will not experience the like of it again.[2]

Along with the over 100,000 killed, much of the city's physical structure was damaged by fire and looting. Magnificent buildings, testament to an age of knowledge and cultural vitality, like the Mosque of the Caliphs and the Shi'i shrine at Kazim, were completely burned, while universities such as the Nizamiyya and Mustansiriyya were badly damaged, their libraries gutted. It is related that many a priceless book was tossed in the Tigris river. The most terrible damage, however, was that which befell the population itself. Those who survived the slaughter faced the prospect of rape and slavery. Here is how one described the scene:

> ... they swept through the city like hungry falcons attacking a flight of doves or like raging wolves attacking sheep, with loose rein and shameless faces, murdering and spreading fear. ... The massacre was so great that the blood of the slain flowed in a river like the Nile. ... With the broom of looting, they swept out the treasures from the harems of Baghdad ... And a lament reached the ears ... from roofs and gates. ... those hidden behind the veils of the great harem ... were dragged like the hair of idols through the streets and alleys; each of them becoming a plaything in the hands of a Tatar monster, and the brightness of the day became darkened for these mothers of virtue.[3]

It is safe to say that though many Christians were spared thanks to Hulago's Christian wife, all Baghdadis suffered badly. Subsequent Sunni writers have claimed, with little justification, that the Shi'i minister, ibn al-'Alqami, treacherously aided the Mongol cause. Whatever action certain Shi'i notables took made little difference in terms of the final outcome. Hulago had both Sunni and Shi'i advisers, and the

---

[2] Quoted in Bertold Spuler, *History of the Mongols, Based on Eastern and Western Accounts of the Thirteenth and Fourteenth Centuries*, New York, 1972, pp. 29–30.

[3] Quoted in *ibid.*, pp. 120–1.

presence of prominent Shi'is like Nasir al-Din Tusi did not prevent the Mongols from desecrating Shi'i shrines or killing such important Shi'i notables as ibn Tawus. In any case, the city's leading Sunni figures soon gave Hulago's authority religious sanction by declaring that a just non-Muslim ruler was preferable to an unjust Muslim. This may have helped to limit the destruction though it shattered the already weakened image of Islamic political authority. Other massacres took place throughout the country notably at Wasit and Mosul in 1262. Most cities, however, quickly submitted and were generally spared. An interesting exception were the Kurds who proved to be among the Mongols' most consistent foes in northen Iraq. In Irbil, for example, even after the submission of the governor, the Kurdish garrison refused to lay down its arms and continued to resist for several years seeking aid from the sultan of Egypt. After the fall of Irbil and the surrounding countryside, Mongol vengeance led to the depopulation of large areas in Shahrazur whose Kurdish inhabitants fled en masse to Syria and Egypt. The advance of Hulago's armies continued westward until they were halted in 1260 at 'Ayn Jalut in Palestine by an Egyptian force.

In many ways, the fall of Baghdad represented a major watershed for the Islamic World and Iraq in particular. While the physical and human damage was great, the psychological effects were far more profound and lasting. Baghdad was not merely one of the greatest cities of the Islamic World but the seat of the caliphate, its most important religio-political institution, a symbol of its unity and protector of the orthodoxy of its faith. The death of al-Musta'sim represented the effective end of this essential symbol even though a shadow caliphate continued for some time in Cairo and Istanbul. Moreover, the caliph's executioners were pagans thus dealing a blow to Muslim pride and religious triumphalism. This gave further impetus to an already developing xenophobic tendency that looked upon the outside world and its culture as hostile and threatening. To this very day Iraqis consider the name of Hulago synonymous with an overpowering calamity and the events of 1258 continue to touch an emotional nerve since they are regarded among the causes of the region's current problems. Little wonder, then, that during the second Gulf War Iraqi propaganda could hardly resist drawing on the imagery of the terrible Mongol invasion. Another important development was the deepening separation of Iraq from Egypt and Syria. Iraq's strong ties with Persia and its separation from the eastern Mediterranean countries were not new, but the continuing Mongol hostility to the rulers of Egypt and Syria, and the frequent wars between them, broadened the divide. Lastly, Mongol rule effectively undermined the dominant position of the officially sanctioned orthodox or shari'a-minded Sunni Islam, opening the way for the spread of Shi'ism and various brands of popular Islamic tendencies.

The Il-Khanate

For the next three centuries Iraqi history forms a confused picture of weak central authority, division, a rapid succession of dynasties, and numerous invasions. The vast Mongol Empire was divided into autonomous territories that gradually gained complete independence. The territory ruled by Hulago and his descendants, known as the Il-Khanate, included Persia, Azerbaijan and Iraq. Tabriz eventually became the capital with Baghdad reduced to a provincial center. Northern Iraq was governed from Mosul. Every-day administrative tasks were placed in the hands of a governor (usually, but not always, of Persian origin), but final authority lay with the Mongol military commanders stationed at the important cities. Under the governorship of 'Ata Malik al-Juwayni, who administered Baghdad for over two decades after the invasion, the city showed signs of limited recovery. Some of the buildings were repaired, a number of scholars returned, trade picked up, and a tolerable taxation system implemented. Nevertheless, the overall picture was one of decline which continued well into the sixteenth century. The ruling group, now composed of nomads, were eager to transform large areas of agricultural land to pastures and to milk the peasants for all they were worth regardless of long-term damage. Taxes increased dramatically, particularly in the countryside. In addition to raising the old land and poll taxes the

Il-Khans instituted a number of commercial and extraordinary taxes that were usually collected in advance several times a year. This tax burden was not shared equally. In some areas the peasants paid as much as 66 per cent of their harvest, usually in kind, while the urban areas suffered less.

The people of Iraq had to also contend with increasing feudal-like practices and chronic instability that bound the peasants to the land, encouraged political fragmentation, and discouraged trade and long-term investment. Most serious of all was the deterioration of the irrigation system of canals leading to a rapid reduction in the size of cultivated land. Such economic deterioration, when accompanied with ruthless exploitation and periodic massacre of peasants, was bound to affect the demographic picture. Although the decline of the population started much earlier than the Mongol invasion, the general decline and instability that followed accelerated this process. In addition to the blood-letting and adverse conditions in agriculture already mentioned, malnourishment, epidemics and flight all contributed to the complete depopulation of large areas. In one estimate, the province of Diyala in central Iraq, including Baghdad, declined from about 400,000 in 1100 to only 60,000 after the Mongol invasion. Lamenting this state, Juwayni, who was patronized by the early Il-Khans, wrote:

> ... every town and every village has been several times subjected to pillage and massacre and has suffered this confusion for years, so that even though there be generation and increase until the Resurrection the population will not attain a tenth part of what it was before.[4]

Baghdad, which still struggled to retain part of its economic and cultural luster, declined in size and importance behind Tabriz, the new Il-Khanid capital and center of international trade in Azerbaijan.

---

[4] Quoted in David Morgan, *Medieval Persia, 1040–1797*, London, 1988, p. 79.

Baghdad and Basra were particularly hurt by the shift in trade routes further east. Prior to Mongol rule, the lucrative trade with India went through the Persian Gulf and Basra to Baghdad and the Mediterranean. During the Il-Khanate and its successors, this route was gradually replaced with the Hormuz-Tabriz axis through Persia. In addition, the Il-Khans' continuous wars with the Sultanate of Egypt and Syria interrupted the long-established commercial ties of Iraq with the Mediterranean. There is no doubt that Iraq's incorporation into the huge Mongol realm fostered greater trade links with Persia and Central Asia. This, however, did not make up for the decline of the India and Mediterranean trade. To make matters worse, corruption and mismanagement left the state completely bankrupt by 1294. In response, paper currency notes called the *ch'ao*, an idea imported from China, were introduced to replace the increasingly scarce metal coins. The new unfamiliar notes were completely rejected by the public. Within a short time the whole scheme had to be abandoned but not before causing confusion and bringing all trade to a standstill in Baghdad. The general economic decline is best summed up by the state revenue figures as quoted by al-Qazwini. Notwithstanding the higher taxes, state revenues fell from about 30 million dinars during the reign of the Caliph al-Nasir (1180–1225), to only 3 million in 1336.

Mongol rule had an important impact on Iraq's sectarian relations. For over 40 years most of the Il-Khans were shamanists and it appears that Nestorian Christians, in particular, benefited from the overthrow of Muslim authority. The jizya tax was removed, new churches were built, some Christians acted as ambassadors of the Il-Khans to the Europeans, and they were no longer barred from high offices with authority over Muslims. In Irbil, for example, a Christian, Taj al-Din Mukhtas, was appointed governor and the community witnessed a period of growth and prosperity. Christian highlanders were recruited to form auxiliary forces to help to control the mountainous areas of the Jazira region. By the end of the century, as the Il-Khans gradually adopted Islam, these early gains were often violently rolled back. In

1295, three churches were destroyed by the Mongols and in 1310 mob attacks ultimately led to the elimination of the entire Christian community there. Similar developments took place in Baghdad with early signs of prosperity followed by mob attacks and flight. The Jews also benefited from the removal of the jizya tax and in 1283 a Jewish physician from Mosul, known as Sa'd al-Dawla, was appointed finance minister. Taking advantage of the Il-Khan's patronage Sa'd al-Dawla had his two brothers appointed governors of Baghdad and Mosul respectively and other relatives were placed in important posts throughout Iraq. Though he served the Il-Khans competently, balancing the books and increasing tax returns, his arrogance earned him enemies who, after the death of his patron in 1291, had him executed. The demise of Sa'd al-Dawla triggered widespread attacks against Jews in Baghdad, Mosul and other cities. The conversion of the Il-Khan Ghazan to Islam in 1295 marked a particularly bad time for non-Muslims. He reinstated the jizya, ordered the destruction of many churches and temples, established separate dress codes for Jews and Christians, and tended to turn a blind eye toward mob violence against them. Many converted to Islam, but Christians usually fled to the countryside causing their numbers in urban areas to remain low up to the late nineteenth century. The Jews, more accustomed to periodic waves of persecution, weathered the storm and remained an important part of the urban population in most Iraqi cities up to the mid-twentieth century.

The Shi'is also benefited from the blow to Sunni Islam. Shi'i influence in the courts of the Il-Khans remained substantial, and Hilla, the center of Shi'i scholarship at this time, was spared the devastation that rained on other cities during the Mongol advance. Ghazan's conversion was to Sunni Islam but he still had a high regard for Shi'ism, as demonstrated by his recurrent visits to the shrines at Najaf and Karbala. His successor, Khudabanda, actually converted to Shi'ism in 1309 making it the official religion of the Il-Khanate until his death in 1316. In general, the relations between Sunnis and Shi'is, which had been tense and often violent during the preceding centuries, greatly improved under the Il-Khans. The threat that Islam as a whole received at the hands of the early Mongols pushed the two sides closer together. This was reflected among scholars by a decline in the number of polemical works directed at one another, the use of a more respectful tone when they did debate, and, more importantly, extensive borrowing of each other's ideas. Among Sunnis the virtuous roles of 'Ali and the family of the Prophet were highlighted to the point where some, while not accepting the notion of divine inspiration, agreed that 'Ali was superior to the first three caliphs. Shi'i influences were particularly strong among Sunni mystics (sufis) who emphasized 'Ali's esoteric knowledge and even adopted some Shi'i practices. For Shi'is, the most important impact was the progressive integration of Islamic mysticism, which had been dominated by Sunni scholarship, into Shi'i beliefs.

The conversion of the Mongols to Islam marks a remarkable, though not completely surprising, turn of events. As with their kinsmen in China, the Mongol Il-Khans ended up adopting the culture and mannerisms of the sophisticated societies they ruled. This was a gradual process of assimilation in which Ghazan's conversion in 1295 was an important point. Initially, they were prone to favor mystical sufi Islam over the shari'a-minded schools. Ghazan's conversion was part of an effort at creating a more centralized state in which the alienation between rulers and ruled would be ameliorated, and improved productivity could yield higher tax returns. Under the direction of his prime minister, Rashid al-Din, a broad set of reforms were introduced, chief of which was the regulation of taxation. Other reforms included the digging of canals, improved security for traveling merchants, the standardization of weights and measures, the reopening of the mints at Wasit, Hilla and Basra, a more cohesive system of justice based on the Islamic shari'a, and the centralization and regulation of the *iqta'* grants. These reforms, though impressive on paper, enjoyed only limited success because of the general inability of the state to enforce them. In fact, the death of Ghazan in 1304, ushered in a period of factional struggles spearheaded by the two main competing households of the Chopanids and the Jalayirids. The Il-Khan Abu Sa'id, who assumed effective control in 1327, was able to bring back some semblance of central control, but his death without heirs in 1335 marked an intensification of factional conflicts and the eventual fragmentation of the empire. Lastly, it should be mentioned that the Il-Khans adopted Persian culture and became enthusiastic patrons of the arts. During their time, Chinese and Central Asian taste and decorative vocabulary came into the Middle East transforming the existing architectural traditions and revitalizing the arts of book illustration. A distinctly Central Asian design is evident in many of the shrines of the period, such as the domes of Dhu al-Kafal (built in 1316) and the Suhrawardi shrine (1334), both of which resemble the Buddhist pagoda structures found in and around Mongolia.

Jalayirid and Turkoman rule

As the Il-Khanate slowly fell apart and various claimants rapidly succeeded one another, Iraq came under the control of Hasan Buzurg and his Jalayirid household. The Jalayirids were a prominent Mongol family who had accompanied Hulago to Baghdad. Under the leadership of Hasan Buzurg's son, Shaykh Uways (r. 1356–74), the Jalayirids formed an independent state which expanded to include most of Azerbaijan. The Jalayirids were unable to reverse the overall decline of Iraq but they are remembered for a number of important architectural projects such as the mosque and *khan* of Marjan in Baghdad. Among the administrative practices that had an adverse effect at the time was the selling of offices, including those of important governorships. Several uprisings and invasions interrupted their rule. Soon after the death of Shaykh Uways, a bloody struggle erupted between the Sultan Jalal al-Din and his two brothers, the governors of Baghdad and Basra. Not long after this the country had to contend with two invasions by Timur Lang, the great conqueror from Samarkand. Timur's conquests were, in some cases, more destructive than those of the Mongols. In

1393, he spared the population of Baghdad because most of the notables welcomed him in the hope that he would bring relief from the abuses of Jalayirid rule. In 1401, however, he was forced to reconquer the city and this time a general massacre followed. Timur's second conquest was far more devastating than even that of Hulago a century and a half earlier. In addition to the physical destruction and the lives lost, a large number of skilled workers and scholars – the basic foundation of economic and cultural production – were forcibly transported to Samarkand. This time the city failed to recover even a portion of its past stature. While greatly diminished from its heyday under the 'Abbasids, Baghdad continued to represent an important economic, political and cultural center throughout the period of the Il-Khans and the Jalayirids. After this last blow, however, it sunk to the position of a secondary provincial town with little to offer except memories of past glories.

Timur conquered a huge area from Delhi to Damascus but was unable to consolidate this territory into a lasting empire, which duly fell apart after his death in 1405. The Jalayirid ruler, who escaped before Timur's advancing army, returned to Baghdad in 1405 and attempted some repairs. But at this point, weakened by the Timurid onslaught, the Jalayirids did not last much longer. In 1410, a Turkoman federation known as the Qara Qoyunlu ("Black Sheep") seized most of Iraq. The Qara Qoyunlu were a nomadic people whose pastures extended from Mosul (which fell under their control intermittently) to the region of Van to the north. Despite previous hostilities, they formed a tenuous alliance with the last Jalayirid ruler to oppose the Timurid invasions. In the tumultuous climate of the time, this alliance soon broke down and the last Jalayirid leaders were pursued to the south where they continued to exercise authority over Hilla, Wasit and Basra until 1432. Among their strongest allies in northern Iraq were the Kurds, especially those of the Bidlis clan, who figured prominently in the administration and military. During Qara Qoyunlu rule, Iraq sunk to new levels of misery and poverty. Regional rivalries, particularly between Baghdad and Mosul, intensified, as did the level of decentralization in general. The founder of the dynasty and conqueror of Iraq, Qara Yusuf, was noted for his cruelty, which he applied regardless of the victim's social or religious standing. In 1417, in a fit of anger, he ordered that the qadi of Baghdad, the 70-year-old Taj al-Din Ahmad, have his nose cut off for his insolent behavior. According to one contemporary: "The sons of Kara Yusuf altogether are the wildest people God has created, in their days the lands of Iraq and Persia and the town of Baghdad have been ruined."[5] This level of misrule accelerated the de-urbanization of Iraq, especially with respect to Baghdad and Basra.

The Qara Qoyunlu period witnessed a rise, albeit in a confused manner, of various Shi'i tendencies among broad sections of the population. This Shi'i ferment also affected sections of the ruling group. Jahan Shah (r. 1439–67), whose reign marked the apogee of Qara Qoyunlu power, showed some favor to Shi'ism issuing coins with both Shi'i and Sunni inscriptions. His brother, the governor of Baghdad, is said to have converted to Twelver Shi'ism in 1444. Shi'ism, however, remained, as it had in the past, strongly imbued with an ideology of popular protest. When the Qara Qoyunlu were evicted from Iraq between 1467 and 1469, their successors adopted a staunch Sunni outlook. The new rulers of Iraq were yet another Turkoman tribal federation from Eastern Anatolia known as the Aq Qoyunlu ("White Sheep"). Their primary pasture grounds were centered between Diyar Bakr and Amid, just west of Qara Qoyunlu territory. The two tribes had, in fact, been rivals for many generations. In Diyar Bakr, the Aq Qoyunlu took revenge on the Kurdish allies of their rivals by exterminating their leading families. Under Uzun Hasan they conquered, in addition to Iraq, most of Azerbaijan and Persia. The Aq Qoyunlu proved to be the last of the great nomadic dynasties to exert such broad

---

[5] Quoted in E. Ashtor, *A Social and Economic History of the Near East in the Middle Ages*, Berkeley, 1976, p. 268.

control over Iraq. Within the next 50 years, the region would witness the rise of stable empires capable of using new military methods to enforce a high degree of order. The first sign of this change came in 1473 when Uzun Hasan's nomadic cavalry were soundly defeated by the artillery of the rising Ottoman state. Despite this defeat, the Aq Qoyunlu continued to govern Iraq up to 1508. Their rule brought a degree of order to Baghdad and toward the end they instituted a number of reforms designed to reduce the power of the nomadic chiefs in favor of greater central control. Chief among these reforms was the full implementation of the shari'a at the expense of tribal customary law. This was bound to stir up resistance within both the ruling group and the lower classes hastening the fall of Turkoman rule.

Turkoman dominance had important long-term consequences for the economic and social development of Iraq. Feudal divisions reached their highest point during this period where the old *iqta'* estates became a hereditary grant. In the past, the reigning sultan could revoke and reassign a land grant. Under the new conditions of weak central authority, the landholder won the right to administer his estate almost free from any state interference. In periods of relative stability this might have resulted in greater investment in the productive forces of the land. In the conditions of fifteenth-century Iraq, however, such authority only led to increasing disintegration, savage exploitation of the peasantry and the further decline of agricultural productivity. Trade also continued to suffer. Under the Jalayirids the ordinary commercial tax amounted to 2.5 per cent. During the Turkoman period it reached 10 per cent, despite an overall decline in Iraq's share of the East–West transit trade. The weak central government and the decline in agriculture and trade encouraged the development of the pastoral sector and, concomitantly, a rise in the power of nomadic and semi-settled tribes. These tribes did not only represent the invading Mongols and Turkomans, but, more importantly, the indigenous Arab and Kurdish peoples. Under the dual pressure of a rapacious central government and roaming armies of pillagers, peasants had to place themselves under the protection of large tribal federations such as the Khafaja and Muntafiq of the middle and lower Euphrates, the Banu Lam and Rabi'a along the Tigris, and, in the north, the Kurdish tribes of Bilbas, Jaf and Harki. Soon the tribes dominated the countryside and most of the towns, leaving their stamp firmly fixed upon the nature of Iraqi society up to the present. Well into the nineteenth century about three-quarters of the people of Iraq still had strong rural tribal affiliations.

The instability and low productivity of the time brought famine and disease in their wake. In 1342/3, a famine affected the entire region and was followed by several others throughout the fourteenth and fifteenth centuries. The bubonic plague, known as the Black Death in Europe, struck Iraq in the summer of 1347 and was still raging in 1349. Precise information on its demographic impact is lacking, but it is known to have carried off more than one-quarter of the population of Europe and there is no reason to believe it was less severe in Iraq. Subsequent epidemics were recorded for 1394, 1416, 1425, 1431, 1436, 1438 and 1470. The combination of poor security and declining economic fortunes led to the complete abandonment of several cities. Basra, Baghdad's primary outlet to the sea and one of the most important ports of the Medieval world, was in the process of being abandoned when ibn Batuta, the great Moroccan traveler, visited in the mid-fourteenth century. Threats from the desert tribes, the silting up of canals, and the expansion of the marshes pushed its inhabitants to move closer to the Shatt al-'Arab river, where modern Basra now stands. Wasit, the capital of the Umayyad province and a center of minting, was attacked by Shi'i rebels in 1438, 1440 and 1442. In 1454, after yet another sacking, the population dispersed to other towns. Even Hilla, the important center of Shi'i scholarship, was not spared. Ironically, it was Shi'i tribes who, in 1453, sacked and burned it to the ground.

The Musha'sha' challenge

In the face of such disasters indigenous uprisings were bound to develop. True to their time, all such movements expressed themselves through religious ideas, usually some form of messianic Shi'ism. By far the most powerful of these protest movements was the so-called Musha'sha' rebellion of the mid-fifteenth century. The founder of this movement was Muhammad ibn Falah, a descendent of the Prophet and a disciple of one of the leading Shi'i scholars of fifteenth-century Hilla. Ibn Falah was strongly influenced by mysticism and messianic notions, both of which had been spreading throughout the post-Mongol Middle East. In 1436, having been expelled from Hilla for his unorthodox views, he and his small number of mystic followers found refuge among the Arab tribes of the marshes around Wasit. There he convinced the leaders of several tribes, particularly the Banu Sulama and Tayyi', to unite under his authority. Initially, he won over their loyalty by claiming esoteric knowledge and the mystical ability to perform supernatural acts, both of which earned him the title of *al-Musha'sha'*, meaning the "Radiant". With time, he came to declare that he was the Mahdi, the one who will lead Muslims to victory over injustice prior to the Day of Judgement. His son, Mawla 'Ali, took these ideas a step further by claiming to be the incarnation of the spirit of 'Ali, the first Imam of Shi'ism. It is interesting to note that this movement had much in common with the Zanj and Qarmatians of the ninth and tenth centuries. In addition to its Shi'i overtones it also emphasized the plight of the poor and condemned the tyranny and hypocrisy of the rich landowners. Like its predecessors, the Musha'sha' movement was based in the marshes of southern Iraq, a large, inaccessible region where rebels can easily find refuge. These marshes continued to act as a refuge for various opposition groups, until Saddam Husayn's regime drained the swamps ending a way of life that had continued unchanged since the ancient Sumerians.

While such notions might have won over some, it was ibn Falah's and his son's ability to organize successful raids which cemented his leadership. As his raids proved lucrative, more recruits joined the growing movement. Initially he attacked the landlords around Wasit, but after suffering a defeat there he turned south and took Huwayza which became his primary base. As the Qara Qoyunlu weakened, the Musha'sha' launched raids on Wasit (which he ruled intermittently), Basra, and even around Baghdad. Najaf was sacked and the shrine of 'Ali was looted. In 1453, Hilla was destroyed and its countryside continued under the control of ibn Falah until shortly after his death in 1466. Travel was so insecure that even the pilgrim caravans to Mecca were not spared. Ibn Falah's successor, Sultan Muhammad, tried to consolidate the fledgling state through more permanent control of territory, the appointment of governors and the regular collection of taxes. His authority spread throughout southern Iraq all the way to the environs of Baghdad. To enhance his image in the cities, he attempted to attract respected Shi'i scholars to his court in Huwayza. In turn, the presence of such scholars as Shams al-Din Astarabadi helped to moderate Musha'sha'i views, drawing it closer to mainstream Twelver Shi'ism. The independence of the Musha'sha' state came to an end through its gradual incorporation into the Persian Safavid Empire during the early sixteenth century. This was the only indigenous movement to challenge the power of the Turkoman dynasties but, even in its heyday, it remained limited to the countryside, unable to develop a strong backing in any of the important urban areas.

Urban organizations

During the Mongol and Turkoman periods, the urban centers of Iraq developed their own means of responding to the problems of tyranny and insecurity. There, exploitation was not as severe as in the countryside and radicalism not as popular. The preference, for most people, was to protect their community through various methods of mutual aid. Since the usual state-supported services, like the police and the judiciary, grew progressively weaker community groups attempted to fill the vacuum. Different types of social organizations, which had appeared much earlier, took on new roles and moved to the forefront.

Certainly the most prominent were the associations of *sharifs*. The sharifs, or *sayyids*, were those who had a recognized claim to being descendants of the Prophet and whose lineage guaranteed them a high social standing. In addition to their honorable lineage, the sharifs were normally men of learning and wealth who enjoyed broad privileges including exemption from most taxes. Their activities on behalf of the poor, such as distributing free meals during the month of Ramadhan or coming to the aid of families in need with gifts and favors, gained them a solid popular backing. The sharifs came to form an important bloc, organized within associations, with individual members exercising influence in their neighborhoods. The head of these associations was called the *Naqib al-Ashraf*. The associations acted as guardians of the religious shrines and played a role in the administration of neighborhoods, resolving disputes, managing relief work to the poor, and acting as representatives of the people when called upon. During the Mongol conquest, for example, the Shi'i sharif, Majd al-Din Muhammad ibn Tawus, acted as Hilla's chief representative and negotiated its peaceable surrender. The same occurred a century and a half later at Mosul during Timur Lang's siege of the city. Its *Naqib al-Ashraf*, Nasir al-Din 'Ubaydullah al-A'raji, again successfully negotiated an amicable surrender.

The position of *Naqib al-Ashraf* was, in theory, filled through an appointment by the ruler after consulting with the leading sharifs. In practice, this only occurred when the ruler was firmly in control. To bring some stability to these associations the *Naqib al-Ashraf* gradually came to be dominated by only one or two families. In Mosul, the al-A'raj family normally held the post while the Rifa'i family were the recognized leaders at Basra. Since Baghdad was the seat of government, the association had a more difficult time establishing its autonomy and the sharifs remained without a recognized leader for long periods at a time. Nevertheless, the Gaylani family continued to wield substantial authority particularly within the large quarter of Bab al-Shaykh. During the Ottoman period they finally gained official recognition as the hereditary holders of the *Naqib al-Ashraf* office in Baghdad. The associations of sharifs were naturally influenced by the forces affecting the different cities. In Baghdad and Basra, for example, sufism played an important role in determining the leadership. Thus, in Baghdad, the Gaylanis were also the leaders of the mystical Qadiriyya order, while at Basra the Rifa'is were the leaders of the Rifa'iyya order. At Najaf, a seat of Shi'i learning, the sharifs who controlled the associations came from the Shi'i scholars, while those at Karabala' usually belonged to one of the two tribal federations which dominated the town.

Another important social organization which played a prominent role during this time were the sufi orders or brotherhoods. During the post-Mongol period, orthodox, or shari'a-minded Islam received a paralyzing blow both to its leading figures (the execution of the caliph and a number of leading shari'a scholars), and to its main patron, the Islamic state. To an extent, the defeat of the caliphate was also a defeat for the exponents of its ideological base. This is not to say that shari'a scholars were completely discredited after the Mongol conquest, but certainly the new conditions in which they functioned limited their influence. To fill the void many people sought out the assistance of sufi mystics. The sufis had always retained the reputation of remaining close to the popular classes with their public displays of going into trances and performing supernatural feats, their asceticism and self-denial, and their dedication to charitable activities. Their focus on allegorical tales and a generally more flexible approach to religious interpretation appealed more to the common people than the legalistic arguments of the shari'a scholars. The premise of esoteric knowledge, central to sufi thinking, allowed for the development of a strong, intimate master–disciple relationship characterized by an unquestioning obedience and even veneration of the sufi master. In addition to the disciples, a large number of people regularly attended the mystics' liturgical sessions (usually held on Thursdays), in special lodges known as *zawiyas*, seeking emotional fulfillment and acceptance in an age of uncertainty and danger. As a result a powerful bond was established which cut across class and communal lines, acting as a unifying factor in society. At the center of these fraternities were the sufi shaykhs whose opinions were held in high esteem and were essential to the functioning of communities.

Iraq was the first place within the Islamic world where sufi orders developed. In addition to the previously mentioned Qadiriyya and Rifaʻiyya orders, there were a number of orders whose disregard for orthodox Islamic sensibilities offended many scholars. Among the most unorthodox were the Qalandariyya who had a large lodge in thirteenth-century Baghdad known as the Qaladarkhana. Its followers tended to openly disregard the shariʻa and were known to practice alchemy, fortune-telling and the preparation of magic potions. Another order, which was particularly popular among the Turkomans, was the Mawlawiyya, known for its practice of "whirling" to achieve a trance. Their sessions, sometimes accompanied by the beating of drums and music, attracted huge crowds but few dedicated followers. During the fifteenth-century, the Naqshabandiyya order, originating in Central Asia, gradually made inroads among the Kurds of Mosul and Shahrazur. Leaders of this order would later play important roles in the Kurdish nationalist movement of the twentieth century.

Sufi orders had a special relationship with the numerous guild associations. Prior to the Mongol invasion the economic activities of the various artisans, craftsmen and small shopowners, were, to an extent, regulated by the state. After the decline in the power of the central state, more of this regulatory burden had to be sustained by the urban classes themselves. The *asnaf*, as these guilds were known, developed slowly reaching their full maturity during the latter part of Ottoman rule in the eighteenth and nineteenth centuries when they would again submit to central government control. The early development of the *asnaf* was greatly influenced by the *futuwwa* organizations of the late ʻAbbasid period. Much of the vocabulary used for the different positions within the guilds, or ceremonies, like those of the induction of new members, resembled those of the *futuwwas*. In addition to regulating the various economic activities of the trades, including the collection of taxes for the authorities, they also functioned as social institutions fostering a strong sense of group identity.

The *asnaf* were normally organized in a hierarchical fashion with an elected *shaykh* at the helm assisted by a treasurer and secretary. As with the sufi orders, the leadership of the *asnaf* soon developed into a hereditary post monopolized by the prominent families. The shaykh oversaw the administrative and economic functioning of the guild and acted to resolve disputes between its members. He also represented the interests of his members in meetings with other guilds or the authorities, and in ceremonial functions like festivals and parades. Below the shaykh there were at least four other levels starting with the master of the trade and ending with the simple servant. A partial list of the *asnaf* of Baghdad included those of the butchers, cooks, millers, bakers, weavers, tailors, dyers, tanners, silver- and goldsmiths, sword-makers, brick-layers, eye physicians, sailors, paper-makers, book-binders, carpenters, brokers, night-watchmen, porters, blacksmiths and saddle-makers. Sufi orders often overlapped with the *asnaf* so that, at times, it was difficult to distinguish one from the other. Most of the *asnaf* would start their meetings with a couple of hours of sufi liturgy before settling down to deal with the practical issues confronting their trade. Sufi shaykhs were very often also the leaders of some of the *asnaf* and the hierarchies of both groups tended to overlap. Notwithstanding their religious character, many of the *asnaf* included non-Muslim members. The most normal feature, however, was for the reflection of religious divisions in the division of labor. The commerce in food items, for example, was controlled by Muslim merchants while the money-changers were mostly Jews. In addition, some of the trades were dominated by particular tribes from the surrounding countryside. During the late Ottoman period, most of the porters of Baghdad were affiliated to the Al Bu Mafraj tribe, the cooks usually came from the Banu 'Izz, the makers of reed mats were dominated by the Ja'ayfur and the butchers by the Mahdiyya.

Iraq under the Safavids

During the fifteenth century, the Shi'i and sufi ferment of the post-Mongol period came together through the rise of the Safavid movement in Azerbaijan. Originally, this movement, which would rule Iran and expand Shi'i influence in the area, was a sufi order, the Safawiyya, founded by Safi al-Din in the early fourteenth century. Over the course of the next two centuries it would develop political ambitions and a strong emphasis on the veneration of 'Ali and the twelve Imams. By the time the 7-year-old Isma'il inherited its leadership in 1494, the Aq Qoyunlu state was in disarray as rival claimants fought over the throne. Isma'il, at this time, was not merely considered a sufi shaykh demanding absolute obedience, but also a leader with divine attributes. This highly unorthodox movement had a core following of Turkoman tribesmen known as the *Qizilbash*, or "Redheads", due to the red caps they wore. Their fanatical devotion and fearless participation in battle, allowed Isma'il to defeat the last of the Aq Qoyunlu rulers and take Tabriz in 1501. There he was crowned shah and proclaimed Twelver Shi'ism the official religion of his empire. Iran, at this time, was predominantly Sunni and Shi'ism had to be imposed by force. Leading religious figures were obliged to curse the first three caliphs and proclaim the new faith in public or face brutal reprisals, including execution. This policy, which eventually converted Iranian society to Shi'ism, was in full swing when Isma'il sent his general, Lala Husayn Beg Shamlu, to conquer Baghdad in 1508. For the Safavids, Iraq was not only important for strategic reasons. The existence there of the major Shi'i shrines at Najaf, Karbala, Kazim, and Samarra, made its control an important source of prestige and legitimacy. The Safavid entry into Baghdad was accompanied by a massacre of many of the leading Sunni figures and the desecration of Sunni shrines like the Abu Hanifa Mosque. Christians were also singled out for persecution and within a short period they were completely wiped out of the city. This was followed with an advance on the south where Basra surrendered without a fight and the Musha'sha' state swore allegiance to the new Shi'i empire. Despite the importance of the Shi'i shrines Safavid control of Iraq remained tenuous.

There is little doubt that the Safavid empire was poised to dominate Iraq and the heartland of Islam were it not for the Ottoman Turks. The Ottoman Empire was the heir to the Seljuks. Having started as a small principality in central Anatolia in the late thirteenth century, they expanded steadily at the expense of the declining Byzantine Empire. Despite a major defeat at the hands of Timur Lang in 1401, they continued to expand, and in 1453 they scored one of Islam's greatest victories by taking Constantinople. The Ottomans were eager to portray themselves as the leaders of Sunni Islam, the heirs of the 'Abbasids, carrying the new religion into infidel Europe at a time when the other major Sunni state in Egypt was in decline. For them, Shi'i Islam was not merely a heresy, but a threat to their image as the unrivaled leaders of the Islamic world. When the Safavid state was established, a direct military confrontation was inevitable. Safavid influence had reached eastern Anatolia and in 1511 and 1512 major Shi''i revolts broke out against Ottoman rule. The Ottoman Sultan Selim "The Grim" responded with a brutal repression of the revolt followed by a massive invasion of Safavid territory. The two great empires representing the main competing branches of Islam met in 1514 at a site called Chaldiran in Azerbaijan. In some ways, the ensuing battle resembled the Ottomans' victory against the Aq Qoyunlu in 1473. With their superior numbers and weaponry, notably field artillery and hand guns, they secured a decisive victory against the Qizilbash and their young God-king.

Shah Isma'il escaped and the Safavid Empire survived to fight another day but the line dividing Ottoman Sunni influence from that of Persian Shi'ism was drawn. Sultan Selim occupied Tabriz for a while but eventually had to withdraw. Mosul, Shahrazur and Diyar Bakr fell under Ottoman control and, in the next two years, Syria and Egypt followed suit. In return for their support, Sultan Selim allowed the Kurds of Shahrazur to establish a number of autonomous principalities such as Baban, Suran and Bahdinan. The rest of Iraq remained under Safavid control even though its hold grew progressively weaker. Rather than ruling Iraq directly, the Safavids recognized the leaders of the Kurdish Mawsillu tribe as the governors of Baghdad. In 1526, a rival Mawsillu leader by the name of Dhu al-Faqar Nukhud Sultan, defeated the Safavid governor of Baghdad, Ibrahim Khan, and declared his allegiance to the Ottoman Empire. Apparently, Dhu al-Faqar was a popular ruler maintaining his hold on central Iraq for over two years before the Safavid Shah Tahmasp recaptured Baghdad in 1529. Shah Tahmasp brought Iraq under direct Safavid administration and it appeared that the country would soon be fully integrated into the empire. The Ottomans, however, were encouraged by the support which Dhu al-Faqar was given and, in 1533, Sultan Sulayman, known in the West as "the Magnificent", set out at the head of a large army to conquer Iraq. On 18 November 1534, he was presented with the keys of Baghdad by its leading Sunni notables and entered the city to the general acclaim of the population. The Ottoman sultan was eager to avoid destruction and unnecessary sectarian strife. He ordered his troops to camp outside the city walls and made a point of visiting both Sunni and Shi'i shrines promising peace and justice to all. Despite this show of good-will, Ottoman conflicts with Persian rulers in the following centuries continued to adversely affect Sunni-Shi'i relations.

Iraq's entry into the Ottoman orbit represented the end of a tumultuous period which witnessed an overall economic and demographic decline, increasing fragmentation, and the rise of tribal power throughout the country. This weakness was highlighted by repeated invasions from abroad which prevented the rise of an indigenous force capable of bringing some order. This sorry state contrasted sharply with the inhabitants' image of the prosperous past which continued to represent a source of pride for the small urban elite. Despite the threat of complete fragmentation, Baghdad continued to act as an administrative and cultural center with ties to the various parts of Iraq. The battle of Chaldiran and the subsequent campaign of Sultan Sulayman inaugurated a new epoch where Iraq found itself situated between the two main powers of the Middle East. Iraq was often the battlefield on which the two empires repeatedly collided. More importantly, the relatively peaceful relationship between Sunnis and Shi'is which had developed during the preceding period was threatened as the Ottoman–Safavid struggle increasingly took on a religious character.

chapter three

THE FIRST THREE CENTURIES OF OTTOMAN RULE, 1534–1831

The Ottoman conquest of Iraq seems to have been welcomed by broad sections of the urban population, especially the notables. Many Shi'is were undoubtedly concerned about the Sunni character of the new rulers, but this was not something to which they were unaccustomed and Sultan Sulayman's gestures and promises of tolerance went a long way toward allaying their fears. In addition, the Shi'is were no different from their Sunni, Jewish or Christian compatriots in longing for a more stable, secure rule. This, the Ottomans seemed well poised to provide. By the time of Iraq's incorporation into the empire, Ottoman rule extended from Hungary to Yemen, and from Algeria to Tabriz. It included the holiest cities of Islam and was already renowned for its efficient administration and tolerant legal tradition. It formed a vast trading area with generally low taxes and relatively secure roads. At the center of this empire stood the great metropolis of Istanbul, one of the most populous, economically productive and affluent cities of its time, exuding a confidence worthy of its role as an imperial capital. Claiming to be the heirs to High Islamic traditions of governance, the Ottomans habitually compared themselves to the 'Abbasid caliphs, a symbol which continued to fill Iraqi notables with a strong sense of pride. Aleppo, one of the empire's major cities at this time, was fast becoming an important trading partner of northern Iraq even before the conquest of Baghdad. Under the Ottomans, Iraq was gradually reoriented away from Persia and Central Asia toward Anatolia and the Mediterranean.

Imposing the new order

Notwithstanding this early optimism, three centuries of recurring invasions, internal anarchy and economic impoverishment could not be brought to an end so easily. After his entry into Baghdad, Sultan Sulayman was spared the need to move further south through news of the capitulation of Basra. Throughout Safavid rule, the port city had protected its autonomy under the government of Shaykh Mughamis of the powerful Muntafiq tribe. This autonomy would continue even after Sultan Sulayman received the city's symbolic keys from Rashid ibn

Mughamis, whom he duly appointed governor. Less than ten years later the southern tribes were in full revolt. Fearful of Ottoman attempts at extending their direct rule over the south through the construction of fortresses and more diligent collection of taxes, the Muntafiq and allied tribes, especially those of the old Musha'sha' confederacy, launched raids against government positions. In 1546, the governor of Baghdad, Ayas Pasha, defeated the Muntafiq and brought Basra under direct Ottoman rule. This was followed with a push down the east coast of Arabia where, in 1555, the region of al-Hasa was conquered. While Ottoman governors and tribal shaykhs often cooperated to further trade and security, the conditions for this cooperation had to be renegotiated periodically leading to repeated instances of conflict and instability. This pattern was evident throughout the country but particularly in the south.

The other threat to Ottoman control during this early period was, of course, the ever-present danger from Persia. Following his conquest of Baghdad, Sultan Sulayman launched an attack on Shahrazur which had fallen back into the Safavid orbit. In 1548, he invaded Safavid territory temporarily capturing Tabriz. After additional hostilities, the two empires signed the Treaty of Amasya in 1555, which guaranteed peace for several decades. This treaty is also notable for establishing the boundary in northern Iraq which is still roughly the same today. After the death of Shah Tahmasp in 1574, the Ottomans took advantage of the ensuing struggle in Persia to invade Azerbaijan once again. The newly crowned Safavid Shah 'Abbas, was forced to sign a humiliating treaty in 1589, ceding all of Kurdistan and most of Azerbaijan, including Tabriz, to the Ottomans. After securing his power, he resumed hostilities in 1603 winning back most of what he had ceded. While most of the major battles during this century were in Azerbaijan and parts of Shahrazur, central Iraq did not remain free of danger. Refugees, mostly soldiers fleeing the fighting, poured into Baghdad and other Iraqi cities causing violent outbreaks. Battles were fought near Baghdad in 1586 and 1604 while, in between, the Ottoman governor,

Jighalzada, launched several raids into southern Persia. In 1605, the Persians succeeded in partially blockading Baghdad and in 1616 they sacked the border town of Mandali.

At that time, Iraq was important to the Ottomans as a base from which the defense against the Safavids could be organized. Hence, much of the early construction focused on the strengthening of defensive walls and the building of fortresses and barracks for the reportedly 32,000 troops left behind by Sulayman. This, however, did not prevent other constructive activities. The tone was set by Sulayman himself during his stay when he ordered the building of a new dome and college for the Abu Hanifa shrine, and the rebuilding of the mosque and sufi lodge at the 'Abdul-Qadir al-Gaylani complex. He likewise ordered repairs to the Shi'i shrines at Najaf, Karbala and Kazim. At Karbala the Husayniyya canal was cleared of silt and fields which had lain waste were productive once again. At Basra, Ayas Pasha opened a new mint, repaired the old mosques, constructed a new one, and established a small fleet with a naval arsenal to guard against the raids of maritime Arab tribes and the encroaching power of the Portuguese. New security arrangements allowed the annual pilgrimage to Mecca to recommence and the caravan routes from Aleppo to Mosul, Baghdad and Basra to thrive.

Administrative arrangements

Ottoman control, like that of any other empire of its time, was uneven and followed various arrangements. A general rule of thumb was that direct rule tended to be stronger in the major urban areas growing weaker the further one moved away into the countryside. In the more remote areas the Ottomans found it easier to recognize the local tribal powers in return for peaceable conduct and some form of occasional payment of tribute. Within these tribal lands customary forms of revenue sharing and social justice were followed which often bore little resemblance to the Islamic norms of the central Ottoman state. Technically, the entire land of Iraq was divided into three or four provinces each governed by a *pasha* which, in turn, were divided into local *sanjaqs* governed by *sanjaq-beys*. Taxes, considerably lighter than the preceding period, were of three forms. Taxes on agricultural output were assessed either according to the size of the land or as a proportion of the yield. The urban areas faced a multitude of taxes levied on various activities including sales, import–export, small-scale industries, and the use of shops, baths, caravanserais and roads. Lastly, protected religious minorities, mainly Christians and Jews, paid the *jizya* poll tax. Other extraordinary taxes were often levied as occasions demanded. These taxes were collected in a number of ways either directly by the governors and imperial tax-collectors, or through a system of land assignments similar to the old *iqta'*. Ottoman land assignments varied in size and nature, but the most common was the small rural grant known as *timar*. The timar-holder would maintain order on his estate, collect the various taxes, keeping most of the revenue for his expenses. In return, he was expected to report to the imperial army when called upon, bringing along a specific number of fully-equipped cavalrymen. Like the *iqta'*, these land grants were not held as private property but were often re-assigned to different holders on a regular basis.

Early Ottoman administration saw Iraq divided into four provinces: Baghdad, Mosul, Shahrazur and Basra. As the primary base of organizing the defense against Persia, Baghdad was clearly the most important. While the other provinces were governed by lower ranked pashas, Baghdad's governor was a pasha of the first rank, with the title of wazir. His status was demonstrated during military campaigns with a banner featuring three horse tails.[1] This also allowed Baghdad to exercise some authority over the other provinces. Early on, the pasha of

---

[1] The *togh*, as it is known, was an old Turkish military banner harking back to the Ottomans' Central Asian origins. It featured a white flag with a number of horse tails fastened above it. A *sanjaq-bey* was permitted to raise one horse tail, a "regular" pasha, two horse tails, a pasha of the first rank, three horse tails, the sultan's wazir, five horse tails, and the sultan himself, nine horse tails.

Baghdad had the right to appoint and remove Kurdish princes in Shahrazur. Later, with constant Persian threats and the insubordination of Kurdish leaders, Shahrazur was incorporated within the province of Baghdad. The same was true of Basra, with Baghdad repeatedly being called upon to check tribal revolts, Persian threats, or the province's own secessionist tendencies. By the early eighteenth century, Basra was also placed under the direct administration of Baghdad. Even Mosul, despite its more secure position as an autonomous province, was not completely immune from the growing power of Baghdad. By the late eighteenth century, it had lost most of its territory to Baghdad and faced continuous intervention in its administrative affairs.

Northern Iraq, including Mosul, was the first part to fall under Ottoman administration. Unlike Baghdad or Basra, parts of its countryside were portioned out into *timars*. Other than Mosul city, it included Tikrit to the south and 'Amadiyya to the north. Its mainly Kurdish and Arab population were overwhelmingly Sunni with its previously important Shi'i population dwindling down with time. During the early part of Ottoman rule Mosul had strong administrative and economic links with Diyar Bakr to the west, but this was soon overshadowed by its growing relationship with Baghdad. To the east was the Kurdish province of Shahrazur with its main city of Kirkuk. By the end of the eighteenth century, this was replaced with the new city of Sulaymaniyya. Shahrazur was plagued with conflicts between the tribes who, nevertheless, usually supported the Ottomans against the Safavids. In return for this support the Ottomans recognized their autonomy while allowing the pasha a limited interventionist role before its full incorporation into the province of Baghdad. Basra's distant location and tribal hinterland also made it difficult to govern. An interesting feature of Ottoman rule at Basra during the sixteenth century was the development of a navy capable of challenging the Portuguese in the Persian Gulf. In 1507, the Portuguese under their famous commander, Alfonso de Albuquerque, managed to take the fortress of Hormuz at the entrance to the Persian Gulf. They sub-sequently established a string of trading posts including one at Basra. Even before Sulayman's conquest, an Ottoman fleet from Egypt had sailed near Basra in 1529 , but made no lasting impact. After the con-quest of Ayas Pasha, the Ottoman fleet raided Portuguese positions throughout the Gulf without managing to dislodge them. In 1559, they made a daring but ultimately unsuccessful attempt to capture Bahrain, and in 1581 they temporarily seized Muscat. Eventually, these cam-paigns were called off and only a small fleet was left under the com-mand of a *Qubtan Pasha* to protect the Shatt al-'Arab river.

During the sixteenth century, most of the governors were sent from Istanbul. In the following centuries, however, direct rule eased, open-ing the way for local leaders to enforce their claim over the adminis-tration. What made this task even easier was the tendency of each governor to establish his own local military forces. The pasha was assisted by a *kahya* who acted as his chief executive officer, particularly during the many military campaigns. This post grew in importance during the eighteenth century and was often used as a springboard to the governorship itself. Contingents of imperial troops were assigned to each of the important towns. These troops, known as the Janissaries, were the slave soldiers of the sultan, trained in the use of fire-arms and artillery. Their commander, the *Agha* of the Janissaries, received his appointment from Istanbul and, though technically subservient to the governor, was still considered an instrument of central control on the pasha's power. Originally an elite fully professional force, the Janissaries numbered only a few hundred in Iraq. During the seven-teenth century, their ranks were opened up to local participation increasing their numbers but diluting their discipline and martial spirit. They were also allowed to seek employment outside the barracks further weakening their allegiance to Istanbul and transforming them into local often unruly militias. In Baghdad and Basra their ranks over-lapped with those of artisan guilds, while at Mosul almost all armed men had some affiliation to the Janissaries. Despite its often chaotic and destructive role, Janissary insubordination at times represented the dissatisfaction of sectors of the urban population against government policies.

The other officials appointed directly from Istanbul were the *qadi*, or chief judge, and the *daftardar*, who was the director of finances and responsible for general bookkeeping. The latter also assumed control over an ex-governor's properties until all his debts to the central treasury were paid. The *qadi* cut a powerful figure throughout the Ottoman Empire. Independent of the governor, he presided over the Islamic *shari'a* court which ruled over a wide array of cases including crime, marriage, inheritance, personal wills, market pricing and taxation disputes. He also oversaw the actions of the governor himself making sure that they did not conflict with the *shari'a*. The Ottomans favored the Hanafi school of *shari'a* interpretation, but also recognized courts of the other three schools. In addition to the *shari'a*, the provinces had to also adhere to the various sultanic decrees, *farmans*, and customary law as long as they did not conflict with the *shari'a*. Normally, the *qadi* of Baghdad was considered superior in rank to those of Basra, Shahrazur and Mosul. Each *qadi* had one or two local assistants who, thanks to their familiarity with the town and its conditions, wielded extensive influence. The Islamic court was also assisted by the *mufti* who was consulted in cases requiring legal clarification. The governor of each province was further assisted by an advisory council known as the *diwan* made up of the *Agha* of the Janissaries, *daftardar*, *qadi*, *mufti* and a number of the leading men of the city.

The second Persian conquest

The Safavids remained on the defensive after the campaigns of Sulayman the Magnificent. The death of Shah Tahmasp in 1574 accentuated their predicament, ushering in a long period of internal strife. In 1588, however, the empire gained a new energetic leader in the person of Shah 'Abbas. After some initial losses during the first decade of his reign, he went on the offensive in 1603 and re-established the old territories of Safavid rule with the notable exception of Iraq. The early seventeenth century represented a critical time for the Ottomans. Internally, they suffered from provincial rebellions, a bankrupt treasury and weak central rule, while externally they were on the defensive in Europe with even Istanbul threatened by sea. As the shah campaigned in Azerbaijan, a steady stream of Persian pilgrims to the shrines at Najaf and Karbala, as well as numerous sympathizers from among the local Shi'i notables, kept him well informed of developments in Iraq. In 1605, rebellious Janissaries had practically ruled Baghdad, keeping out Ottoman reinforcements for several years. The action was repeated, with far greater consequences, in 1619 when one Bakr Subashi, a ruthless and ambitious Janissary officer, rose to become the city's most powerful man. His power, typical of the time, was based on a combination of loyal well-armed followers reinforced with ties of patronage, and a series of alliances with important families and guilds. He held the city in the grips of terror, overcoming an attempt by the Ottoman governor, Yusuf Pasha, and some of the notables to get rid of him. After brutally killing his enemies, including the governor and *mufti*, he faced an Ottoman army sent to re-establish government authority. During the siege that followed, Bakr Subashi sent the keys of Baghdad to Shah 'Abbas in return for assistance and his appointment as the new Safavid governor of Iraq. As the shah approached to claim the city in 1623, Bakr changed sides once again but this time he was unable to hold out and was eventually executed.

After taking Baghdad, Shah 'Abbas repeated what his great grandfather had done a century earlier by launching an attack against Sunnism. He ordered the destruction of the two prominent symbols of Sunni Islam, the Abu Hanifa and al-Gaylani shrines. This was accompanied by the execution of a number of prominent figures including the *qadi* of Baghdad. Still, the fact that Sayyid Darraj, the guardian of the shrine at Karbala, a respected Shi'i scholar, and an ally of the Safavids, courageously protected the lives of many Sunni notables, shows that intercommunal ties were not completely undermined. In any case, this anti-Sunni campaign soon eased up, and while Shi'i notables now occupied the previously Sunni-dominated government posts, a sense of guarded normalcy slowly returned. During their 15-year rule, the Safavids encouraged trade with Persia (particularly silk), and the Shi'i shrines received new endowments. Once again, however, their hold was tenuous. Mosul and Basra remained in Ottoman hands though the latter only nominally. In 1625, and again in 1629, Persian armies failed to take Basra thanks to the leadership of its governor, the unified resistance of its population, and the support of many of the surrounding Arab Shi'i tribes.

The return of Ottoman rule

Despite their difficulties in Europe, the Ottomans continued to work for the restoration of their rule over Baghdad. In 1625/6 and again in 1629/30, Ottoman troops besieged the city only to be thwarted by the stiff resistance of Safavid defenders. By 1632, however, Sultan Murad IV had succeeded in consolidating power and addressing many of the immediate dangers. In 1638, he set out at the head of a large army and, after a difficult siege of forty days, took Baghdad. The chivalry demonstrated by Sultan Sulayman during the Ottomans' first conquest was now a thing of the past with Sultan Murad ordering a general massacre of all Persians, including the prisoners. There is some reason to believe that he may not have had any choice in this matter. In one story, illustrating the hatred that had built up between the two rival empires, an Ottoman soldier refused to abide by the Sultan's initial promise of amnesty because he had lost his father, brother and uncle in previous wars with the Safavids. There are some reports that the massacre also included a number of Shi'i residents, but apparently these were quite limited.

During the following year the Ottomans entered into a series of negotiations with representatives of the Safavid shah aimed at establishing a lasting peace. This was finally achieved on 17 March 1639, with the signing of the Treaty of Zuhab (also known as the Treaty of Qasr-i

Shirin). Unlike its numerous predecessors,[2] this treaty went into greater details, specifying the border particularly in the northern part of the country. The treaty also guaranteed safe passage to pilgrims from Persia wishing to visit the Shi'i shrines in Iraq. For the Kurdish Jaf tribe, however, this treaty was disastrous since the border split its territory between the two empires. During the nineteenth and twentieth centuries, when the border was more thoroughly enforced, the Jaf tribe's struggle to maintain its unity came to form a cause of instability in the area. The other problem was that the Treaty of Zuhab ignored the question of the southern borders near Basra, particularly along the marshes and the Shatt al-'Arab river. Nevertheless, the treaty did ensure a peace which lasted into the next century.

Peace abroad had little effect on internal political stability. The period from 1638 to 1704 was one of numerous factional struggles particularly in Baghdad. The problem for the Ottomans was that Iraq was too distant to warrant a major investment in direct rule, but, at the same time, allowing governors too much local autonomy was considered risky in terms of maintaining even nominal control. The result was a disturbing pattern of shifting governors, not granting any the time to enact meaningful policies. During this period Baghdad had no less than 24 governors who were constantly harassed and threatened by local groups particularly the Janissaries. In 1646, for example, the Janissaries raised havoc when they suspected the governor, Ibrahim Pasha, of favoring the development of an alternative local militia. In 1655, the governor was chased through the streets like a common criminal and, eventually, had to flee as a result of another Janissary uprising. The problem was made all the more grave with the factional conflicts in Istanbul itself. About half of the governors of Baghdad fell victim to these struggles losing their lives in the process. Such an atmosphere, at times, caused governors to behave rashly such as

---

[2] Previous treaties which delineated the borders of Iraq were signed by the Ottoman and Safavid Empires in 1555, 1568, 1590 and 1613.

Husayn Pasha (r. 1644) who was nicknamed "the Insane", or Musa Pasha (r. 1648) whose oppressions drove many of the inhabitants out of the city. At other times it encouraged insubordination with several governors refusing to give up their post for fear that this would be followed with an execution. Political instability also made the recurring natural catastrophes of the time all the more difficult. In 1649 and 1693, floods destroyed parts of Baghdad, and in 1690, the plague struck wiping out much of the population. Despite these conditions, a number of governors did score some notable achievements. The walls were repaired, a number of canals near Baghdad (notably the Dujayl Canal) were cleared of silt deposits, and a number of religious buildings (such as the Abu Hanifa and al-Gaylani mosques) and caravanserais were rebuilt.

Local rule in Basra and the impact of the tribes

Despite the Ottoman conquest of Basra in 1546, various tribal confederacies continued to dominate southern Iraq. The long history of Shi'ism in the area reinforced their sense of independence from the Sunni Ottoman government, and the great swamps and marshes between Baghdad and Basra continued to act as an effective barrier to central control. During the seventeenth and eighteenth centuries a series of new migrations from north central Arabia added to the power of the tribes. Beginning as early as the late fifteenth century, large waves of Najdi tribes, probably driven by drought, moved into Iraq and Syria. Among the earliest were the 'Anayza and Zafir confederacies, followed later by the Shammar, Mutayr and the Banu Lam. Their entry unleashed numerous intertribal conflicts but also increased the number and power of the tribes as a whole. As proud of their independence as ever, they formed ever-larger confederacies and repeatedly challenged Ottoman authority. Among the most famous tribal leaders of this period was ibn 'Ilayan, shaykh of the Jawazir tribe, who attacked caravans and besieged Basra in 1549. His followers repeated the attempt to capture the port in 1566 and 1596. One campaign after another failed to score a decisive victory against the Jawazir and their allies leading to a decline in commerce and growing urban dissatisfaction with the governor's rule. Around 1625, the Ottoman governor of Basra, frustrated by his inability to rule, sold the governorship to an official by the name of Afrasiyab, and left the city to manage its own affairs. His one condition was for continued allegiance to the Ottoman sultan.

Not much is known of this interesting period, but it is clear that Afrasiyab's rule successfully developed an understanding between the governor, the urban notables (most importantly the merchants) and the surrounding tribes. While not free of conflict, particularly with some of the tribes, Afrasiyab was able to establish a relatively stable, autonomous, political dynasty which lasted until 1668. Under the governorship of his son 'Ali, and grandson, Husayn, Basra enjoyed prosperous trade, a rise in construction activity and a cultural renaissance of sorts. The city's security was enhanced with the building of a strong defensive wall which successfully withstood several Persian attacks. It was also during the Afrasiyab period that Basra established commercial relations with the English and Dutch trading companies and renewed its relations with the Portuguese.

This success increased the ambitions of the Afrasiyabs who sought to expand their territory down the Arabian coast to al-Hasa and north at the expense of Baghdad. The people of Basra who had supported the Afrasiyabs so steadfastly, turned against them when their ambitions threatened to upset the city's limited but amicable relationship with the Ottoman authorities in Baghdad. It would appear that while the influential merchant community applauded local autonomy, they still preferred the security of the sultan's realm to the risky prospect of full independence. In 1653, when Ottoman troops approached Basra, the governor, Husayn Pasha Afrasiyab, was unable to secure the support of the inhabitants and had to flee. The same attitude, however, was not true of the surrounding tribes who feared the extension of Ottoman authority and rallied to the Afrasiyab cause. The Afrasiyabs did manage to return as governors of Basra but, by 1668, fresh troops from

Baghdad finally ended the rule of this local dynasty. Tribal opposition to Ottoman control, however, continued to be fierce and, in 1694, Basra came directly under the rule of the Muntafiq tribe and its shaykh, Mani' ibn Mughamis. It was not until the Ottomans had gained a respite in Europe after the signing of the Treaty of Karlowitz in 1699, that they were able to mount an effective campaign which brought Basra under the direct control of Baghdad. The different attitudes taken by the urban inhabitants and the tribes concerning Ottoman control and the limits of local autonomy were generally uniform throughout Iraq. The notable exception being the Shi'i towns of Najaf and Karbala where Sunni rule continued to be deeply resented.

Economic and social developments

In general, this first period of Ottoman rule in Iraq benefited overall economic and social development. Gradually, and not without serious setbacks due mainly to the recurrence of epidemics and floods, production and trade increased, the population grew, and cities expanded. Ottoman officials conducted several cadastral surveys to assess land productivity and the nature of taxation. In theory, the sultan was the guardian of all the land known as *miri*. In addition to the division of this land into *timars*, government officials were sometimes assigned to collect taxes directly from the peasants. These officials (often the governors themselves) were either salaried or, more commonly, tax-farmers. Some families sought to establish greater rights over the land and escape taxation by registering it as a religious endowment or *waqf* and arranging the contract in such a manner as to allow most of the proceeds to return to the family. Another form of land-holding, which was quite rare in Iraq during this period, was *mulk*, or land held in absolute freehold. Some notable families who had received recognition for their services were granted *mulk* allowing them basically the same rights as those associated with private property. Most of the tribal lands were officially classified as *musha'*, or lands held in common. The manner in which the tribes put these lands to use varied greatly with some set aside for the benefit of the shaykh and his guest-house, while others were divided among peasants and herders. Each tribe referred to its traditional territory as its *dira*.

The rising cost of the military in the seventeenth century and the constant struggle of local notables for greater economic influence, led the Ottomans to expand the practice of tax-farming, *iltizam*. Normally, the right to collect the taxes of a certain land was auctioned off to the highest bidder. This provided local notables with new opportunities which they soon took full advantage of. Early on, most tax-farms were limited to one year. By the eighteenth century, however, the notables had won the right to hold tax-farms for life with the right of inheritance (*malikana*). A similar process evolved in the tribal lands where, in some areas like the lower Tigris, shaykhs and prominent tribesmen gradually won individual rights (*lazma*) over certain lands. Peasants normally entered into share-cropping arrangements with their overlords, whether tax-farmer or tribal shaykh. In theory, the rate of taxation and type of taxes allowed were strictly regulated by the central government and supervised by the local *qadi*. In practice, however, the tax-farmers and tribal shaykhs used every means available and any excuse possible to squeeze as much as they could out of the peasantry so that it was rare to find a peasant family living above mere subsistence. Also, while this period certainly represented a vast improvement over its predecessor, the wars with Persia and the regular campaigns of the central government against tribal insubordination, limited the development of the countryside.

Most of the land-holders lived in the cities, which, at this time, grew in size and population. Between the late sixteenth and the late eighteenth century Baghdad's population increased from around 68,600 to 80,000, Basra and Mosul grew from 20,000 to 40,000, and various growth rates were also noted for Kirkuk, Irbil, Najaf and Karbala. Cities benefited from the gradual development of trade. The sixteenth and seventeenth centuries marked an important increase in maritime trade supported by the establishment of powerful land empires in India and the Middle East, and by the participation of European fleets. During the first half of the eighteenth century, the Dutch and Portuguese presence gradually faded leaving the English East India Company as the main European commercial power in the Persian Gulf which formed the basis for later political dominance. Basra's status as Iraq's primary outlet to the sea was greatly enhanced by this trading activity and a new customs house brought in much revenue. The chief exports from Basra included dates, Arabian stallions and specie. Imports, such as Indian textiles and spices, Yemeni coffee, Batavian sugar and numerous other items, were transported to Baghdad and Persia either through the rivers or by caravans. Large camel caravans, some numbering as many as 4000, also linked Basra to Aleppo, while smaller ones traveled down the Arabian coast. Caravans and river boats also traveled between Baghdad, Mosul, Kirkuk, Damascus, Diyar Bakr, Isfahan, Mardin and various other cities in Anatolia and Persia. The functioning of internal trade required a delicate balance between the interests of the merchants, the Ottoman authorities and the tribes. Various arrangements and forms of revenue sharing were negotiated and renegotiated (interrupted by many rebellions) depending on the route and the period in question. Often, merchants had to pay customs dues to the authorities when approaching the main cities, and some form of tolls to the tribes guaranteeing safe passage when crossing their territories.

The relative stabilization and revival of trade under the Ottomans boosted local industries. While the wars with Persia were often destructive, they too encouraged some manufacturing. Most towns had wool, cotton or silk textile workshops, but the most important center for textile manufacturing during this period was Mosul. Associated industries such as dyeing and embroidery also flourished. Baghdad, which was the chief base of military actions against Persia, became a center of gunpowder production with 16 such factories by the late eighteenth century. These industries, in addition to the many tra-ditional manufacturing shops, continued to organize their activities through guild associations which, under the Ottomans, came to be more strictly regulated than before. As in agriculture, tax-farming was also applied to urban activities including the collection of customs dues. Tax-farmers were usually already men of great influence and wealth such as merchants, local government officials, religious leaders ('ulama) and even some tribal shaykhs (like those of the 'Ubayd), whose diras were in close proximity to the cities. The leading 'ulama had additional access to wealth through their role as administrators of religious endowments. The introduction of tax-farming (especially the lifetime tax-farm) acted as a strong incentive for these classes of notables to strengthen their ties with one another. Ties of money-lending and the pooling of resources were strengthened by marriage alliances. By the end of the eighteenth century, such social ties with the tribal shaykhs were also becoming more evident. The power of the urban notables was demonstrated politically with the rise of local dynasties such as the Afrasiyabs of Basra, the Babans of Shahrazur and the Jalilis in Mosul. At Baghdad, the eighteenth century saw the development of a military oligarchy supported by the land-holding classes. Their influence, however, was tempered not only by the central Ottoman government which still demanded its share of the local revenues, but also the lower classes who were always ready to create havoc if pushed too far.

The new wealth of the cities (modest when compared to other Ottoman regions) is still apparent in the numerous public buildings constructed during this time. Funded either by the governor's family or through private patronage, their architectural designs, while not uniform, point to a certain cultural autonomy in the Iraqi provinces. In most of the Ottoman domains a certain architectural style can be detected particularly in the construction of the mosques with their characteristic thin pencil-like minarets, flatter domes and front canopies. This style never took hold in Iraq where the Persian forms predominated in most of the country. The most recognizable feature of this style is the use of blue tiles particularly to cover the domes and minaret tops. In shrines, such as those in Najaf and Karbala, gold tiles were also used. In Mosul, a wholly indigenous style, represented with the use of decorative bricks in minarets, continued an old tradition going back to 'Abbasid times. Increasing patronage seems to have also been behind a rise in literary activities, particularly the writing of local histories and biographical dictionaries.

The religious communities

The Ottomans, building upon older Islamic customs, recognized the autonomy of a number of monotheistic religious communities as sep-arate *millets*. Most religious communities benefited from the overall economic improvement. Members of the small Mandaean gnostic community, having disappeared into the marshes of southern Iraq since the late Abbasid period, appear to have trickled into the city of Basra to eke out a living as poor artisans, boat-builders or carpenters. By 1625, they participated in the defense of the city against Safavid attacks despite the non-violent nature of their religion. The con-dition of the Jews, who had always been visible in urban life, also improved. By the end of the eighteenth century, a number of promi-nent Jewish merchants acted as chief bankers for the governors in Baghdad, Mosul and Basra. One Rabbi Jacob Gabbai of Basra played a leading role in 1775/6 by raising funds for the support of Ottoman troops facing yet another Persian offensive. His efforts were recog-nized in 1780 by the Ottoman sultan who honored him with a special decree and exempted him from paying state taxes. By the end of the century, another Jewish leader by the name of 'Abdullah ibn Yusuf, was elevated to one of the governor's most influential advisers in Baghdad. The most important Jewish community was still in Baghdad reaching as much as 20 per cent of the city's population by the early nineteenth century. Their numbers seemed to have increased during the late seventeenth century through the arrival of Jewish immigrants from Iran escaping religious persecution. Living in their own separate quarter, most were poor but many became successful merchants, shop owners and financiers. During the early nineteenth century, a certain

Heskel Gabbai was one of the wealthiest men in Iraq. His abilities caught the eye of the sultan and earned him the post of chief treasurer in Istanbul. This tolerant atmosphere, however, did not always guard against all forms of oppression. During the reign of Dawud Pasha (1817–31) some of the Jewish bankers fell foul of the Baghdad governor's favor. One Sassoon ben Salih bar David was forced to escape to India where he later made a fortune and became the founder of the celebrated Sassoon family of entrepreneurs in England. It would be wrong, however, to take this incident as evidence of a general anti-Jewish policy on the part of this governor since his close circle of advisers continued to include other prominent Jews. Muslim merchants also suffered from such oppressions, which were often motivated by political and financial considerations rather than religious bigotry.

The most important developments in the condition of Christians in Iraq during this time were the growth of the Armenian community and rising Catholic influences. The Nestorian Church, which had spread throughout Asia, received a major blow during the late fourteenth century when Timur Lang destroyed much of its presence east of Iraq with the exception of India. In 1551, the Nestorian patriarch John Sulaka, after converting to Catholicism in Rome, returned to northern Iraq and established a loose union between his followers and the Vatican. During the next three centuries, additional agreements drew the Chaldeans, as these Catholic converts were known, closer to Rome. The patriarchs of the Chaldean Church were initially based in Mosul but subsequently moved to Baghdad. Nevertheless, many of Iraq's Christians, spread out in numerous villages around Mosul, remained true to the Nestorian Church, which now came to be known as the Assyrian Church. The Catholics received additional support when, in 1628, Shah 'Abbas allowed the Capuchin Fathers to build a church in Baghdad. In 1638, a Carmelite mission was established in Basra followed by another in Baghdad in 1721. Due to Islamic injunctions, these missionaries had to limit their activities to non-Muslims in the hope of winning converts mainly from among the Mandaeans and non-Catholic Christians. By the early nineteenth century, around 10 per cent of the population of Baghdad was Christian. The Armenians, who appeared during the early Ottoman period, successfully defended the independence of their church. In 1604, Shah 'Abbas transferred large numbers of Armenian merchants and their families from their homeland to his new capital of Isfahan. Thanks to his favorable treatment, they soon became the Safavid Empire's most important long-distance merchants with links stretching as far as western Europe, Russia, India and China. Through their control of the lucrative Persian silk trade to Ottoman lands, members of this community came to settle in Baghdad, Mosul and Basra during the seventeenth century. At Basra, they were among the leading merchant communities trading with India and Aleppo and the main competitors of the Jews.

Sunnism was the only officially recognized Muslim faith in the Ottoman Empire. In Iraq, this guaranteed Sunni notables a monopoly over the government and judiciary. Despite this, there were no direct efforts at eliminating Shi'ism (as was done in Syria and Anatolia for example), since this would have certainly invited powerful resistance which the Ottomans were not in a position to control. Instead, the Shi'is simply withdrew into their own communities and institutions. This isolation should not be taken too far. There were, for example, numerous cases of neighborhoods with a religiously mixed population, Sunni-Shi'i merchant cooperation, or tribes with members from both sects. Safavid influence remained strong in Najaf and Karbala where Shi'i scholars and notables craved the support of a powerful patron. Such support was distinctly absent among the Shi'i tribes of the south who despised state control, regardless of its religious nature. These tribes, along with the location of Najaf and Karbala at the edge of the Arabian desert, encouraged the conversion to Shi'ism of many of the Najdi tribes, which were moving into Iraq in the seventeenth and eighteenth centuries, thereby adding substantially to the overall Shi'i population. In the Shi'i urban centers, this period saw the development of the position of *mujtahid*, or a recognized authority permitted to give an opinion on matters of Shi'i law. Under the guidance of the *mujtahids*, who soon formed the leadership of the community, Shi'i Islam became more "orthodox" by moving away from the influences of *sufi* mysticism. Since Shi'i scholars were always in close contact with their counterparts in Iran, this development undoubtedly encouraged, and was in turn strengthened by, Safavid moves to limit the power of the sufi groups. At the same time, however, it came to encourage popular rituals peculiar to its tradition such as public mourning for the martyrdom of Husayn and the visitation of the tombs of the 12 Imams and their descendants. The dominant position of the *mujtahids* was challenged by the rise of the so-called Akhbari school which cautioned against the danger of excessive flexibility in interpreting the law. In this manner, the Akhbaris were actually much closer to Sunni views on the limits of interpretation. Though the Akhbaris eventually lost their influence, their adherents were particularly strong in Iraq.

Of all the numerous religious communities in Iraq, perhaps the one that suffered the most at the hands of the Ottomans were the Yazidis. The origin of the Yazidis goes back to the early tenth century and Kurdish tribal resistance to 'Abbasid control. One such movement expressed its resistance by praising the Umayyads, especially the Caliph Yazid ibn Mu'awiya (hence the movement's name). Yazidi cohesion was strengthened in 111 with the arrival of the mystic Shaykh 'Adi ibn Musafir, a descendant of the Umayyad family. Over the next three or four centuries the community's beliefs gradually evolved into an independent religion with elements of Islamic sufism and pre-Islamic Iranian traditions. Erroneously thought to be devil-worshipers, they were repeatedly attacked by Muslim Kurdish tribes and Ottoman forces driving many out toward the Caucasus and Syria. Nevertheless, important Yazidi communities continued to exist especially in the Shaykhan and Jabal Sinjar regions near Mosul.

Baghdad's autonomy under the mamluks

While overall economic and social progress was evident throughout the country, political instability continued to plague the Ottoman governors. In 1704, the sultan appointed Hasan Pasha, one of his most skillful administrators, to finally bring the troublesome province of Baghdad under control. The new governor faced a truly daunting task. Persia still represented a constant threat, Arab and Kurdish tribes were as powerful and aggressive as ever, an increasing number of the rural population were Shi'i, and the Janissaries continued to act as an independent militia in the cities. Hasan Pasha's strategy was to build an independent power base using imported Georgian mamluks who soon formed a separate military caste. They were usually brought in as children, converted to Islam and enrolled in special schools which emphasized military and religious education. Each "class" had no more than 200 mamluks who, over the course of their service, developed a strong bond with one another as well as with their master. Hasan Pasha was also able to convince the sultan that a long tenure in office was essential if the province was to be brought under effective control. He was thus able to secure his rule for 20 years after which it passed to his son, Ahmad who governed until 1747. Istanbul had less of a reason to fear the development of local rule during this period since the empire was generally at peace and Hasan Pasha had had a distinguished career as a loyal servant.

The new mamluk army proved quite capable whether in the battlefield or in administration. Tribal insubordination, both in the south and among the Kurds, was kept in check through regular, forceful campaigns. These campaigns were destructive to the countryside but did secure tribute from recalcitrant shaykhs and kept them from growing too strong. As a result, not only did security improve to the benefit of trade, but it also provided Hasan Pasha with the opportunity to expand Baghdad's direct control over Basra and much of the area around Mosul including Kirkuk and Mardin. He also succeeded in playing a much greater role in determining the choice of the paramount shaykhs of the tribes. By the early nineteenth century, the governors of Baghdad had secured an area roughly the same as that of modern Iraq with the notable exception of Mosul and its immediate hinterland. Trade improved thanks to the elimination of several taxes and the construction and repair of a number of caravanserais. The legitimacy of Hasan Pasha and his son was further enhanced through their generous endowments and the construction of a number of religious buildings. At Baghdad, Ahmad Pasha reduced the power of the Janissaries by deporting some of their regiments to Mosul and elsewhere. Delighted by these policies, the leading merchants, land-holders, religious leaders, and other urban notables, rallied enthusiastically behind the new mamluk-based regime and encouraged it to adopt a more autonomous posture. This was particularly true of Ahmad Pasha whose annual payments to Istanbul were reduced to a mere token and all important appointments, including that of the *qadi* and *daftardar*, were handled from Baghdad.

Ahmad Pasha, even more than his father, increased the number of Georgian mamluks in his government and took care to form family ties with his leading officers. Soon after his death in 1747, his son-in-law and most trusted mamluk, Sulayman, secured the governorship with the help of the mamluk army and the local notables. The Ottomans had little choice but to recognize his claim since they were hard-pressed in Europe once again and in no position to forcibly install their own candidates. On several occasions, officials sent from Istanbul were murdered before even reaching the city. Sulayman (r. 1750–62), known as "Abu Layla" or "Of the Night", because of his night-time raids against the tribes, was the first mamluk governor of Baghdad. For the next 80 years, the governorship would pass from one mamluk officer to the next despite their ferocious power struggles and Istanbul's constant attempts to dislodge them. Nevertheless, the mamluks continued to recognize the sovereignty of the sultan by proclaiming his name on coins and during the Friday prayers. And the sultan's official confirmation of the legitimacy of a governor continued to play an important role in securing the claims of one candidate against those of his rivals. The reign of Sulayman the Great (r. 1780–1802) is generally seen as the height of mamluk power with over 12,500 full-time slave soldiers and an additional 20,000 to 50,000 armed men when needed. During his reign, Janissary threats became a thing of the past, and construction activities, economic production, and literary output were all on the rise. The hegemony of Baghdad over other parts of Iraq was noted in 1784 by the establishment, in the heart of Kurdish territory, of the new city of Sulaymaniyya, named after Sulayman the Great. The strong links between the mamluk leadership and the notables of Baghdad were evident just prior to the appointment of Sulayman the Great. In 1779, the Ottomans were prevented from installing a non-mamluk governor only by the collective action of the people of Baghdad led by the urbanized shaykhs of the 'Ubayd tribe. This relationship, however, did have its tense moments. The mamluks, being of recent slave and foreign origin, never fully managed to become accepted as members of the indigenous notable classes. Baghdadis often referred to the mamluks as having "a broken eye", meaning that they were ashamed of their background. This may explain how Sulayman Abu Layla's wife, 'Adila Khatun, who hailed from a distinguished family, was able to command authority and even hold court independently of, and at times in opposition to, her husband.

The Ottoman–Persian wars of the eighteenth century

The Ottomans were willing to put up with Baghdad's growing autonomy as long as it continued to check the threat from Persia. This threat reappeared after the collapse of Safavid rule in 1722. Initially, the Ottomans saw this as an opportunity to expand their domain and ordered Hasan Pasha to invade the region of Hamadan. Though this campaign was initially successful, the Ottomans were soon on the defensive when Nadir Shah Afshari reunited the country and invaded Iraq in 1732, 1733, 1735 and 1743. The wars of Nadir Shah placed Iraq, once again, in the role of the Ottoman first line of defense with Mosul, Baghdad and Basra repeatedly suffering from long sieges, and the countryside decimated by the advancing armies. In the end, the cities, depending mainly on their own resources, held firm and the border again returned to that outlined by the Treaty of Zuhab. There were, however, important differences with previous Ottoman–Persian wars in that the size of Nadir Shah's armies, particularly during the campaigns of 1743, were much larger and better equipped (and thus more destructive), than anything seen before. Also, unlike his Safavid predecessors, Nadir Shah made a serious attempt to win over the Sunni population by proposing the acceptance of Shi'i Islam as a fifth school of interpretation (the Ja'fari school) within the Sunni tradition. In this regard, he sponsored a conference at Najaf designed to iron out the differences between the two branches and to basically permit Shi'ism within the Sunni fold. This interesting experiment, which might have resolved the great schism within Islam, ultimately failed. The participants, a collection of Sunni and Shi'i scholars, did agree to a common statement in which the "extremist" Shi'i practices were condemned and the Ja'fari school was recognized. Soon after this, however, both sides reverted to their traditional positions refusing to budge or to trust the other's promises.

Nadir Shah's murder in 1747, and the collapse of his state did not bring an end to the conflict. During the following decades southern Persia was united under Karim Khan Zand, a devout Shi'i who soon did away with Nadir's pro-Sunni policies. Though generally reluctant to go to war, Karim Khan was drawn to Iraq by the rivalries within the rising princely family of the Babans in Shahrazur. He was also covetous of the wealthy port of Basra which had strong commercial links with southern Persia. The fighting in Shahrazur resulted in stalemate, but Karim Khan's army was able to take advantage of a devastating plague to occupy Basra. The plague, which struck in 1773, wiped out about one-third of the population and left the city vulnerable to tribal attacks. While the plague still raged, an Englishman, who witnessed the event, wrote the following lines:

> Neither it is in our power sufficiently to describe to you the horrid scene that we had hourly before our eyes and the dreadful accounts which we dayly received from Bussora. ... the inhabitants were carried off in such number that for several days very few could be found who were daring enough to pay the last duties to their departed friends and relations ... the creek which runs through the town ... was covered with clothes and beds of deceased persons, and numbers of baskets with dead bodies were seen floating up and down in it undirected but by the wind and tide – the dead were probably the owners, and had been suddenly struck whilst they were earning their dayly substance.[3]

Three years later, after a brutal siege which lasted more than one year, Karim Khan's army entered the exhausted city. The Persian occupation lasted three years during which trade declined and many merchants fled to other parts of the Persian Gulf, notably to the small port of Kuwait. What made the situation worse was that these wars coincided with the rise of the puritanical Wahhabi movement in central Arabia. Taking advantage of Baghdad's preoccupation with the Persians, they raided deep into Iraq with attacks on Basra, Najaf and Karbala. The most destructive of these raids was the one on Karbala in 1802, where 3000 inhabitants were slain and the venerated shrine of Husayn looted and destroyed. Other than the material destruction and anxiety that these wars left behind, a strong case was made to the Ottomans for the benefits of local leadership with ties to the powerful notable families. In addition to mamluk rule of Baghdad and Basra, Mosul came under the governorship of a local Arab family. The Jalilis were even more successful in building a military–administrative apparatus that was dependent, almost entirely, on their province's own

---

[3] Quoted in Thabit A.J. Abdullah, *Merchants, Mamluks and Murder: The Political Economy of Eighteenth-Century Basra*, Albany, 2001, pp. 52–3.

resources. In addition to urban notables they formed strong alliances with the surrounding tribes, especially those of Tayy. Their success was most ably demonstrated during Nadir Shah's siege of 1743. Faced with overwhelming odds, the city repelled the invasion thanks to the ability of its leaders to effectively mobilize its population and resources. Unlike the rest of Iraq, Mosul never became a direct dependency of Baghdad though by the early nineteenth century Baghdad's hegemony was clearly on the rise.

Dawud Pasha and the end of mamluk rule

The last of the mamluk pashas was perhaps the most controversial. A deeply religious man and a respected scholar in his own right, Dawud Pasha ascended the governorship in 1816 after a turbulent power strug-gle. His reign, which lasted until 1831, witnessed the early develop-ment of two factors which would shape much of Iraq's modern history: more effective central state control and the expansion of British econ-omic influence. He has often been compared to his more illustrious contemporary, Muhammad 'Ali Pasha of Egypt, as a reformer who moved Iraq toward complete independence from Ottoman rule. Possibly influenced by the military reforms in Cairo and Istanbul, and by his own regional ambitions, his initial focus was on strengthening the army. A French military adviser was brought in to oversee the training of the troops (now numbering some 20,000), the remaining Janissaries were completely integrated into the standing army, a modern munitions factory, constructed by European engineers, was built, and a number of other military-related industries were estab-lished. State revenues increased thanks to an improvement in agricul-tural production, more efficient taxation, and regular campaigns against the tribes. An interest in broadening these modest reforms was evident through the establishment of textile factories and the country's first printing press. Unlike Muhammad 'Ali of Egypt, how-ever, Dawud Pasha did not broaden the base of his army through gen-eral conscription nor did he overhaul the bureaucracy. Also, the scale of Dawud Pasha's industries cannot be compared with Muhammad

'Ali's mammoth projects. Nevertheless, during his reign Baghdad witnessed a more vibrant cultural life and his court became a magnet for scholars and poets from Basra to Mosul.

Dawud Pasha was gravely concerned with the growing power of the English Resident in Baghdad. Early British contacts at Basra, going back to 1635, did not raise much concern. As representatives of the East India Company, their original interest was limited to trade. In 1723, a permanent trading house (called a "factory") was established at Basra and upgraded, in 1763, to the company's main agency in the Persian Gulf. Due to their growing control of India and its trade, British commercial influence in Basra grew rapidly during the eighteenth century. In 1767, the company signed a treaty with Sulayman the Great which provided for British naval protection of Basra's trade. A greater role in the port's commerce and security, coupled with Baghdad's financial indebtedness to the company were the early foundations of British political influence. By the end of the century, British representatives were also present in Baghdad and, in 1802, a consulate was opened. The most powerful consul during Dawud Pasha's time was Claudius James Rich. Appointed to his post in 1808, the *baliyawz*, as he was known, came to be regarded as the second most powerful man in the province. In 1821, outraged by Rich's meddling, Dawud Pasha forced the consul to leave the country. British interests, however, had become so important that scarcely a year went by before a new consul was cordially received.

By 1830, Iraq was at a cross-roads. The Ottomans, now under the command of the energetic Sultan Mahmud II, were determined to bring the provinces under direct control. To achieve this end, Sultan Mahmud inaugurated a period of broad reforms designed to strengthen the army and the state. On the other hand, Dawud Pasha's policies had positioned the country on the verge of complete independence. When the Ottoman envoy, Sadiq Effendi, demanded that Dawud relinquish his post he was duly strangled. As Dawud Pasha prepared his troops to meet the oncoming Ottoman army led by 'Ali Rida Pasha, a terrible plague struck Baghdad in April, 1831. At its height the epidemic was claiming as many as 1500 lives a day with an accompanying destruction of social order. Just when it seemed as if the worse was over, the Tigris broke its banks in the northern part of the city resulting in the collapse of a section of the citadel and the complete ruin of whole neighborhoods. According to the Carmelite missionaries in Baghdad at the time:

> ... the water entered the city, and destroyed an incalculable number of houses which fell on their owners and occupiers, turning into graves instead of dwellings. As though these two disasters, the plague and the flood, were insufficient, robbers and looters spread into the city, breaking into houses and stealing what they found in the way of jewels, ornaments or other valuable household goods.[4]

The extent of this damage was still evident some 20 years later when the population of Baghdad had yet to recover its pre-1831 level. Despite this, there is no indication of widespread demands for Dawud's surrender on the part of the city's notables. After some hesitation, Dawud, sensing the futility of resistance, turned himself over to the new governor, and was later pardoned by the sultan. News of the end of mamluk rule of Baghdad encouraged the growing anti-Jalili faction in Mosul. While the autonomy of Mosul had brought many notables great rewards, there was also concern at the gradual monopolization of power and wealth in the hands of the Jalili family. In 1834, after a series of uprisings, the Ottoman army seized the city and ended a century of autonomous local government.

The imposition of direct Ottoman rule in Iraq inaugurated a period of important development. During the sixteenth and seventeenth cen-

---

[4] Quoted in Charles Issawi (ed.), *The Fertile Crescent, 1800–1914: A Documentary History*, Oxford, 1988, p. 102.

turies, Ottoman rule, as imperfect and unstable as it was, helped to foster the growth of a powerful urban elite composed mainly of a land-holding gentry, wealthy merchants and religious leaders. By the eighteenth century these classes were powerful enough to take advantage of the empire's problems in Europe to promote local autonomous rule. In Baghdad and Basra, where tribal power was particularly strong, stable rule required an independent base of imported slave soldiers. At Mosul, however, the province was able to manage its affairs through the leadership of one of its own families. Historians have debated endlessly whether the mamluk period established the foundations of the modern Iraqi state. As academic as this question is, it is not impossible to assume that had nature not intervened in such a destructive manner, Dawud Pasha could have resisted the Ottoman army in 1831 and imposed an agreement similar to the one that gave Muhammad 'Ali and his descendants effective independence in Egypt. One factor which mitigated against local support for independence was the constant fear of another Persian invasion. While the Ottomans were happy to see Iraqi cities defending themselves without major assistance from Istanbul, locally, some form of ties were still preferred. Ideally, the notables would have liked weak ties with respect to taxation, revenue distribution and provincial policies, and strong ones with respect to military assistance against Persian threats. For the ordinary Iraqis, it must have seemed like fate had played a cruel joke by placing them between the two rival states. This is best summed up by a popular Iraqi saying which apparently originates from this time: "Between the Persians and the Turks, what a calamity!" At any rate, the conflict's impact on sectarian divisions and the resultant Sunni domination of the government continued to affect the nature of Iraqi political development over the course of the next two centuries.

chapter four

THE TANZIMAT AND YOUNG TURK PERIOD, 1831–1918

As in other parts of the Middle East, the two main forces that affected Iraqi history during the nineteenth century were the growing powers of the centralizing Ottoman state and the region's integration into the European-dominated world economy. Both of these processes were already evident, on a smaller scale, in the preceding period, particularly during the mamluk and Jalili periods.

Problems of consolidation

The task of firmly integrating Iraq into the Ottoman Empire proceeded slowly during the first four decades after the end of mamluk rule. While this was somewhat simpler in Mosul, the Ottomans still lacked contacts and a solid base of local support throughout the country. Military campaigns continued well into the final third of the century before all of the cities were brought under control. Tensions with Persia, now reunified under the Qajar dynasty, remained high with sporadic fighting along the northern border. The threat of all-out war was narrowly averted through the mediation of Britain and Russia. Using the Treaty of Zuhab as a rough reference point, both sides agreed, in the 1847 Treaty of Erzerum, to a clearer delineation of the border. This, however, did not prevent regular incursions, claims and counter-claims and disagreements over the interpretation of the treaty. In the meantime, the relationship with the tribes became even more strained with Ottoman attempts at pitting one tribe against the other and encouraging rival claimants to the leadership within each tribe. Still fearful of the development of autonomous tendencies, they reverted to the policy of limiting the governor's tenure. In a system which still depended on networks of patrons and clients rather than a professional bureaucracy, the frequent change in governors greatly hampered effective rule. Elements of such a bureaucracy, however, were not long in arriving. In Istanbul, there was growing conviction that the empire's weakness in dealing with the European powers required significant reform designed to centralize authority. Between 1839 and 1876, a series of reforms, known collectively as the *Tanzimat* (regulations), were applied. While some aspects of the reforms, such as the establishment of a constitution in 1876, were liberal in form, the primary beneficiary of the Tanzimat was the army. This "military-led modernization", however, had broad ramifications on various sectors of society. In the words of Malcolm Yapp:

> Money to pay for the army had to be raised by taxes and loans. In turn a larger and more efficient administration was required to mobilize the empire's resources. Educational reform was needed to produce the necessary officers and bureaucrats.[1]

For Iraq, the most important aspects of the Tanzimat had to wait until 1869. Nevertheless, some changes were evident earlier. The remnants of Dawud's army with that of 'Ali Rida's forces formed the nucleus of the modernized Ottoman Sixth Army stationed in Baghdad. Limited conscription to this army gradually expanded to include Mosul and Basra in addition to Baghdad. Over time, the Sixth Army came to be dominated by local Iraqis with the exception of its commanding officers. Thus, while the Ottomans divided Iraq into three provinces once again, the army, and its frequent use to bring order throughout these provinces, helped to strengthen the ties between the different parts of the country. For many Iraqis of modest backgrounds the army, even at this early stage, represented a means of upward mobility. By 1912, there were an estimated 1200 Iraqi officers serving in the Ottoman army; the largest group from the Arab provinces. The most notable name here was Mahmud Shawkat who, by 1910, was one of the most senior commanders in the Ottoman army and later went on to become the empire's Prime Minister. The lower ranks of the bureaucracy were also drawn from local elements like Turkish-speakers from Kirkuk, Georgians from the old mamluk families, and some from the influential notable families. Shi'i participation was still negligible as almost all of these new bureaucrats and army officers were Sunnis. Up to that

---

[1] Yapp, Malcolm, *The Making of the Modern Near East, 1792–1923*, London, 1987, p. 109.

point, almost all the schools available had a limited curriculum which emphasized religious education. During the nineteenth century a number of missionary schools were opened providing a broader curriculum with a strong emphasis on science, math and languages. Probably the best of these early "modern" schools in Baghdad was the one founded by the Alliance Israelite Universelle in 1865. Many of the subjects taught were new to the country, like classes in English, French, Mathematics, Chemistry and Science. Most of its teachers came from London and Paris. While this school benefited the Jewish community above all, it also opened its doors to a limited number of Muslims and Christians. Missionaries also played a role in increasing literacy through the introduction of modern printing such as the Dominican printing press in Mosul which opened in 1860. Communications were improved with the use of steamships between Baghdad and Basra reducing the return trip from one month to 10 days. In 1861, a telegraph service was established between Baghdad and Istanbul and in the following years it reached all of Iraq's major cities. Some work was also done to improve the quality of roads.

Early resistance to centralization

The attempts of the state to extend its power were met with stiff resistence every step of the way. In 1832, a rebellion broke out in Baghdad itself led by the *mufti* 'Abdul-Ghani Al Jamil followed by another in Basra led by remnants of the old mamluk soldiers. As can be expected, however, the most stubborn resistence came from the tribes and the urban Shi'i establishment. In 1843, the governor of Baghdad, Najb Pasha, sent a force to bring Najaf and Karbala under central control. For the past decade, the two Shi'i cities had fallen under the control of semi-mafiosi gangs reminiscent of the medieval 'ayarun of Baghdad. The main difference between the two was that in Karbala these gangs had grown to such an extent that they were able to win over the support of many merchants, land-holders and religious leaders who feared central Ottoman control. When the Ottoman army arrived they faced a population who, despite their many differences, were unified under the leadership of the urban gangs. The taking of the city was accompanied by a great loss of life and the desecration of the shrines. Similar occurrences took place in Najaf nine years later. In addition to appointing a Sunni governor to both cities, the Ottomans attempted to stamp out Shi'i jurisprudence by appointing a Sunni *qadi*. The second measure soon failed but the two cities would never enjoy the same degree of autonomy. The sacking of Karbala in particular, contributed to the straining of relations with Persia and a period of religious persecution during which Shi'is were forced to conceal their beliefs and rituals. Other campaigns were directed against the Kurdish principalities particularly the one in Jabal Sinjar where the fiercely independent Yazidi religious community resisted well into the 1870s.

Resistence to Ottoman control also gained some encouragement from the governor of Egypt. Muhammad 'Ali Pasha, who governed Egypt between 1805 and 1848, had gradually established the foundations of an independent state which could effectively challenge the Ottoman sultan. In 1832, news of his invasion and annexation of Syria had a profound impact on Iraq. Some favored an alliance with Muhammad 'Ali as a tactical measure meant to promote greater local autonomy. The shaykhs of such powerful tribes as the Shammar, 'Uqayl and Zubayd, all declared their allegiance to Muhammad 'Ali, as did the governors of 'Ana and Hit. The most dangerous rebellion, however, was led by Yahya al-Jalili who attempted to gain Egyptian support for his claim to the governorship of Mosul. Mosul continued to clamor for an alliance with Egypt until 1839 when it was finally brought to heel.

Integration into the world economy

Early centralization, modest up to this point particularly when compared to other parts of the empire, was accompanied by a rapid increase in commercial ties with Britain. Prior to the opening of the Suez Canal and the discovery of oil in southern Persia, Britain's interests in Iraq were mainly related to communications with India. While the trade of Basra was important for certain parts of India, Iraq's strategic location at the head of the Persian Gulf was of more interest. During the late eighteenth and early nineteenth century, London's correspondence with India often went through the "Great Desert Route" from Aleppo to Basra before being despatched by sea. Thus, Iraq was seen as an extension of British interests in India. To further develop this interest, the Bombay government sent a number of expeditions between 1830 and 1860 to determine the feasibility of navigation in the Tigris and Euphrates rivers. In 1831, Francis Chesney's work on the Euphrates was completed, soon to be followed by H.B. Lynch's expedition along the Tigris. Lynch later formed the Euphrates and Tigris Steam Navigation Company which operated two steamers for regular travel between Baghdad and Basra. The British vessels competed favorably with the Ottoman steamers since they had a better reputation with respect to dependability of service. By 1862, regular steamship service was established between Basra and Bombay. Around this same time, a telegraphic link was also established with India but a proposal to build a railway line through Iran and Iraq never materialized.

With improved communications the volume of Basra's shipping rose steeply. Between 1864 and 1869 the number of Ottoman ships docking at Basra climbed from 552 to 1105, while those of Britain went from 27 to 52. The opening of the Suez Canal in 1869 made possible a direct link with Britain further enhancing commercial growth. By the end of Ottoman rule, Iraq had become largely dependent on Britain for its foreign trade. In 1913, two-thirds of Iraq's imports came from Britain and its possessions in India, with almost half of its exports going the other way. British ships also dominated the so-called local "carrying trade". By 1896, British vessels carried more than ten times as many goods between Basra and the Arabian peninsula as did the native Arab or Ottoman vessels. In addition to improved communications, the trade with Britain received encouragement through low customs duties regularly secured through effective diplomatic pressure. Despite several earlier attempts by the Ottomans to raise duties, they remained relatively fixed at around 8 per cent until 1907.

The reforms of Midhat Pasha

While Ottoman governors did their best to extend central control, the full impact of the Tanzimat reforms did not reach Iraq until 1869. That year two events marked a significant departure from the past: the opening of the Suez Canal and Midhat Pasha's assumption of the governorship of Baghdad. The former brought Iraq much closer to Europe allowing for direct trade and facilitating the integration of the country into the world economy. The latter brought one of the Ottoman Empire's most distinguished and energetic reformers. During his short term (1869–72), Midhat Pasha introduced far-ranging reforms designed to modernize the bureaucracy, raise overall economic standards, improve education and firmly bind the country to the rest of the Ottoman Empire. Though he was the governor of Baghdad, he oversaw the reforms (particularly in administration and land proprietorship) throughout Iraq. As he had done in his previous posts in the Balkans and Anatolia, Midhat Pasha approached his task with great zeal and integrity. Notwithstanding the fact that most of his grandiose plans failed completely, Iraqis still fondly speak of how this honest governor was forced to sell his watch to pay for his journey back to Istanbul. According to the English representative, his first act was to inform the leading notables of his plans:

> His Excellency addressed the assembly telling his audience that he had come hither with an earnest desire to benefit the country and enrich the people – that he proposed to introduce many changes and reforms which he hoped would be beneficial, changes, which perhaps at first they might not altogether approve but which they would appreciate when they had experienced the advantage that would accrue to them therefrom.[2]

Perhaps the most successful of Midhat Pasha's reforms was the application of the empire's *Vilayet* Law of 1864. This law was designed to

---

[2] Quoted in Issawi, Charles (ed.), *The Fertile Crescent, 1800–1914: A Documentary History*, Oxford, 1988, p. 115.

define and standardize the empire's provincial administration and to make the state more accessible to the ordinary people. Under Midhat's supervision, the borders of the three Iraqi provinces (*wilayahs*), with their various subdivisions, were mapped out. Each administrative division (the lowest being the neighborhoods and villages) was governed by an appointed official, often a local notable or tribal shaykh, assisted by a council which included, for the first time, a number of elected representatives. In Baghdad, about half of the council members were elected with usually two of these being non-Muslims (one Jewish, the other Christian). These councils, especially the council of Baghdad, later formed an important institutional base of the early Iraqi state.

The administrative reforms were accompanied by a rather grand plan aimed at transforming the nature of land-holdings and settling the nomadic tribes through the application of the Ottoman Land Law of 1858. This law, basically designed to eliminate tax-farming, also envisaged an increase in productivity and improved tax collection. While the state technically continued to own the land, the actual cultivators were to be given titles (the so-called *tapu* deed), where they would have almost the same rights as private owners. Nomadic and semi-nomadic tribes were promised substantially lower taxes should they register and settle. To enact this land reform, Midhat established a Land Commission which began issuing *tapu* deeds in selected areas of the country. In a few locations, notably around Baghdad and the date groves around the Shatt al-'Arab river, land registration did produce beneficial results. In most regions, however, the peasants were left worse off than before. Most of the peasants of Iraq had strong tribal allegiances and codes of behavior that often recognized only communal ownership of the land and the shaykh's role as the guardian of this land. In addition, past experience suggested that any government registration campaign was certain to be a prelude to conscription or taxation. Lastly, despite the administrative reforms, the peasants were powerless and had virtually no influence on the Baghdad government or, specifically, the Land Commission which was plagued by inefficiency and not immune from corruption. Through a combination of custom, fear, intimidation and ignorance the vast majority of *tapu* lands ended up being registered under the names of a few shaykhs, notables and urban merchants. Gradually, many of the tribesmen were transformed into tenant farmers. On paper, it appears that one of the greatest beneficiaries of land registration was the Sa'dun family, the paramount shaykhs of the large Muntafiq confederacy. Though they had difficulty enforcing their claims, they still ended up with the lion's share of *tapu* deeds in the south. The land grants, however, also had the effect of fracturing the family's solidarity and their ability to effectively lead their tribes. The primary effect of the land registration reforms then, was the acceleration of the process of privatization or semi-privatization and centralization of land proprietorship, both of which had started during the preceding century. It is not clear how much land was ultimately registered as *tapu*, with estimates varying between 10 and 20 per cent of the total cultivated area. In any case, the government soon realized the shortcomings of the plan and by 1881 the issuing of new deeds was halted and even reversed.

Other reforms, which greatly affected tribal relations, included those in irrigation, transportation and military conscription. Throughout the last decades of Ottoman rule, the government manipulated the water flow of the irrigation canals to reward or punish selected tribes causing massive migrations and intertribal conflicts. Often the target of these efforts was the Khaza'il confederacy around the Middle Euphrates region. This tribe had risen to prominence during the mamluk period under their famed shaykh, Hamad, who successfully kept central authority at bay. Midhat Pasha inflicted a severe blow to the Khaza'il during his military expedition of 1869, but the real penetration of central authority into their lands occurred only after the construction of the Hindiyya barrage in 1913. This effectively controlled the water which irrigated the Khaza'il's rich rice fields, placing them under the mercy of the Baghdad government. Canals were also used for transportation and communication but more modern means were also developed during this time. In addition to the expansion of steam navigation and the telegraph system, modern roads were constructed, a postal service was established, Basra's port facilities were upgraded and a tramway linked Baghdad with nearby Kazim. The Ottoman Sixth Army was bolstered through a cautious extension of conscription to the countryside. Making full use of his post as the commander of this army, Midhat enforced his authority throughout the Iraqi provinces and even extended it to Kuwait and down the Arabian coast as far as modern Qatar. Local officers for the Sixth Army were recruited and trained in two newly founded military schools. The urban police forces were also enlarged from a total of about 800 to more than 6400.

General secular education received a boost during the last decades of Ottoman rule. In addition to the two military schools, Midhat Pasha established a technical academy, a secondary school designed to produce civil servants, and several elementary schools, all of which were free. This was followed, in 1899, with a junior high school for girls and, in 1900, a primary teachers' academy. With the exception of the Law College (opened in 1908), post-secondary education was not available in Iraq. By the end of Ottoman rule, Iraq still lagged behind other regions of the empire with only slightly over 100 schools, five of which offered secondary education. Nevertheless, literacy, especially in the urban areas, witnessed modest but consistent growth. This increase in literacy fueled the demand for publications. In 1869, Midhat established a new printing press which produced various publications including textbooks and the country's first official newspaper, *al-Zawra'*. The vast majority of urban development schemes were applied to Baghdad. He ordered the dismantling of the city walls, parts of which were built in 'Abbasid times, to facilitate urban growth and provide bricks for new constructions. A bridge was built across the Tigris, the city gained its first water supply system and its first paved streets. Several new government bureaus and public facilities were opened such as the census and commerce bureaus, the city's first savings bank, a new hospital (completed in 1879), an orphanage and a public park. The area which received the least amount of attention was industry. Even though Midhat aimed at encouraging production by abolishing a number of taxes, the country remained woefully short of modern machine-operated industries. With very few exceptions industrial production continued to take place as it had for centuries, through small shops using man or animal power.

Social transformation

Iraq's integration into the world economy and the centralizing reforms of the state had a profound impact on society. Perhaps the most important changes, with respect to the future development of the Iraqi state, occurred in the countryside. The land reforms accelerated processes, clearly evident during the mamluk period, whereby class divisions were deepened and tribal ties somewhat undermined or transformed. Within a few decades, a growing number of shaykhs and *aghas* (Kurdish chieftains) became great landowners, closely associated with the state. In the past, their authority was primarily based on their leadership abilities particularly in times of war. The change in land tenure brought with it new power relationships which were now based on ownership claims secured, ultimately, by the Ottoman Sixth Army. The once proud tribesmen felt increasingly resentful of their new status as tenants with share-cropping and semi-feudal arrangements. Since many of the new landowners, whether tribal chieftains or urban notables, were usually absentees, subchiefs (*sirkals*) were increasingly used to organize production. This had the effect of further alienating the shaykhs from the peasants and encouraging a greater hierarchy of power within the tribes. Some shaykhs, like the Sa'duns, actually secured official government posts to cement their new relationship to the state. Shaykh Nasir al-Sa'dun was considered a strong ally of Midhat Pasha who appointed him district-governor of the Muntafiq lands. In 1870, as part of the government's policy to encourage settlement, he founded the new town of Nasiriyya and, in 1876, he was further rewarded with the governorship of Basra. His close relations with the government gave rise to jealousies and charges of betraying tribal loyalties. When relations soured a few years later the Ottomans were able to take advantage of his weakened authority over the tribesmen to score a decisive victory over the Muntafiq from which they would never recover their past independence. Similar developments took place with respect to the Shammar and other tribes. The weakening of tribal bonds, however, should not be overstated. Many powerful tribes in the more inaccessible marshes of the south or the mountains of the north refused to cooperate with the government and generally maintained their cohesion. Much of the cultivated land was owned directly by the sultan, rather than the shaykhs, and administered by government agents. More importantly, even in areas where traditional tribal relations were affected, they did not necessarily dissolve but were transformed, within a new setting, into relations of patronage fostered by a common tribal heritage. In the words of one Baghdadi notable of the time:

> To depend on the tribe is a thousand times safer than depending on the government, for whereas the latter defers or neglects repression, the tribe, no matter how feeble it may be, as soon as it learns that an injustice has been committed against one of its members readies itself to exact vengeance on his behalf.[3]

Despite the contradictory results of the land reforms and the social disruptions which they caused, there were some very real advances made. The roaming nomads, who had been the scourge of Iraqi prosperity since the thirteenth century, declined noticeably from 35 per

---

[3] Quoted in Batatu, Hanna, *The Old Social Classes and Revolutionary Movements of Iraq: A Study of Iraq's Old Landed and Commercial Classes and of its Communists, Ba'thists, and Free Officers*, Princeton, 1978, p. 21.

cent of the population in 1867 to 17 per cent in 1905. This was accompanied by an increase in permanent settlement for the same years from 41 to 59 per cent of the population. Population estimates for the same years point to a significant rise from 1.25 million to 2.5 million. This was partially due to the end of the major plague epidemics which used to strike the country periodically, but there is also strong evidence that agricultural production grew steadily with new lands being cultivated. Much of the increase in production was driven by accessibility to the international market with exports (mainly dates, wheat and barley) climbing from 89,000 pounds sterling in 1864 to around 2,700,000 by the end of Ottoman rule. The shift to commercial agriculture brought new value to the land and tended to intensify the competition between the Ottoman authorities, the indigenous notables and the local cultivators over the control of the land. The concomitant rise in imports had a destructive impact on some of the local industries, particularly textiles and copperware, and their guild organizations.

Secular education slowly produced a new type of native elite who, despite their small numbers, still managed to fill important posts in the administration. While most of these educated professionals were Sunnis with strong ties to their traditional communities, they still posed a threat to the established urban classes who had hitherto wielded unchallenged local authority through their religious influence. Not surprisingly, it was elements of these traditional classes, notably the sayyids, who initially led the way in opposing Ottoman centralization in the cities. The tensions between Istanbul and the elites of Iraq, however, were quite complex, played out in events that often led to contradictory results. An illustrative case affected the religious scholar and sayyid Abu Thana' al-Alusi. After the fall of Dawud Pasha, al-Alusi rose to the powerful position of chief *mufti* of Baghdad. For the next decade and a half, al-Alusi remained loyal to the Ottoman state and even defended its centralizing efforts in the face of criticisms expressed by the competing Gaylani family of sayyids. In 1847, a new governor unceremoniously stripped al-Alusi of his lucrative *waqf* income and removed him from the muftiship of Baghdad. He journeyed to Istanbul to seek justice but received little sympathy from the Ottoman central government whose minister of finance reportedly told the petitioning religious leaders: "There are no livelihoods for you in the Treasury; your livelihoods are to be found in Paradise."[4] In many instances, the notable classes proved quite resilient in maintaining their positions and limiting the influence of the central state. The Gaylanis of Baghdad, who were generally more conservative than the Alusis, remained untouched and even managed to increase their *waqf* income. Another example is the role which Mustafa Chalabi al-Sabunchi played in Mosul. Seemingly unaffected by the presence of Ottoman governors and officials, this wealthy notable practically ruled the city between 1895 and 1911. Among Shi'is, however, the reforms had little impact on the status of their religious leaders. Despite the imposition of direct Ottoman rule over Najaf and Karbala, Shi'i autonomy kept the community somewhat insulated. This autonomy was even enhanced with the further centralization of the religious leadership. The rise of the Mujtahids during the preceding century paved the way for the development of a single recognized leader for the entire Shi'i community. This occurred during the mid-nineteenth century when the Mujtahids of Iraq agreed to defer, in matters of religious practice and law, to the opinion of the wisest among them. Such a leading Mujtahid was called the *Marja' al-Taqlid* or "source of emulation". The first paramount *Marja' al-Taqlid*, recognized as such in both Iraq and Iran, was probably Shaykh Murtada al-Ansari of Najaf who soon emerged as one of the wealthiest and most powerful men in Iraq.

Probably the community that benefited most from the reforms and the

---

[4] Quoted in Hala Fattah, "Representations of Self and the Other in Two Iraqi Travelogues of the Ottoman Period", in *International Journal of Middle East Studies*, vol. 30, no. 1, Feb. 1998, p. 66.

growing ties to Europe were the Jews. Throughout the Ottoman period many Jews had become wealthy merchants and financiers and their numbers, especially in Baghdad, had given the community an important status. In 1908, their numbers in Baghdad were considerable even when compared to the Sunni and Shi'i populations, as is evident from the following contemporary estimate[5]:

Sunni Muslims	40,000
Shi'i Muslims	50,000
Christians	7,000
Jews	53,000
Total	150,000

Jewish merchants were among the first to take full advantage of the growing import-export trade with Europe. By 1926, when the Baghdad Chamber of Commerce was first opened, the majority of its members were Jewish. Another important fact was that one of the driving ideologies of the Tanzimat reformers, "Ottomanism", stressed citizenship and equality before the law regardless of religion. While this "liberal" side of the Tanzimat was partially interrupted in 1878 by the autocratic and pan-Islamic rule of Sultan 'Abdul Hamid II, reforms aimed at the secularization of the state resumed thereafter. For non-Muslims, these reforms opened up new avenues for advancement, especially in public service and law. Among the many Jews who practiced law during the late Ottoman period, Sassoon Heskel would later become Iraq's first minister of finance.

The Young Turks, nationalism and oil

In 1876, the Ottoman Empire faced a number of grave threats. Nationalist uprisings spread throughout its Balkan territories, the treasury was completely bankrupt, European military intervention

---

[5] Issawi, Charles (ed.), *The Fertile Crescent, 1800–1914: A Documentary History*, Oxford, 1988, p. 124.

seemed likely and the sultan was weak and incompetent. A number of officials, including Midhat Pasha, secured the abdication of the sultan and forced the successor, 'Abdul Hamid II, to consent to a constitution with a representative assembly. The constitution and the assembly were seen as institutions that could protect the empire from an unscrupulous monarch. Yet the Ottoman parliament, which had a few representatives from the Iraqi provinces, barely functioned for two years. Its inability to deal effectively with the growing crisis in the Balkans allowed Sultan 'Abdul Hamid to dismiss parliament, suspend the constitution and establish absolutist rule. To an extent, 'Abdul Hamid's long reign represented a reaction against the more liberal and secular pronouncements of the reformers rather than the main centralizing goals of the Tanzimat. The sultan came to place renewed stress on his role as the caliph of all Muslims and made increasing use of pan-Islamic ideology as the foundation for the unity of the empire and its alliances abroad. In response, a coalition of various disaffected groups (known collectively as the Young Turks), including army officers, liberal-minded intellectuals and civil servants, formed a number of secret societies opposed to despotism and favoring the restoration of the 1876 constitution. Among the most important of these societies was the Committee of Union and Progress (CUP). In 1908, a rebellion in the army forced 'Abdul Hamid to consent to the Young Turks' demand for the restoration of the constitution. A year later, he was deposed with effective rule passing to a CUP-dominated parliament.

In Iraq, the population remained generally unaffected by the political changes occurring in distant Istanbul. Some of the Kurds of Iraq were recruited into 'Abdul Hamid's new irregular frontier forces known as the *Hamidiyya*. These forces were active during the 1890s in brutally suppressing Armenian rebellions which also affected the Assyrian Christians of south-eastern Anatolia. Since the *Hamidiyya* forces were organized along tribal lines, the state's penetration of Kurdish society did not weaken tribal structures, nor did it lead to a significant development of Kurdish nationalism. Throughout Iraq, a number of Sunni religious figures gained through the more favorable treatment of 'Abdul Hamid's court. But, for the educated elite, it was the ideological struggles that left the deepest impact. Islamic revivalism, emboldened by 'Abdul Hamid's pan-Islamic policies yet critical of his despotism, found its most distinguished Iraqi representative in the figure of Mahmud Shukri al-Alusi. A member of the distinguished family of sayyids, al-Alusi was widely respected for his impeccable reputation as a religious scholar of high integrity. In his numerous works he expressed familiar themes of the Islamic revivalist movement, known as the *Salafiyya*, which emphasized the compatibility of Islam with scientific progress and sought to restore religious practice to its pristine origins during the time of the Prophet and the early caliphs. Quite illustrative of the contradictory relations that these Muslim thinkers had with 'Abdul Hamid, Mahmud Shukri al-Alusi was exiled in 1902 for attacking the "superstition" of some sufi groups and for "sedition" because of his Wahhabi leanings. The ideas of secularism and equality as expressed by the Young Turks also had an impact on Iraqi thinkers. Men like the poet Jamil Sidqi al-Zahawi wrote moving works on the plight of the poor and called for an end to the subjugation of women. Many of his poems urged religious equality and indirectly helped to promote a national consciousness, as in the following lines:

> Christians and Jews have lived in one spot
> with the Muslims, they are all brothers[6]

The fall of 'Abdul Hamid's rule opened the way for the appearance of political parties and publications. In this regard, Iraq was no different from other regions of the empire with the publication of over 50 newspapers and the establishment of a multitude of political organizations and clubs expressing a broad spectrum of ideas. Among these groups

---

[6] Quoted in Yusuf Rizq-Allah Ghunayma, *Nuzhat al-Mushtaq fi Ta'rikh Yahud al-'Iraq*, second edition, London, 1997, p. 260.

were local chapters of the CUP and its opponent the Moderate Liberal Party. The Shi'is, long absent from the political stage in Iraq, were gradually drawn into the debates not only by the Young Turks' renewed emphasis on secularism, but also by the political develop- ments in neighboring Iran. In 1906, a popular movement in Iran chal- lenged the power of the shah and succeeded in establishing a constitutional government with an elected parliament. Thanks to direct telegraph and postal links, the Shi'is of Iraq, particularly the Mujtahids, closely followed the news from Tehran and Tabriz and par- ticipated in the ensuing political debates. The Shi'i centers of Iraq also contributed to the success of the Iranian Constitutional Revolution by providing a safe haven for leaders to organize an effective movement.

Seventeen men represented the Iraqi provinces to the 1908 Ottoman parliament. Most, like Sayyid Talib al-Naqib of Basra and Sayyid 'Ali 'Ala' al-Din al-Alusi, a cousin of Mahmud Shukri al-Alusi, came from old notable families. In Istanbul, they found themselves naturally drawn to representatives from the other Arab provinces of the empire. Sharing the same language and culture, they also discovered a sense of solidarity based on the commonality of many of their pressing prob- lems. This budding nationalism was supported through the spread of Arabic language publications from Cairo, Beirut and Damascus, and through the development of Arab literary societies. Scholars like the linguist and historian Father Pere Anastase, poets like Jamil Sidqi al- Zahawi and Ma'ruf al-Rasafi, writers like Ahmad al-Shawi and 'Abdul- Muhsin al-Kazimi, and literary clubs like the National Scientific Club in Baghdad, all glorified Arab history, literature and culture. In addition to Sunni intellectuals, this early expression of cultural nation- alism also drew in Shi'i, Jewish and Christian participation and helped establish bridges between Iraq's many religious communities.

Politically, the early nationalist movement did not go beyond the demands for greater autonomy. There was resentment at Arab under- representation in parliament and some Iraqis established connections with the Ottoman Administrative Decentralization Party and the Freedom and Accord Party, both of which opposed the CUP's centralizing policies. Two Iraqis were also present at the Arab Congress of 1913 in Paris, which raised similar demands for greater provincial autonomy and the protection of the Arabic language. Within a few years of the 1908 Revolution, the Young Turks began to clamp down on the recently gained freedoms. The CUP's goal of molding the numerous peoples of the empire into a single nation regardless of religious affiliation soon gave way to ethnic and cultural discrimination. The single nation was to be Turkish and a policy of cultural "Turkification" gradually came into effect during the close of the Ottoman period. Throughout the Arab provinces this was met with stiff resistance. Intellectuals now came to entertain the notion of political separation as the only way to protect Arab interests. Once again, the literary societies played an important role in resisting cultural Turkification. While the National Scientific Club in Baghdad tended to support Arab autonomy within the empire, Mosul's Scientific Society and Basra's Reform Society expressed clear secessionist ideas. Probably the most vocal demands for independence at this time came from Basra's ambitious Sayyid Talib al-Naqib who aspired to form an Iraqi state under his rule. The closure of many of these clubs and the intimidation or imprisonment of their leaders only radicalized the movement and drove it underground. The most important of these secretive societies was the Covenant Society (al-'Ahd) which drew most of its members from Arab army officers and called for the independence of the Arab provinces. Though its founder was an Egyptian, Iraqi officers, such as Nuri al-Sa'id, Yasin al-Hashimi, Ja'far al-'Askari and Jamil al-Midfa'i, dominated its membership and later played important roles as the early leaders of the independent state of Iraq. Despite these activities, nationalism at this time was neither as developed nor as popular in Iraq as it was in Syria or Egypt.

While the CUP government was promoting Turkish nationalism at home, it also tried to counter British, French and Russian influence through closer ties with Germany. During 'Abdul Hamid's reign, an old idea of building a railway linking Iraq with Europe was revived by a German firm. In reaction to the rise of such a rival, Britain formed an agreement, in 1899, with Shaykh Mubarak al-Sabah of Kuwait under which the tiny principality would receive assistance and protection in return for British control of its foreign policy, including any possible agreements on the extension of the proposed railway to Kuwait. In 1903, the Ottoman government agreed to a concession for the so-called Berlin-to-Baghdad rail line. The concession also awarded the Germans mineral rights along the line. Fearful of German ambitions in the area, the British initially sought to sabotage the agreement. Later, Britain dropped its opposition with guarantees that the final Baghdad-to-the-Persian-Gulf link would be constructed by a British firm and terminate at Basra. In the Anglo–Ottoman draft convention of 1913, Britain also agreed to withdraw from its 1899 agreement with the shaykh of Kuwait and recognized the principality as an autonomous Ottoman *qada'* (district) linked to Basra. With the commencement of World War I only a tiny section of the line, between Baghdad and Samarra, was actually completed. British interests in the region had risen considerably in 1908 with the discovery of oil in Iran, not far from the border with Ottoman Iraq. In 1914, the Anglo–Persian Oil Company began to export refined oil from Abadan, just across the Shatt al-'Arab river. When the British navy decided to convert its fleet from coal to oil fuel, the government sought to secure control of the Anglo-Persian Oil Company and duly acquired a 51 per cent share. There was high hope that oil would soon be found in Iraq and in 1912 a British-dominated consortium, the Turkish Petroleum Company, was formed for that purpose. Iran's oil was a major factor in Britain's renewed attempts to settle the Ottoman–Persian border dispute along the Shatt al-'Arab. With Russia, pressure was exerted on the Ottoman and Persian authorities to accept a protocol, signed in 1913, which defined the border in a much more detailed manner. Once again, the Ottomans won recognition of their sovereignty over both banks of the Shatt al-'Arab though Persia was awarded sovereignty over its anchorage which extended into the river.

War, occupation and secret agreements

In August 1914, the First World War broke out among the major powers of Europe. Fearful of Russian ambitions, the Ottomans, after much deliberation and hesitancy, made their fateful decision to join the war on the side of Germany in early November. Long before the Ottoman entry into the war, Britain was preparing an expeditionary force to invade southern Iraq from India. Given its strategic and economic interests in the region, few were surprised when British forces landed at Fao on November 6, 1914, barely one day after the formal declaration of hostilities. Yet while the British took Basra without much of a fight, their conquest of Iraq was anything but easy. During this campaign they suffered over 100,000 casualties and damages worth more that 200 million pounds sterling. Initially, they had intended only to secure the province of Basra, which they did by early December. Encouraged by the early success, however, they pushed further north toward Baghdad only to be driven back by the Ottoman Sixth Army to Kut al-'Amara in November 1915. After a siege of five months, the British, under the command of General Townshend, surrendered unconditionally. This humiliating defeat convinced the War Office of the need for reinforcements and General Stanley Maude was sent in to assume overall command. A new offensive succeeded in capturing Baghdad in March 1917, and by the end of the war in November 1918 British troops were just to the south of Mosul. The city was taken a few days after the signing of the Armistice of Mudros, which had guaranteed an end to all hostilities between the Ottomans and the Allies.

The war had opposite effects on the northern and southern parts of the country. Basra suffered little damage during the operations and its economy prospered with increased shipping from India. British engineers worked on expanding and modernizing the port's facilities to better handle the heavy traffic. Efficient troop movement required the construction of new roads and rail lines and the economy received a boost through demands for greater food production and an increase in employment opportunities. Baghdad suffered from the loss of its economic outlet to the sea and the increasingly burdensome Ottoman conscription. Mosul was not far removed from the destructive battles that raged in eastern Anatolia. During much of the war, Russia and Britain encouraged the Armenian and Assyrian Christians of Anatolia to rebel against Ottoman rule. Such uprisings led to widespread massacres eventually causing many Assyrians to flee to northern Iraq. The sudden appearance of these refugees, and their recent history of brutal conflict with the Muslim Kurds, created much resentment which continued to fester for many decades to come.

As the war progressed the English sought agreements with numerous parties to help bring about a speedy victory. In 1914, the shaykh of Kuwait was recognized as an independent ruler under British protection. In 1915, agreement was also reached with Sharif Husayn, the governor of Mecca, according to which he would declare an Arab revolt against the Ottomans in return for British support for Arab independence in Arabia and the Fertile Crescent. Whether this amounted to a unified kingdom or not remained unspecified. Exceptions were made with respect to certain parts of this territory. Regarding Iraq, the British put forth their concerns in the following manner:

> With regard to the *vilayets* [provinces] of Baghdad and Basra, the Arabs will recognize that the established position and interests of Great Britain necessitate special administrative arrangements in order to secure these territories from foreign aggression, to promote the welfare of the local populations, and to safeguard our mutual economic interests.[7]

---

[7] Quoted in P.M. Holt, *Egypt and the Fertile Crescent, 1516–1922: A Political History*, Ithaca, 1966, p. 266

It was widely assumed that the "special administrative arrangements" implied British advice and assistance or, perhaps, some sort of protection agreement. The vagaries notwithstanding, the revolt was declared in 1916 under the able leadership of Sharif Husayn's son Faysal. Faysal's forces included a significant number of Iraqi officers who had left the Ottoman army to join the nationalist cause. Most of these officers, like Ja'far al-'Askari, (who actually assumed overall military command) and Nuri al-Sa'id, were members of the Covenant Society. The revolt succeeded in tying down Ottoman forces and, toward the end of the war, capturing Damascus.

At the same time that the British were formulating their agreements with Sharif Husayn and his son Faysal, they were secretly negotiating with the French over the future of the Arab territories. In 1916, the French and British negotiators, Charles Picot and Mark Sykes, agreed to divide the Fertile Crescent after the conclusion of the war. France was to get the territory of modern Lebanon, Syria and Mosul, while Britain would receive Baghdad, Basra and the territory stretching from there to parts of coastal Palestine. Despite the various qualifications there is little doubt that Iraq was promised independence in the correspondence with Sharif Husayn, but received no such recognition in the Sykes–Picot Agreement. To further complicate matters, General Maude, upon his entry into Baghdad, had unequivocally declared that the British had arrived as "liberators not conquerors". To placate Arab fears once the provisions of the Sykes–Picot Agreement became known, the British and the French made a joint declaration promising independence based on the self-determination of the peoples themselves. In the end, however, none of these agreements seemed to matter when faced with the reality of who, at the end of the war, actually controlled the territories in question.

The nineteenth century saw a steady extension of urban hegemony over the countryside for the first time since the collapse of the Abbasid Caliphate. While Iraq was hardly unified during this period, Baghdad continued to act as a center to which Mosul, and especially Basra, gravitated. The Ottoman Tanzimat, with its emphasis on centralization and the development of the Sixth Army stationed in Baghdad, further promoted the dominant role of the city. Iraq's integration into the world economy was spearheaded by growing British commercial interests, particularly after the opening of the Suez Canal in 1869. These interests took a qualitative leap with the discovery of oil in nearby Iran and the strong prospects of discovering more of this precious commodity in Iraq. Socially, centralization tended to push the old notable classes and tribal shaykhs toward accommodation with the state, while the economic influences from abroad had the effect of promoting the interests of the commercial classes. Both of these processes encouraged secularization, thereby creating more opportunities for the non-Sunni communities. Far from being all-conquering processes, the expansion of the state and European economic penetration faced stiff resistance which eventually altered the intended results of their promoters. Midhat Pasha's land policy, for example, was successfully derailed from its intended goal of creating a large class of peasants with usufruct rights over their lands, into one which promoted the rise of big landowners and share-cropping relations. In addition, among some intellectuals of the pre-war period this resistance was gradually expressed in the form of a nationalist movement.

chapter five

MANDATE AND MONARCHY, 1918–1958

After World War I, the territory of Iraq under British military control contained a number of peoples divided by ethnicity, religion and tribal loyalty. Of all the Ottoman provinces in the Middle East, those in Iraq had demonstrated a strong resistance to centralized rule. Despite the reforms of the nineteenth century, the region was also one of the least developed in the empire. According to the best available estimates, the population of Iraq at the end of the war numbered some 2.5 to 3 million. While the Arabic-speaking population constituted a solid majority of 75–80 per cent, this group was deeply divided between Sunnis and Shi'is on the one hand, and along several tribal confederacies on the other. The Kurds, plagued with tribal divisions and inhabiting the most inaccessible part of the country, constituted about 15–20 per cent with most of the remainder being Turkomans, Persians and Assyrians. Muslims, 55 per cent of whom were Shi'i, formed 90 per cent with Christians, Jews, Mandaeans and Yazidis making up the rest. The Jews were especially important in Baghdad forming about one-third of the city's population. Tribes, such as the 'Anayza, Shammar and Jubur, still engaged in violent feuds. The country had one major city in Baghdad (population about 200,000) and two smaller ones in Basra and Mosul (each about 50,000). Around 80 per cent of the people lived in the countryside with few having ever ventured outside the region around their village. The country had no mechanized factory industries and only 5 per cent knew how to read and write. By the end of the war there were only around 200 students enrolled in secondary-level schools. The new boundaries, drawn up after the war, forced Iraq to reorient itself away from what had once been the Ottoman Empire. Both Anatolia and Syria suddenly became different countries with new borders separating communities and disrupting centuries-old trade routes. While these issues represented formidable obstacles, perhaps the greatest asset to the establishment of the modern Iraqi state was the long history of the centrality of Baghdad and the gradual extension of its hegemony over the rest of the country including Sulaymaniyya and parts of Kurdistan.

In general, the Iraqi response to the British invasion was one of initial neutrality later progressing into active resistance when it became clear that a long-term occupation was developing. Nevertheless, there were different reactions among the cities. Basra, which had a long history of interaction with Britain and benefited from the presence of the army, generally cooperated with the expedition. Even the massively ambitious Sayyid Talib al-Naqib, who wielded great influence in the city, did not oppose the invasion at the beginning. Baghdad remained quiet with its notables not yet sure what to make of the new situation. The Kurds of Sulaymaniyya initially cheered the new conquerors in the hope that they would pave the way for greater Kurdish autonomy or even independence. Very soon after the end of the war, however, they began to actively oppose the British presence. The only cities which, from the start, resisted the British were the Shi'i centers of Najaf and Karbala. During the war, many Mujtahids raised the banner of *jihad*, or holy war, against the non-Muslim invaders. In 1918, fearing that the new rulers of Iraq threatened not only Shi'i independence but the Islamic religion as a whole, a number of notables in Najaf helped form the Islamic Revival Society, one of the first post-war political organizations. The following year, several Sunni and Shi'i figures met to form The Guardians of Independence, the first specifically Iraqi nationalist society. No popular anti-Ottoman movement developed during the war and most Sunni notables continued to honor the name of the sultan even after the war. Once again, the only exception was in Najaf and Karbala where uprisings against Ottoman rule did take place.

Post-War British policy

Among British officials there was general agreement as to their country's prime interests in Iraq being, first and foremost, oil, and the establishment of some entity, or entities, which would facilitate British control over this valuable commodity. What this entity should be, however, was very much in dispute. Toward the end of the war, two schools of thought were already quite discernible. The so-called "Eastern School", championed by Arnold Wilson, the country's Civil Commissioner, sought to extend the British policies of India to Iraq. This meant the establishment of direct colonial rule with efficiency being the primary consideration and little attention given to local participation in governance. Wilson argued that such a policy would not only ensure British vital interests but also serve the loftier goal of spreading modern civilization among the backward peoples of Asia. This was, after all, the age when European imperialism was justified with notions of the "White Man's Burden" and the "Civilizing Mission", and Wilson firmly believed that Iraq could become a glorious example of the progressive nature of British rule. He was, however, under no illusion of the investments required for such a vision and he repeatedly urged London to be prepared for a long stay. While this policy initially had the upper hand, it was constantly challenged by the rival "Western School" formulated by the Arab Bureau in Cairo. Proponents of this policy, such as the famous T.E. Lawrence, argued that British interests were better supported through indirect control over friendly Arab governments. They believed that Wilson's policy was too costly and likely to lead to Arab resentment and animosity and preferred to maintain influence through advisers and treaties.

Nevertheless, Wilson pushed on with his program and by 1920 there were almost 3000 British officials manning government offices. Iraqis were excluded from any meaningful positions and the Ottoman elected councils were eliminated. Since the center of state development were the cities, this policy was particularly harmful to the urban notables even though Wilson did go out of his way to demonstrate his respect for certain men of influence. In the countryside it was quite different. Eager to win over the support of the tribal shaykhs, the British sought to actually enhance their powers. As one British officer noted in 1919: "We must recognize that it is primarily our business not to give rights to those who have them not, but to secure their rights to those who have them."[1] This was done through the Tribal Criminal and Civil Disputes Regulation of 1916. Under this law tribal shaykhs who were willing to demonstrate their loyalty to the new order, were given full judicial, administrative (including tax collection) and policing rights over their territory. This policy had the effect of reversing the erosion of tribal power, evident during the late Ottoman period, and promoting many whose shaykhly claims were questionable. In some areas, especially along the Tigris south of Baghdad, a strong base of support for the British developed among the rural elite. In this regard, another official wrote:

> The shaikhs were in most cases directly dependent on the civil administration for the positions they held; realising that their positions entailed corresponding obligations, they cooperated actively with the political officers.[2]

British intentions notwithstanding, the shape of the new state was also molded by the active resistance to their rule. This was already taking a more determined form through demonstrations and the assassination of a British officer in Najaf. Even in Kurdistan, where the population had initially welcomed the British, signs of tension were evident. Due to its inaccessibility, the strategy here was to allow for a greater degree of self rule. In 1918, Shaykh Mahmud Barazanchi, the head of the Qadiriyya sufi order and an influential tribal agha, was appointed governor of Sulaymaniyya. Soon, the ambitious Barazanchi, supported by a number of tribal aghas, sought to free himself of British patronage and set up an independent Kurdish state. The British were forced into military action and Barazanchi was sent into exile. As with other parts of the country, northern Iraq grew more restless with uprisings and the

---

[1] Quoted in Marion Farouk-Sluglett and Peter Sluglett, "The Transformation of Land Tenure and Rural Social Structure in Central and Southern Iraq c. 1870–1958", in *International Journal of Middle East Studies*, 15 (1983), p. 504.

[2] *Ibid.*, p. 496.

assassination of a number of British officers. Turkey, which still laid claim to the province of Mosul, encouraged the opposition.

The final straw came in 1920 when the newly established League of Nations, meeting at San Remo in Italy, declared that the Fertile Crescent should be parceled out into a number of "mandates". Syria (including modern Lebanon) was entrusted to France, while Britain received the mandates for Iraq, Jordan and Palestine. France had agreed to give up its claim on Mosul, promised to it in the Sykes–Picot Agreement, in return for a share of the province's oil. The mandates were justified in the following manner:

> Certain communities formerly belonging to the Turkish Empire have reached a stage of development where their existence as independent nations can be provisionally recognized subject to the rendering of advice and assistance by a Mandatory until such time as they are able to stand alone. The wishes of these communities must be a principal consideration in the selection of the Mandatory.[3]

In essence, the mandate was nothing but a cover for colonialism. Certainly the wishes of the people in Iraq were never seriously con-sidered. An American suggestion that a commission of enquiry be sent in "to discover the desires of the population" was rejected. Later, when this commission (known as the King–Crane commission), did go it was not allowed to function in Iraq and its findings for Syria and Palestine were completely ignored. If any further confirmation was needed of the Allies' "right of conquest" approach to governing the Middle East, it was amply demonstrated in Syria shortly after the San Remo conference. Most of Syria was under the control of Faysal's Arab government. In a desperate effort to prevent a French invasion, Faysal convened a National Congress in Damascus which rejected the

---

[3] Quoted in Justin McCarthy, *The Ottoman Peoples and the End of Empire*, London, 2001, p. 176.

decisions of San Remo and declared the independence of Syria (understood at that time to include Syria, Lebanon, Jordan and Palestine) under a constitutional monarchy. Faysal was then elected as the country's first king. A smaller congress, composed mainly of Faysal's Iraqi officers, also convened in Damascus to declare the independence of Iraq with Faysal's brother, 'Abdullah, as king. Both congresses agreed that the two countries should be federated in some manner. The "Iraqi Congress" was hardly representative, nor was 'Abdullah even keen on adopting its claims, yet it was significant because it formed another nationalist center willing to challenge British rule. In fact, as the French prepared to invade Damascus, many of these Iraqi officers established a base at Dayr al-Zur, on the border with Iraq, to help support the developing anti-British movement.

The rebellion of 1920 and the birth of the Iraqi state

As news of the San Remo conference became known, the country appeared to be on the verge of a massive uprising. The mandate was denounced in almost every public place, be it in the mosques or the coffee-houses of Baghdad. Sunnis and Shi'is demonstrated a rare sense of solidarity by sharing their places of worship to mobilize the population. Oddly enough, Wilson brushed aside such concerns, treating Iraqi delegates who came to see him with conceit and arrogance. The uprising began with street demonstrations in Baghdad followed by armed tribal revolt in the middle and lower Euphrates region. Kurdish tribes also took advantage of the disturbances to press the British in Mosul. As the rebellion reverberated throughout the country, Karbala and its environs emerged as the bastion of the anti-British movement. Arab nationalist flags and agitational pamphlets were produced in the city and distributed to the rest of the country, while leading religious figures like Ayatollah Shirazi urged Muslims on with calls for a jihad. Traditional taboos did not prevent women from playing important roles as well, such as smuggling arms, collecting donations and acting as messengers. There is little doubt that the Great Rebellion of 1920, as it came to be known, demonstrated a clear manifestation of early Iraqi nationalism. A sense of unity developed, albeit briefly, between Sunnis and Shi'is, urban and rural peoples, and the numerous tribes, especially in the Euphrates region. The British responded with a brutal repression in which the Royal Air Force (RAF) and large-scale reinforcements used mustard gas on the tribal armies.

Weaknesses soon appeared within the rebel camp. The tribes of the middle and lower Euphrates region eagerly joined and eventually led the struggle, but they doggedly resisted any attempt at the establishment of an overall revolutionary leadership. Many urban Sunni notables refused to back the rebellion for fear that it might lead to an increase in Shi'i power. Likewise, the Shi'i shaykhs along the lower Tigris who had benefited from British largesse and were known for their extensive land-holdings, opposed the uprising with some even committing their tribal forces. In Kurdistan the rebellion never fully developed since Kurdish nationalists and tribal leaders were still suspicious of Arab leadership. Nevertheless, the rebellion, which lasted from July to October, cost the British more than 450 lives and 40 million pounds sterling. About 10,000 Iraqis, mostly tribesmen, were killed. During this same period, developments in neighboring Syria also affected the course of events in Iraq. Having been granted the mandate of Syria, France sent its forces against Faysal's young Arab kingdom, defeating his army and occupying Damascus in July 1920. The immediate result of this was the return of most of Faysal's Iraqi officers to their country where some participated in the Great Rebellion.

Despite its eventual defeat, the Rebellion of 1920 dealt a decisive blow to Wilson's plans of direct rule over Iraq. The widely respected Sir Percy Cox returned to Baghdad to assume the post of High Commissioner and resolve the problem of British rule. In a full reversal of Wilson's policy, Cox set up an Iraqi interim government under the leadership of Sayyid 'Abdul-Rahman al-Gaylani, one of the most respected Sunni notables of Baghdad. Members of the government did reflect a desire to include the various Iraqi communities but Shi'is were again under-represented. In 1921, under the chairmanship of Winston Churchill, the Colonial Secretary at that time, a conference was held in Cairo to discuss Britain's policies toward its possessions in the Middle East. It was decided that an Iraqi government, under British tutelage, be created provided that it "be constitutional, representative and democratic". After some debate Faysal, the exiled king of Syria and leader of the Arab Revolt against the Ottomans, was invited to assume the leadership of the new state of Iraq. Faysal was considered the ideal candidate because he could satisfy several interests while remaining loyal to the British. Being a descendant of the Prophet from the Hashimite clan, he was thought acceptable to the traditional Muslim elements. His nationalist credentials were established through his revolt against the Ottomans and his leadership of the Arab government in Damascus. Throughout these difficult trials he demonstrated effective, moderate leadership winning the respect of his followers. At the same time, he was expected to favor cooperation with Britain because, as a non-Iraqi, he lacked a solid domestic base and had already suffered at the hands of France for challenging the authority of a European power.

Before accepting the Iraqi throne, the 30-year-old Faysal insisted on a national referendum which was hastily arranged and yielded a rather dubious 96 per cent in favor. This result was hardly representative since Sulaymaniyya and much of Mosul (still claimed by Turkey) did not participate. Kirkuk returned a no vote, at Basra many supported the claims of the exiled Sayyid Talib al-Naqib, and among the Shi'is, most of the Mujtahids denounced the whole affair. Nevertheless, under British guard and a band playing "God Save the King", Faysal was enthroned as the first king of modern Iraq on 23 August 1921. The lack of enthusiasm was obvious: in their Friday prayers, Sunni religious leaders continued to mention the names of the caliph and the sultan before that of the new king. Faysal did receive a boost when Mustafa Kemal abolished both the sultanate and the caliphate by 1924, but in Kurdistan his authority was challenged by the inexhaustible Mahmud Barazanchi who returned from exile in 1922 and proclaimed himself king of an independent Kurdish state. From his city of Sulaymaniyya he passed laws, collected taxes and issued stamps until the RAF again drove him out and re-established Baghdad's control.

The enthronement of Faysal meant a certain readjustment of Britain's position in the country. Instead of the despised status of the mandate, Faysal insisted on a formal treaty spelling out the relationship between the government of Iraq and Britain. In effect, the Treaty of 1922 incorporated all the terms of the mandate system in the form of a bilateral agreement. Britain directly administered the defense and internal security of the country while all other ministries and departments were required to accept the presence of British advisers and inspectors wielding veto power. In addition, the Iraqi government had to pay half of the cost of the British Residency. Regardless of this treaty, the League of Nations continued to formally refer to Iraq as a mandate territory.

Developments under the mandate

The new government faced a truly daunting task. Throughout its history, multi-communal Iraq has not been an easy country to govern. As part of the Middle East, the new country suffered from the post-war turmoil that affected the entire region. More importantly, Faysal had to build a nation with one eye firmly fixed on his British protectors and the other on a populace deeply resentful of its continued subjugation by a foreign power. Drawing up the exact borders of the new state proved extremely taxing. A resurgent Iran under Reza Khan (later Reza Shah Pahlavi) refused to even recognize the Iraqi government until 1929. While fundamentally the tensions between the two states were caused by the competition for regional supremacy, the immediate problems centered around three issues. First, the border region in Kurdistan remained a source of contention. The rugged terrain and constant tribal migrations mitigated against a clear delineation of the boundary. Second, Iran's military occupation of the area of Khuzistan in 1925, with its Arab majority and tribal ties across the border, further soured the relationship. Lastly, Iran continued to object to Iraq's claim of sovereignty over the entire Shatt al-'Arab, demanding, instead, that the border run through the mid-point of the river. Despite several embassies, including a visit by Faysal to Tehran, these issues were left unresolved by the mandate government.

The country's borders with its southern neighbors were settled in the 'Uqayr conference of 1922 organized by Percy Cox. The meeting also included 'Abdul-'Aziz Al Sa'ud (the future king of Arabia), representatives of the Iraqi monarchy, and a British officer representing the shaykh of Kuwait. With Cox practically dictating the final settlement, the border was drawn with Arabia in favor of Iraq. On the other hand, Iraq's claims of sovereignty over Kuwait (at that time a very poor country) were rejected. The monarchy's failure to secure Kuwait meant that the Iraqi state was almost land-locked, contributing to its future economic difficulties. But the most dangerous question of the time was that of the border with Turkey. Mustafa Kemal's new republic made a concerted effort to gain control of the province of Mosul. They argued that since Mosul was occupied by British forces after the Ottoman Empire had already signed the armistice, its annexation to Iraq represented a violation of that agreement. In addition, they argued that the Kurds were culturally akin to the Turks and called for a referendum to settle the question. Many Kurds, fearing the division of their people among Turkey, Iran and Iraq, favored the Turkish argument, though it is impossible to say whether they formed a majority. The British argument was based on the historic and administrative ties between Mosul and Baghdad. Legalities notwithstanding, the matter was ultimately decided by the facts on the ground. The British army controlled the province and the Turks were not willing to fight for it when they had just recovered from a terrible war with Greece. For the British, Mosul was important for its oil and the viability of the young state of Iraq. The influential Sunni notables of Baghdad and Basra were also eager to include Mosul because of its Sunni population which could counterbalance the Shi'is of the south.

The eventual settlement of the Mosul question was intricately tied up with the nature of Iraqi–British relations. Iraqi nationalists, such as the Shi'i minister Ja'far Abu al-Timman, fought tooth and nail for effective independence. Even Faysal, who was beholden to the British for his position and depended greatly on British advisers such as Gertrude Bell, did not always act according to the consul's wishes. The Mosul question, however, served to strengthen the hand of Britain. In return for its assistance Britain demanded that Iraq agree to a 75-year oil concession with the British-dominated Turkish (later the Iraqi) Petroleum Company. The government had been demanding a 20 per cent share in the company, but fearing the loss of Mosul it eventually gave in and was left with no shares in its country's most important economic asset. In 1925, as a result of British pressure, the League of Nations awarded Mosul to Iraq on condition that the Kurds be guaranteed control over their local government and the right to use their own language. Though Baghdad often flouted these rights, they were, nevertheless, unique to the Kurds of Iraq and absent in both Turkey and Iran. From this point on the government tended to cooperate fully with the British. At times, the tension caused by the growing popular appeal of the nationalists and the government's reluctance to challenge British hegemony, proved too much for the early Iraqi statesmen. A powerful man like 'Abdul-Muhsin al-Sa'dun, who hailed from a distinguished family of sayyids, was driven to such despair that he took his own life. In what might have been his suicide note he lamented over the fact that the country was too weak to win its independence while the people still expected the government to do so.

Internally, no one had any doubt about the difficulties involved in forging a national identity among Iraq's many communities. As late as 1933, Faysal wrote:

> In Iraq, there is still – and I say this with a heart full of sorrow – no Iraqi people but unimaginable masses of human beings, devoid of any patriotic idea, imbued with religious traditions and absurdities, connected by no common tie, giving ear to evil, prone to anarchy, and perpetually ready to rise against any government whatever. Out of these masses we want to fashion a people which we could train, educate, and refine ... .[4]

According to the 1925 constitution, which basically remained intact throughout the monarchy, Iraq had a two-chamber parliament and an independent judiciary. The king held important powers including those of vetoing any legislation, dismissing parliament and calling for new elections. Elections were effectively controlled and martial law periodically declared to ensure that the state remained firmly in the hands of a rather small elite. Between 1922 and 1958, when the monarchy was overthrown, 10 elections were held and 59 cabinets formed. Rarely, however, did these interruptions represent anything more than a reshuffling of posts. Throughout the monarchy, the political elite remained rather stable, dominated by ex-Ottoman officers and a number of urban notables. The most durable politician of the monarchy was Nuri al-Sa'id, the pragmatist *par excellence*, who assumed several cabinet posts including that of Prime Minister. Faysal, conscious of the need to broaden his political base, tried to include Shi'is and Kurds by promoting a number of them (along with the token Jews and Christians). Both the Sunni elite and the British resisted the initiative and made sure that the Shi'is remained woefully under-represented. Sunni dominance was also evident in the provincial governments even in Shi'i dominated areas.

To help foster a sense of nationhood, Faysal appointed Sati' al-Husri, an ardent pan-Arabist of Syrian origin, to the post of Director General of

---

[4] Quoted in Batatu, Hanna, *The Old Social Classes and Revolutionary Movements of Iraq: A Study of Iraq's Old Landed and Commercial Classes and of its Communists, Ba'thists, and Free Officers*, Princeton, 1978, p. 25.

education. The curriculum which al-Husri developed promoted Iraqi patriotism but also sought to instill a sense of belonging to the broader, mainly Sunni, Arabic-speaking world. Arab nationalism, in many ways, represented an ideological rejection of colonialism and division. It sought to foster pride in a glorious past, an attribute necessary for national development. By highlighting the Arab identity of the country, however, al-Husri tended to alienate the Kurds and Shi'is. While the former feared the loss of their national identity in an enlarged Arab state, the latter were equally concerned about their reduction to a minority in a Sunni country. For Faysal, the most important instrument of nation-building was the army. He claimed that the government could do little when it possessed only 15,000 rifles compared with the estimated 100,000 rifles available to the tribes. In spite of his repeated appeals for the creation of an adequate force, the British, fearing nationalist influence, insisted on keeping the army at the ludicrously low number of 7500 men throughout the mandate period.

In addition to their ability to control the government through advisers and the RAF, the British consciously promoted the power of loyal tribal shaykhs. The Tribal Criminal and Civil Disputes Regulation of 1916 was included within the constitution. This greatly limited the power of the central government. The dubious nature of the elections and near absolutist power of the shaykhs in the provinces, guaranteed the dominance of parliament by the big landowners. Over the period of the monarchy parliament passed several laws which enhanced semifeudal relations in the countryside, centralized land ownership and tilted development in favor of agriculture at the expense of industry. In the urban areas, family and personal status law (including inheritance) continued to be handled by the Islamic shari'a courts. These followed separate traditions with the most obvious differences being those between the Sunni and Shi'i courts.

Though the nationalist opposition was weak, fragmented, and focused on a number of ambitious individuals, it did manage to keep the pressure on the government. The central issue, of course, was Britain's dominant role which it described as an "unnatural condition" blocking development. In 1929, a new Labor government in London invited Iraqi representatives to negotiate a new treaty with guarantees for independence. Under the forceful leadership of Prime Minister Nuri al-Sa'id, the Anglo–Iraqi Treaty of 1930 was signed. It was to last 25 years and provided for the independence of Iraq within two years of its ratification. The treaty also sought to create a "close alliance" between the two countries largely by protecting Britain's dominant role in the country. This was achieved by granting Britain the right to veto all foreign policy decisions, a monopoly over the training and equipment purchases of the army, and the right to use Iraqi territory in times of war. The RAF would remain in two bases at Habaniyya near Baghdad and Shu'ayba near Basra. Iraq also agreed to uphold Kurdish national rights in the north. The treaty was bitterly opposed by the nationalists who believed it truncated Iraq's sovereignty while many Kurds and religious minorities feared that the withdrawal of Britain might leave them unprotected. This fear, in fact, did materialize when the government began to replace local Kurdish officials and enforce the use of Arabic in schools. Once again, Shaykh Mahmud Barazanchi appeared to lead a rebellion in 1930, and once again the British helped to crush it. This time, however, Barazanchi's leadership suffered a decisive blow and a new generation began to look toward Shaykh Ahmad Barazani and his brother Mulla Mustafa of the rival Naqshabandiyya sufi order. In spite of these challenges, the treaty was pushed through parliament and, in October 1932, Iraq formally achieved its independence.

The Independent Kingdom

There is little doubt that the formal independence of Iraq in 1932, and its admittance to the League of Nations the same year, signaled an important step in the history of the modern country. The government, however, continued to suffer from a legitimacy crisis with many, especially the younger generation of educated professionals, far from happy with the country's subservience to Britain. For this generation, the question was not only one of patriotic pride. Britain was seen as a force that supported a narrow political elite and the shaykhly classes in the countryside – a condition that undermined economic and social development, keeping the country weak and backward. Shi'is and Kurds were especially wary of the continuing Arab Sunni hold on central power.

The most important institutional change after independence was the growth of the army. One of the first decisions taken by the new kingdom was to expand the army through the conscription law of 1934. The army was a natural haven for nationalist ideas. Officers, almost all of whom were Sunni, saw themselves as the Prussians of the Arab world, admired Mustafa Kemal's achievements in Turkey, and took great pride in their independent spirit. In 1933, under the command of General Bakr Sidqi, the army was called on to clamp down on Assyrian armed bands in the north. Most of these bands belonged to the so-called Iraqi Levies, a British-controlled force of Assyrians independent of the Iraqi army. Despite being disbanded they rejected Baghdad's control and refused to turn over their arms. The campaign resulted in a massacre of some 300 unarmed Assyrian villagers, yet was still drummed up as a patriotic victory against British mercenaries. The illness and death of Faysal in 1933, and the succession of his young and inexperienced son Ghazi, weakened the monarchy and provided more opportunities for the army to play a role in the political life of the country. In 1936, Sidqi staged the first of many military coups. Rather than assume a direct hold on government, which it was still too weak to maintain, the army played the role of political arbiter changing one cabinet for another. In the inter-war years, Iraqi politics became much more divisive and unstable with various factions allied to different military officers. Political differences were often settled through palace intrigues and, most damaging of all, by resorting to the age-old tactic of inciting tribal revolts.

For the British and their allies in Iraq, there were many reasons to be concerned. Other than the rise of the army and the resulting political instability that it fostered, the British were particularly worried about the position of the monarchy itself. King Ghazi was considered rash and ill-tempered. Perhaps more important, he showed clear signs of pan-Arabist sympathies with strong pronouncements in support of the Palestinian uprising against the British and his repeated claims to sovereignty over Kuwait. As the war with Hitler grew near, Ghazi appeared to be reaching out to Germany by encouraging pro-Nazi elements. Nuri al-Sa'id, a steadfast supporter of Iraqi–British ties, is believed to have investigated the possibility of removing Ghazi in favor of another Hashimite. When Ghazi died in an automobile accident in 1939, many Iraqis raised questions about British involvement. Since Ghazi's son, Faysal II, was still a minor, his uncle, 'Abdul-Ilah, was appointed regent. Though they disagreed on many issues, Nuri al-Sa'id and 'Abdul-Ilah formed a solid pro-British leadership which would dominate Iraqi politics for the remainder of the monarchy.

In spite of these difficulties, a weak government finally agreed to a border settlement with Iran in 1937. The Iraqi–Iranian Frontier Treaty, also known as the Sa'dabad treaty, recognized Iraqi sovereignty over the entire Shatt al-'Arab, but conceded part of the waterway around the Iranian oil-exporting port of Abadan. Other important achievements of this time included the resolution of border disputes with Syria, the completion of irrigation works along the Tigris, the opening of an oil pipeline to the Mediterranean port of Haifa, and the completion of the last rail link between the Persian Gulf and Europe.

The Opposition

The singular failure of the monarchy was its inability to create a vision for the identity of the new nation. In the struggle between competing visions, two opposing tendencies appeared among the country's young educated elite. Both benefited from the limited freedom of the press that existed during much of the monarchic period. The first, Arab nationalism, was primarily a reaction to colonial rule. It argued that modern Iraq, along with the rest of the Arab countries, was an artificial creation. Its "natural" identity cannot be separated from that of a single Arab nation stretching from Morocco to the Persian Gulf. The most important features of this nation are its language and common historical experience. Arab nationalists focused on the political goal of uniting the Arab countries as the essential step to bring about progress. The development of the Arab–Zionist conflict in Palestine attracted great concern in Iraq and provided the Arab nationalists with a powerful argument in favor of Arab solidarity. Arab nationalism, however, tended to alienate the Kurdish and Shi'i populations. It also neglected to provide much attention to the country's pressing internal problems since all other concerns were to be relegated in favor of the broader goal of Arab unity. This view was opposed to one that favored a specifically Iraqi nationalism. It argued that far from being a mere creation of colonialism, the country and its people had roots that go back to ancient Mesopotamia and the dawn of history. While not opposed to greater regional integration or even Arab political unity, Iraqi nationalists focused most of their attention on the internal problems of the country such as urban development and the oppressive conditions in the countryside. Iraqi nationalism had more success attracting support outside the Arab Sunni population, but it was also criticized for seeming to accept the colonially imposed borders and for neglecting Arab solidarity. Both tendencies were critical of the government's elitism and its dependency on the British. During the inter-war period, political parties were merely instruments of individual notables through which they pursued their interests. It was not until the war was over that ideological concerns truly began to form the basis of political parties.

The oldest organized groups of the monarchy were the various clubs that sprang up in Baghdad, Mosul and Basra during the 1920s. The pan-Arabist Muthana Club in Baghdad, was particularly important because it attracted a number of army officers. It was also the precursor to the Independence Party, founded after World War II. Though the leader of the Independence Party was a Shi'i, the far majority of its members were urban Sunni Arabs. The other important pan-Arabist party was the Ba'th (Renaissance) Party, originally formed in Syria. It emerged in Iraq in the 1950s attracting a number of teachers and students but generally remained quite small until the fall of the monarchy. Among the groups which emphasized Iraqi nationalism and a program of social reforms was the National Democratic Party (NDP), formed in 1946, led by the charismatic Kamil al-Chadirchi. With roots going back to the Ahali club of the 1930s, the NDP had a basically social-democratic ideology calling for independence, democracy, land reform, and the establishment of a social safety net. The best organized party was the Iraqi Communist Party (ICP). Formed in 1934, it is the oldest Iraqi political party still active today. The ICP had its roots in the intellectual socialist circles and the early labor movement of the late 1920s. Iraqi society, dominated by big landowners and with a growing population of landless peasants and shanty-town dwellers, was particularly receptive to notions of class struggle and social justice. Many Iraqis, motivated by anti-British nationalism, were also drawn to the Soviet Union which emerged as a power challenging Western capitalist hegemony. In addition, the culture of popular movements mobilized under the banner of egalitarianism and social justice was not foreign to Iraq, especially in the south where the ICP was particularly strong. With its emphasis on secularism and internationalism it attracted elements from all of Iraq's various communities including the Kurds. Under its semi-legendary leader, Fahd, who took over in 1941, the party became a major opposition force with a tight organization and dedicated leadership.

Initially standing somewhat aloof but later supporting the Iraqi nationalists were the various groups that made up the Kurdish nationalist movement. During the inter-war period, most of the Kurdish nationalist activities were led by tribal or religious leaders like Shaykh Mahmud Barazanchi. During the 1930s this leadership switched to the Barazani family of the Naqshabandiyya sufi order. The most important figure here was Mulla Mustafa Barazani who, in 1945, organized a tribal rebellion against government intervention in provincial Kurdish administration. Once again, the British RAF came to the rescue of Baghdad forcing Mulla Mustafa and his fighters to flee across the border to Iran. There they played an important role in the establishment of the Kurdish Republic of Mahabad which fell to Iranian arms in 1946. While Mulla Mustafa was seeking refuge and eventually finding it in the Soviet Union, a number of urban intellectuals opposed to the tribal leadership formed the Kurdistan Democratic Party (KDP). Initially small and restricted to the main urban centers of the north, the KDP would later play an important role in the opposition to the monarchy.

All these tendencies were evident to some degree when World War II erupted in 1939. Within the army's officer corps, the war was viewed as an excellent opportunity for getting rid of the British. The defeat of the Palestinian revolt of 1936–1939 at the hands of Britain and the arrival in Baghdad of Haj Amin al-Husayni, the mufti of Jerusalem and one of the leaders of the rebellion, also inflamed public opinion and encouraged the army to act. Colonel Salah al-Din al-Sabbagh, who played a leading role in the anti-British campaign, exemplified the Arab nationalist views of many officers when he wrote:

> I do not believe in the democracy of the English nor in the Nazism of the Germans nor in the Bolshevism of the Russians. I am an Arab Muslim. I do not want anything as a substitute in the way of pretensions and philosophies.[5]

In April 1941, with strong army support, Rashid 'Ali al-Gaylani, a known Arab nationalist, became Prime Minister. Hoping for military support from the Axis powers, he precipitated a crisis when the government refused Britain permission to move its troops across Iraqi territory as stipulated in the Anglo–Iraqi Treaty of 1930. As the situation

---

[5] Quoted in Marr, Phebe, *The Modern History of Iraq*, Boulder, 1985, p. 80.

with Britain deteriorated toward armed conflict, Nuri al-Sa'id and the regent 'Abdul-Ilah fled the country. With the Axis unable or unwilling to provide the promised support, British troops easily defeated Iraqi forces in May and reoccupied the country. The "Rashid 'Ali movement", though short-lived and completely unsuccessful, contributed to the army's popularity as the vanguard of the nationalist struggle. The subsequent execution of al-Sabbagh also gave the army its symbolic martyr capturing the imagination of many, including the uncle and foster-parent of Saddam Husayn, the future ruler of Iraq. Likewise, the return of Nuri al-Sa'id and 'Abdul-Ilah, under British protection, served only to further alienate the monarchy. In 1934, as if to emphasize its pro-British credentials, the new government declared war on Germany thereby qualifying to become a founding member of the United Nations.

Other than ending in a second British occupation, the Rashid 'Ali movement had another, more ominous effect. Throughout the interwar period, the Jews of Iraq had generally prospered with many making use of their community's fine schools to become an important part of the young country's new educated elite. Jewish doctors, lawyers and teachers were rapidly becoming as apparent as the artisans, shopowners and merchants. Within many Arab nationalist circles, especially in light of the situation in Palestine, Jews were increasingly seen as British or Zionist collaborators and a fifth column in society. During the late 1930s, isolated attacks on Jews were reported, but they had not yet resulted in a major panic. As the Rashid 'Ali government crumbled, however, anti-British feelings threatened to boil over in the streets of Baghdad. Roving bands of paramilitary groups, which sprang up in Baghdad to bolster Rashid 'Ali's government, took advantage of the power vacuum prior to the entrance of British troops, to stage a pogrom known as the *farhud*. By the time order was restored two days later, between 150 and 180 Jews were killed. More notable, an even larger number of Muslims died trying to protect their Jewish neighbors. Sayyid Abu al-Hasan Musawi, one of the foremost Shi'i leaders in

Baghdad, condemned the attacks and specifically forbade his followers from harming Jews or looting their properties. Other than starting the count-down toward the disappearance of one of Iraq's oldest and most educated communities, the *farhud* of 1941 also had a profound political impact. In the years following the war, the government, isolated and sensitive to accusations of betraying Arab solidarity in Palestine, tended to encourage anti-Jewish legislation. With most opposition activities censored, Arab nationalists benefited by the freedom to raise in public the question of Iraqi Jews.

Social and economic developments

The Iraqi government remained unstable and unable to begin any systematic economic development program until 1950. That year, the government decided that an independent development agency was needed. It would be directly responsible to the Prime Minister and thereby immune from the various vested interests. The establishment of the Development Board was followed, two years later, with an extraordinary increase in oil revenues. Thus, in spite of the continuously unstable political climate, the government had great expectations for Iraq's progress.

The first major discovery of oil took place near Kirkuk in 1927. In 1934, commercial amounts were exported through the newly opened pipeline from Kirkuk to Haifa on the Mediterranean coast. State revenues from oil, however, continued to be small due to several factors. First, the country was almost landlocked, making exports difficult and subject to relations with neighboring countries in an unstable region. This became quite clear when, in 1948, the Haifa line was closed due to the establishment of the state of Israel. In addition, the foreign-owned Iraqi Petroleum Company (IPC), which monopolized oil production and sales, was not at that time interested in increasing production levels for fear that it might conflict with its exports from other countries. In 1952, the government succeeded in negotiating a new profit-sharing arrangement with the IPC. Iran's move to nationalize its petroleum industry and Saudi Arabia's new 50/50 profit-sharing arrangement convinced the IPC to sign a similar agreement with Iraq. That same year, oil revenues were further enhanced with the opening of a new pipeline to Banias on the Syrian coast. The following year new oil fields were discovered near Basra. The jump in oil revenues (Table 5.1) from 7.5 per cent in 1948 to 61.7 per cent in 1958 meant that the state was now dependent on a single commodity owned and controlled by foreign interests. Increasing this foreign dependency was the government's stubborn refusal to separate the Iraqi dinar (ID) from its links with the British pound sterling.

Table 5.1 Oil Revenues, 1948–58

Year	Revenues (ID thousand)	Per cent
1948	2,012	7.5
1950	5,286	15.7
1952	37,405	47.0
1954	68,371	65.7
1956	68,859	62.1
1958	79,888	61.7

Source: Batatu, Hanna and Batatu, John, *The Old Social Classes and Revolutionary Movements of Iraq: A Study of Iraq's Old Candid and Commercial Classes and of its Communists, Ba'thists and Free Officers*, p. 106. Copyright © 1978 by Princeton University Press. Reprinted by permission of Princeton University Press.

The policies of the newly established Development Board focused on long-term development with agriculture winning the lion's share of investments. Large-scale projects such as flood control, water storage and irrigation schemes, were favored over short-term projects designed to produce immediate benefits. Such planning was considered prudent use of scarce resources, though in hindsight it is clear that the monarchy overestimated the people's willingness to wait for the promised fruits. At first, the achievements appear quite impressive. New bridges, various public buildings and a new Parliament building were constructed. Funded by oil revenues and loans from the World Bank, a huge flood-control project at Wadi al-Tharthar, north of Baghdad, was completed in 1956. Iraq's area of culti-vated land doubled and the country, long self-sufficient in food production, even began to export barley. Nevertheless, the semi-feudal relations in the countryside acted as a formidable barrier to modern agricultural develop-ment. Fearing a rise in labor costs and, more importantly, the disintegra-tion of tribal allegiances which helped secure their position, the landowners continued to rely on share-croppers rather than wage laborers and the cultivation of new lands rather than increasing productivity through mechanization. Agricultural practices became increasingly more wasteful and productivity per acre actually declined. With the rise in oil revenues agriculture came to produce only 30 per cent of the nation's income even though it employed 70 per cent of the population. This, in addition to the state's declining revenues from agriculture (Table 5.2), led the government to be less sensitive to popular demands for land reform.

Table 5.2 Land revenue, 1948–58

Year	Revenues (ID thousand)	Per cent
1948	3,037	11.3
1950	3,963	11.5
1952	3,051	3.8
1954	2,919	2.8
1956	2,190	2.0
1958	2,229	1.7

Source: Batatu, Hanna and Batatu, John, *The Old Social Classes and Revolutionary Movements of Iraq: A Study of Iraq's Old Candid and Commercial Classes and of its Communists, Ba'thists and Free Officers*, p. 106. Copyright © 1978 by Princeton University Press. Reprinted by permission of Princeton University Press.

What is even more interesting about the figures in Table 5.2 is that while agriculture expanded, the state's share in land revenues declined in absolute terms. This was mainly due to the reduction in land taxes, which, of course, benefited the landed elite. This points to another problem: the accentuation of oppressive relations in the countryside. By 1958, 60 per cent of agricultural land was owned by big landowners and 17 per cent was in the hands of only 49 families. In 1932, a law was passed binding the indebted peasant to the land. Most were reduced to share-cropping arrangements living in mud-huts barely above subsistence levels. Education, health care and sanitation were almost non-existent in the countryside where the average life expectancy of the peasant was estimated at 35–7 years and infant mortality remained very high. By the end of the monarchy, centralization of land ownership, the commercialization of agriculture and the oppression and abject poverty of the peasants, left more than 1.5 million landless (out of a total population of 6.5 million) and forced many to flee to the big cities. In 1958, well over 100,000 rural migrants lived in shanty-towns around Baghdad. The menial labor they found there still provided them with a better life. Nevertheless, in the cities they were also subjected to an alien culture, more visible class differences and the influences of opposition parties. Throughout the monarchy the shanty-town dwellers remained a politically volatile group.

While the state invested heavily in infrastructure development, the economy was overwhelmingly privately owned. Industry remained limited, employing only 7 per cent of the population in 1958 and contributing less than 10 per cent to the national income. Education expanded, especially in the urban areas, where several post-secondary colleges were opened and eventually integrated into a national university. Overall illiteracy remained high, however, at 85 per cent in 1958. Urban growth, as a result of migration and better health care, was significant with Baghdad going from 500,000 in 1947 to 800,000 in 1958. Urbanization and education had a profound impact on the generation gap. During the 1950s, a growing number of professionals educated in the modern schools struggled to come to terms with the traditions and ideals of the older Ottoman generation. On the other hand, the country made important strides in national integration. Urbanization and the extension of state control brought more communities in touch with one another. It was also becoming more common for Shi'is and Kurds to hold important positions in government but, overall, Arab Sunni dominance continued particularly in the army's officer corps and the civil service. Women made significant strides particularly in education. The first women's magazine, *Layla*, was published during the Mandate, with occasional articles urging greater opportunities in education and work appearing in it. The growth of the ICP inspired the formation of several women's organizations after the war, the most important of which was the League for the Defense of Women's Rights. In addition to the League's work for women's rights and child welfare, it also contributed to the overall criticism of the monarchy.

These developments were reflected by the country's vibrant literary and artistic production. The best and most widely read contributions were of the opposition which constantly undermined the ideological base of the regime by criticizing traditional values, political decadence, the lack of democracy, the dependency on Britain and widespread social inequalities. Artists such as Jawad Salim received international recognition, and poets, such as Muhammad Mahdi al-Jawahiri, moved audiences by attacking the evils of the time. His poem, "Lullaby for the Hungry", is typical of his satirical style:

> Sleep, you hungry people sleep!
> The gods of food watch over you.
> Sleep if you are not satiated
> By wakefulness, then sleep shall fill you.
> Sleep, with thoughts of smooth-as-butter-promises,
> Mingled with words as sweet as honey.
> Sleep and enjoy the best of health
> What a fine thing is sleep for the wretched![6]

The Coming of the Revolution

Rashid 'Ali's movement followed by British reoccupation left the regime much weaker. As a result, Prime Minister Nuri al-Sa'id and the

---

[6] In Salma Khadra Jayyusi (ed.), *Modern Arabic Poetry: An Anthology*, New York, 1987, p. 80.

regent 'Abdul-Ilah, moved to appease the opposition by granting greater freedoms. In addition to the weakness of government, the communists benefited somewhat after Germany's invasion of the Soviet Union and the ensuing Soviet alliance with the United States and Britain. The ICP responded by suspending its open agitation against the British. Nevertheless, when licences were given out to several political parties, including the NDP and the Independent Party, the ICP was turned down. This was also a period which saw the formation of several labor unions, most of which were controlled by the communists. Politically, the most sensitive unions were those in the large, foreign-owned or managed industries (ports, railways and oil) where class conflict almost always intertwined with the question of national sovereignty.

These freedoms, however, proved to be short-lived. Foreign, regional and internal factors contributed to repression and the dizzying political developments which eventually destroyed the monarchy. Allied victory soon gave way to the Cold War where the United States and Britain led the way to confront the Soviet Union and the socialist bloc. In this climate, Iraq gained new strategic importance not only for its oil and location, but also as a regional ally in the anti-Soviet crusade. This, naturally, had a negative impact on the government's attitude toward the ICP and other socialist groups. Within the Middle East, World War II brought into clear focus the need for regional economic cooperation. In 1945, Iraq helped form the Arab League which later expanded to include all of the Arabic-speaking countries. Regional cooperation, however, was undermined by the competition between the two main Arab countries, Egypt and Iraq. This was especially evident after the independence of Syria in 1946, when Iraq quickly moved to establish its hegemony over the country. Nuri al-Sa'id proposed the notion of a unified Fertile Crescent, while 'Abdul-Ilah, not wanting to be left out after the king's coming of age, conspired to have himself crowned in Damascus. Fearing the loss of their sovereignty, both Syria and

Lebanon sought Egyptian protection. In addition, looming in the background, the crisis in Palestine, blamed largely on British support for the Zionists, continued to worsen with the accompanying undermining of support for the British-backed government of Iraq. Internally, the calls for social reforms returned, more vigorously thanks to the growth of the ICP, but the new centers of tension were the few large, mostly foreign managed, industries. In 1946, the oil workers at Kirkuk filed for permission to form a union accompanied by demands for wage increases. After their demands were rejected, a strike was called where workers from the two traditionally hostile tribes of the area overcame their differences to face government forces. Though the strike was eventually broken, the incident demonstrates that the opposition to the government also enhanced the process of national integration.

All these factors came to a head in 1948 when the country was shaken by a mass uprising which threatened the monarchy and the prevailing social order. The spark came with the government's proposal to replace the despised Anglo–Iraqi Treaty of 1930 with a new "improved" version. What the British wanted was the right to continue to use Iraqi territory (especially the airbases) in case of crisis, and the sole right to equip and train the Iraqi army. Expecting trouble, Nuri al-Sa'id stepped down as Prime Minister in 1947. His replacement, through the usual dubious elections, was Salih Jabr, a Shi'i of humble family background. Having a Shi'i at the helm of the country for the first time since the seventeenth century created some optimism. These hopes were soon dispelled when Jabr oversaw a new wave of repression where even moderate parties were banned and their leaders imprisoned. In the meantime, the news from Palestine caused more alarm. In November, the United Nations voted to divide Palestine into a Jewish and Arab states. Throughout the Arab world the public was outraged, with Britain, in particular, blamed for this latest, and most severe, blow to Arab independence. The climate, therefore, was hardly favorable for the signing of a new treaty with Britain.

Nevertheless, in January 1948, despite earlier reservations, Jabr signed the new treaty in Portsmouth before heading back home to face the storm.

It seems quite incredible that the Iraqi government would take such an unpopular step especially considering the seething anger over Palestine. In many ways, the signing of the Portsmouth Treaty clearly demonstrates the political elite's alienation from popular concerns. The response came swiftly in the form of student demonstrations first called by the Independence Party. The ensuing crackdown only exacerbated the situation as the demonstrations grew larger drawing support from the workers and the shanty-town dwellers. Soon the ICP emerged as the undisputed leader of the growing uprising later called the *Wathba*, the Leap. Alarmed at the radicalization of the movement (there were even some spontaneous calls for a republic), and the fact that it was winning the support of some of the soldiers, the state ordered drastic measures. On 27 January, 300–400 demonstrators were killed in clashes with government forces. Shortly after, Salih Jabr resigned and the government formally declared its rejection of the treaty. The unrest, however, continued with strikes and demonstrations until May, when the declaration of the state of Israel and the ensuing Arab–Israeli War allowed the state to establish martial law and effectively end the uprising. The wave of repression fell particularly hard on the ICP which suffered the execution of a number of its leaders, including Fahd.

Events following the *Wathba* came in the form of a rapid succession of political crises. The Iraqi army, which participated in the disastrous Arab–Israeli War of 1948 with a token force, returned full of bitterness. Many officers believed that their government was corrupt and subservient to British imperialism and its policies prevented the country from effectively assisting its fellow Arabs in Palestine. Among the younger officers was 'Abdul-Karim Qasim, the future leader of the republican revolution. The events in

Palestine also spelled doom for the country's Jewish community. Throughout the 1940s, harassment of Jews had continued to rise. Pan-Arab nationalists led the way with the government, eager to deflect popular anger, acquiescing to a number of anti-Jewish measures. In 1951, the government agreed to allow the direct air-lifting of Iraqi Jews to Israel. By the following year around 160,000 had arrived in Israel, leaving behind most of their possessions. Only 6000 remained and during the following decade they, too, would leave bringing to an end one of the country's most vibrant and productive communities.

Between 1951 and 1952, two events threatened the stability of every Middle East country and heightened tensions between the two world superpowers. In Iran, which continued to have a strong impact on the Shi'is of Iraq, the nationalist leader Muhammad Mossedagh became Prime Minister. With strong communist support, he was instrumental in passing a law nationalizing the Iranian oil industry and challenged Western interests with promises of further nationalist legislation. The following year, the army led by Jamal 'Abdul-Nasir toppled the monarchy in Egypt and promised to bring about radical social reforms and end the country's foreign dependence. To many people, the issues raised in Iran and Egypt seemed identical to those confronting Iraq and a number of solidarity demonstrations erupted that same year. To weather the storm the regime was badly in need of a new vibrant leadership. The coming of age of King Faysal II in 1953 hardly made a difference. Inexperienced and lacking strong character, he remained under the firm influence of the massively unpopular 'Abdul-Ilah (now the Crown Prince). In the meantime, the government also remained under the control of the same Nuri al-Sa'id. In the streets of Baghdad, revolution was becoming increasingly more probable. The young poet, Badr Shakir al-Sayyab, reflected the anticipation with the following lines:

I can almost hear Iraq storing up the thunder
And massing the lightning in the mountains and the plains,
Until, when men tear away their seal
The winds from Thamud[7] will not leave
Any trace in the valley[8]

As the decade wore on, it seemed that the only response made to opposition demands was more repression administered by a more sophisticated internal security apparatus. But repression, as cruel as it was, when coupled with the continuous material development fueled by the oil revenues, might have actually brought the country out of its crisis were it not for the Cold War and the rising popularity of Nasir. During the early phase of the Cold War the United States adopted a strategy of encircling the Soviet Union through a series of regional alliances. Having engineered the downfall of Mossedagh in Iran, the United States now moved to form such an alliance in the Middle East. In 1955, the United States and Britain helped form what came to be known as the Baghdad Pact, which eventually included Turkey, Iraq, Iran and Pakistan. Nasir, who by now had become president of Egypt and a recognized figure in the Non-Aligned movement, condemned the alliance as another colonial treaty that failed to serve the interests of the region. With one eye on their suspicious people and one on the increasingly popular Nasir, the Arab countries quickly distanced themselves from the Baghdad Pact. As even the most moderate politicians geared up to oppose Iraq's involvement in such an alliance, Nasir threw another bombshell. His popularity had been steadily gaining ground throughout the Arab world after he negotiated the evacuation of British forces, stressed an independent foreign policy, and launched a land reform that effectively eliminated the power of the big landown-

---

[7] A pre-Islamic tribe mentioned in the Qur'an as having been destroyed by God for its evil.

[8] Quoted in Terri Deyoung, *Placing the Poet: Badr Shakir al-Sayyab and Postcolonial Iraq*, Albany, NY, 1998, p. 15.

ers. In 1956, he suddenly announced the nationalization of the Suez Canal. After rather fortuitously surviving an attack by Israel, France and Britain, Nasir's popularity skyrocketed. Here at long last was a hero for the Arab nationalists. He had challenged the might of Britain and its allies and won back the political and economic independence of Egypt.

The response in Iraq was two-fold. The opposition parties again went to the streets with demonstrations and strikes against the Baghdad Pact and in support of Nasir. In addition, a group of mostly junior army officers sought to emulate Nasir by forming a secret Free Officers' Movement with the goal of overthrowing the monarchy. By 1957, the movement had come under the leadership of its highest ranking member, General 'Abdul-Karim Qasim. The monarchy's isolation became almost complete in February, 1958, with the unification of Egypt and Syria in a new United Arab Republic. The government's last-ditch effort to create a rival union with Jordan never really had a chance to materialize. On 14 July, the Free Officers struck with a rapid takeover of the centers of power and communication in Baghdad. Within a matter of hours, the monarchy had completely collapsed.

The modern nation-state in Iraq was built upon foundations already present during the late Ottoman period. Under the British Mandate and the independent monarchy, this process continued at a much faster pace. The state's institutions were refined, the country's borders clarified, material development progressed, national integration deep-ened and a new educated cadre came to hold important positions. While elections and the democratic process in general left much to be desired, political diversity was tolerated to an extent and the press enjoyed periods of significant freedom. In the course of its evolution, however, the state came to rely on an increasingly narrow social base composed primarily of big landowners. Even here contradictions flared up especially after the rise in oil revenues which made the regime less beholden to the interests of the landed elite. The narrow base of the regime alienated the country's growing number of educated middle classes who aspired to a greater share of power and wealth. The power of the landed elite rested on semi-feudal relations and the severe exploitation of the peasantry. The high levels of exploitation, coupled with the rising expectations associated with an increase in oil revenues, led to the radicalization of opposition politics. This radicalization was further intensified through the international and regional climate created by the Cold War and the Arab–Israeli conflict. The tensions were so strong that the military coup of 14 July 1958 quickly triggered a profound social revolution.

chapter six

THE STRUGGLE FOR THE REPUBLIC, 1958–1979

The 14 July coup was quick, well-planned and effective. It required the participation of only a small part of the army and around 200 officers. At around 6:30 in the morning, after surrounding the Royal Palace and taking the radio station, Colonel 'Abdul-Salam 'Arif, Qasim's right-hand man in the coup, announced the downfall of the monarchy to a stunned nation. The army's "Proclamation Number 1" read as follows:

> Noble people of Iraq, trusting in God and with the aid of the sons of the people and the national armed forces, we have undertaken to liberate the beloved homeland from the corrupt crew that imperialism installed. ... The army is of you and for you and has carried out what you desired. ... We appeal to you, therefore to report to the authorities all offenders, traitors, and corrupt people so that they could be uprooted. ... Rest assured that we will continue to work on your behalf. Power shall be entrusted to a government emanating from you and inspired by you. This can only be realized by the creation of a people's republic. ... Accordingly, the [new] national government shall henceforth be called the Republic of Iraq.[1]

As news of the army's actions spread, thousands of people, mainly from the poor neighborhoods and shanty-towns, poured into the streets and headed for the symbols of the Old Regime: the Royal Palace, Nuri al-Sa'id's house, and the British Consulate. Statues of Faysal I and General Maude were smashed in scenes mixed with anger and elation. Being the only effective mass party, the communists were quick to call their members into the streets and had some effect in providing direction to the crowds. There is little doubt that the enthusiastic participation of large numbers of people played an important role in deterring any possible move by troops still loyal to the monarchy. It also seems clear that the crowds, despite their essentially spontaneous and

---

[1] Quoted in Batatu, Hanna, *The Old Social Classes and Revolutionary Movements of Iraq: A Study of Iraq's Old Landed and Commercial Classes and of its Communists, Ba'thists, and Free Officers*, Princeton, 1978, p. 802.

unorganized nature, were moved by a strong sense of national idealism which did not degenerate into sectarian violence or uncontrolled looting. By 8:00 a.m., the king, the regent and most of the royal family were killed. The next morning, Nuri al-Sa'id, the stalwart of the Old Regime, was caught trying to escape and shot dead on the spot. Mobs subjected his body and that of 'Abdul-Ilah to untold mutilations before eventually setting them on fire.

The anger, as intense as it was, remained contained and focused. Still, fearing a complete breakdown of order and loss of control, the officers called for calm. A curfew was issued followed by the declaration of martial law. The nature and role of mass participation on 14 July and in the days that followed, plus the changes brought about by the new regime, transformed the military takeover into a genuine social and political revolution. During the next 10–15 years, Iraq would witness an intense struggle over the new direction of the country. The monarchy was destroyed in a matter of hours, but the nature of the new republic was far from clear.

Revolutionary changes

Like their Egyptian counterparts, the Free Officers of Iraq were of mixed political inclinations. They agreed on the need to overthrow the "corrupt" monarchy, establish a democratic republic, end the country's political and economic dependence, and address the problem of social inequalities, but once they sat down to the business of carrying out these goals sharp differences emerged. In Egypt, similar differences were settled through internal purges. In Iraq, they exploded into violent conflicts. Before the eventual break-up of the ruling group, however, the new government did manage to bring about significant change in a number of areas.

The republic replaced the monarchy with a three-man Sovereignty Council taking the responsibilities of the president until such time as national elections could be held. The council had a ceremonial role with no real powers but its members, a Shi'i, a Sunni Arab and a Kurd, symbolized the intention to establish equality among the country's separate communities. Parliament was dissolved and the temporary constitution specifically declared that Arabs and Kurds were partners in Iraq. Qasim held the offices of Prime Minister, Minister of Defense and Commander in Chief. 'Arif, whose rank was lower than that of several of the Free Officers, was rewarded for his role in the seizure of power with the offices of Deputy Prime Minister, Minister of the Interior and Deputy Commander in Chief. The cabinet included representatives from almost all the opposition tendencies, especially the NDP. Also included was the son of Shaykh Mahumud Barazanchi, the distinguished Kurdish leader. In 1959, Dr Naziha al-Dulaymi, a leader in the women's rights movement during the monarchy, was appointed Minister of Municipalities. She was the first woman in the Arab world to hold a ministerial post. The Communist Party benefited greatly from the general atmosphere of freedom that immediately followed the revolution. Though denied official licencing, they quickly dominated most of the non-government associations. They were most conspicuous, however, in their domination of the "street" through mass demonstrations that gave the revolution a distinctly leftist facade.

Such a representative and overwhelmingly civilian cabinet gave the new government a strong basis of legitimacy and enabled it to enact several reforms. A general amnesty was declared and all political prisoners were released. Exiles, such as the veteran Rashid 'Ali al-Gaylani and Mulla Mustafa Barazani (who assumed control of the Kurdistan Democratic Party), returned to the country. Spending on social welfare programs, such as health, education and the construction of affordable housing, was boosted to twice its allocation under the last budget of the monarchy, while new rent controls also favored the poor. These reforms were not inspired by notions of soviet-style socialism, despite the growing influence of the ICP. Qasim was used to saying on several occasions that the goal of the revolution was to "improve the lot of the poor without jeopardizing a fair standard of living for the rich".[2] Influenced by Qasim's mixed Sunni-Shi'i background, the secular nature of the state received a boost especially in personal status law and education. National integration was enhanced by severely limiting the issues handled by the different religious courts and broadening the scope of equality before a single law. Strict limits were placed on polygamy as a first step toward its eradication. A man's right to arbitrary divorce was outlawed, as was child marriage. Most controversial of all from the point of view of the Islamic shari'a, was a law establishing equality for men and women in inheritance. Education also received a strong boost in funding resulting in higher enrollments at all levels. A new initiative to organize and expand Baghdad University was undertaken with the appointment of Dr 'Abdul-Jabbar 'Abdullah as university president. Dr 'Abdullah, an acclaimed physicist and graduate of the Massachusetts Institute of Technology, was from the minority Mandaean community.

Urban development received priority in all planning, but the most revolutionary reforms involved a complete overhaul of rural relations. To enforce the notion of equality before the law, the old Tribal Criminal and Civil Disputes regulations were abolished. This was followed by the introduction of the country's long-awaited land reform law. Modeled after its Egyptian counterpart, the law set ceilings on land holdings, expropriated land over that ceiling (with compensation), and distributed the expropriated land to landless peasants. Even before the new law was formally passed, peasants in the Kut and 'Amara regions, where the largest estates existed, began to take matters into their own hands by seizing land and burning the financial records of the land-holders. This "second rural revolution" had a much more profound impact on Iraqi society since it basically destroyed the political power of the big land-holders who had been so dominant under the monarchy. By 1971, almost all who lived off agriculture owned some

---

[2] Quoted in Uriel Dann, *Iraq Under Qassem: A Political History, 1958–1963*, New York, 1969, p. 14.

land. Agricultural production, however, suffered. Initially, this was the direct result of the confusion which naturally accompanies radical social transformations. Over the long run it represented a clear shift in favor of urban economic development and greater dependence on oil revenues. In 1960 agriculture represented 17 per cent of GNP, by 1980 this figure had declined to 8 per cent. An exporter of grain during the monarchy, Iraq became a net importer of food, eventually reaching 70 per cent of its domestic needs. The confusion that accompanied the early years of the land reform also boosted the already alarming rural–urban migration.

In industry, nationalizations of any sort were expressly avoided. Instead, the government raised tariffs on imported manufactured goods in order to provide more protection for the national industries. As a result, consumer industries, like Fattah Pasha's blankets, witnessed some growth. A sense of economic nationalism directed the state's policy toward greater control over its resources. This was most apparent with respect to the country's leading industry, oil. After a series of tense negotiations with the oil companies, the government passed Law No. 80, which confiscated 99.5 per cent of the IPC's concession land. The IPC was left with only the Kirkuk fields. The IPC never accepted this law and attempted to strike back by disrupting production. Nevertheless, the law proved to be extremely popular and formed the platform from which Iraq would eventually assume full control over its chief economic asset. Nationalism was also evident when the country moved to take a more independent posture in its foreign relations. In 1959, Iraq withdrew from the Baghdad Pact and the Sterling Area and full diplomatic relations were established with China, the Soviet Union and the socialist bloc. Within the Arab world, Iraq became a major supplier of aid to the Algerian and the nascent Palestinian resistance movements.

Reaction

These reforms caused alarm both within and outside the country. The monarchies of Jordan, the Gulf and Iran naturally feared its republican appeal. Britain was concerned about its oil interests and the United States was alarmed over the growth of the ICP and the expansion of soviet influence. Partly in response to the Iraqi revolution, US Marines landed in Lebanon to shore up the government. Internally, various conservative elements, from monarchists and big land-holders to religious leaders and tribal shaykhs, gradually formed an opposition bloc. Though initially quite weak and intimidated by the popularity of the revolution, they were eventually able to take advantage of the differences within the Free Officers and the growing rift between the two major figures of the regime: Qasim and 'Arif. Nominally, the rift was caused by the question of union with Egypt and Syria. Personal rivalries also played a role. Both Qasim and 'Arif tended to ignore institutions of state and emphasized personal rule in their conduct. In this sense they exposed the most glaring weakness in their inability to establish a stable institutional base for the early republic. Perhaps they did not have enough time, but there is little doubt that, despite their popularity, their organized base of support was extremely narrow and not much was done to expand it. The main base of support for Qasim – who would emerge as the undisputed leader after pushing his rival out – remained limited to elements within the army. Throughout his rule he continued to wear his military uniform and base himself at the Ministry of Defense instead of the Prime Minister's office. Ideologically he was closest to the NDP but most of the NDP members resigned after being disillusioned with the pace of democratic reforms. The communists, with a rapidly expanding popular base, were eager to ally with Qasim but he mistrusted their motives and was not persuaded by their ideology. The ICP was shunned and eventually suppressed, even though it remained loyal to Qasim to the end.

'Arif was a Nasirist, a fervent advocate of Arab unity and an anti-communist. His calls for immediate unity with Nasir's United Arab Republic (UAR) soon became the rallying cry of all the forces opposed to Qasim. Qasim refused immediate unity on the basis that it would subject Iraq to Nasir's dictatorship and called for a more decentralized federation. Whatever the arguments, it is significant that the pan-Arabist camp, having seized power in 1963, failed to bring about the promised union and allowed the matter to fade away gradually. Before that fateful year, Qasim faced a number of coup attempts. Rashid 'Ali al-Gaylani, one of the leaders of the nationalist movement during the monarchy, failed in a coup supported by a number of tribal shaykhs. In March 1959, a military coup openly supported by Nasir was thwarted in Mosul. This was followed by sectarian violence between Kurds and Turkomans in Kirkuk in which a number of communists were implicated. In October, the Ba'th Party attempted to assassinate Qasim as his car drove through Baghdad. One of the participants in this unsuccessful operation (who later fled to Egypt), was Saddam Husayn.

The numerous coups and plots that plagued the regime left their effects on an increasingly suspicious and isolated Qasim. Arrests broadened to even include members of the ICP and NDP and some newspapers were closed. The government also moved to take control of the trades unions though this was not particularly successful. In 1960, after the initial goodwill shown to Mulla Mustafa Barazani, relations deteriorated. The Kurdish leadership, still dominated by tribal aghas, feared the extension of the land reform and central authority to the north. Qasim, for his part, tried to divide the Kurdish nationalists and isolate Barazani. Eventually, war broke out and by February 1961 two-thirds of the Iraqi army was bogged down in the mountains of the north. As the conflict weighed heavily on the country, two regional developments added to the general atmosphere of instability. In Syria army officers seized power and declared the country's withdrawal from the UAR. Though it appeared to vindicate Qasim's refusal to join the failed union, the secession of Syria heightened regional tensions and increased Egyptian animosity. Even more serious was Qasim's attempt, in 1961, to annex Kuwait. That year, Britain granted Kuwait its independence but Qasim refused to recognize the new country claiming, instead, Iraqi sovereignty over the Gulf emirate. British troops were called in later to be replaced by troops from a number of Arab countries including Egypt. While no military operations took place, the Kuwait affair put unnecessary pressure on an already strained country and severely damaged Iraq's relations with its neighbors.

By 1962, Qasim had become the picture of the isolated leader. He never lost his reputation for honesty nor did he use his power to amass great wealth. His undemocratic practices and repressions would soon pale in comparison with those who succeeded him. Still commanding significant popular support but unable or unwilling to organize and empower his followers, he was doomed to fall.

The Ba'th Party

The party that would overthrow Qasim and eventually seize unrivaled control of Iraq, was formed in Syria in 1944. The principal ideological tenets of the Arab Ba'th Party (later called the Arab Ba'th Socialist Party) were laid by Michel 'Aflaq, a French-educated Syrian intellectual. It built on the Arab nationalist movement which emerged in opposition to European colonialism in the inter-war period. Essentially a secular party, it called for the unity of the Arab peoples and independence from foreign rule. With a highly centralized organization, it was to be the vanguard of the Arab people in its struggle for unity and independence. To emphasize its rejection of the "colonial borders" which artificially divided the Arab world, it had a pan-Arab structure. Its leading committee, the National Command, was composed of members from the various Regional Commands. Each "region" represented one of the Arab countries. Ba'thist ideas were brought to Iraq in the late 1940s by Syrian teachers. Among the few early recruits was Fu'ad al-Rikabi, a Shi'i teacher, who later became the first leader of the party in Iraq. It remained small and inconsequential throughout the monarchy but gained some importance after the 1958 Revolution. After the collapse of the UAR, the party underwent several splits eventually crystalizing into two separate and hostile organizations based, respectively, in Syria and Iraq. This situation, formalized in 1966, has remained unchanged today. While both claim to represent the party's authentic line, there are, in fact, few doctrinal differences. The division, rather, has been sustained by the regional rivalry between Syria and Iraq.

Ba'thist ideology is vague and represents a knot of contradictions. It might be useful to analyze it through the party's primary slogan: "Unity, Freedom, and Socialism". "Unity" refers to the belief in a single Arab nation whose foundations are sometimes stated as language and history, but more often it is described as having a semi-mystical "spirit" that defines its essence. This nation spans the area from Morocco to Arabia and Iraq. The unification of this nation is the most important goal to which all other considerations are secondary. Hence the party's other prominent slogan: "One Arab Nation With an Eternal Mission." What this "Eternal Mission" is exactly, remains vague. The party's splits in the 1960s, and its inability to forge a union despite coming to power in the neighboring countries of Iraq and Syria, transformed this goal into an empty slogan. "Freedom" does not relate to political freedoms associated with democratic reforms. Rather, it implies freedom from foreign control. The party, therefore, emphasizes the need to wage an unrelenting struggle against imperialism and zionism, which is imperialism's most dangerous manifestation in the Arab world. This also includes their local agents and traitors. There is a consistent use of militaristic language and the picture of a relentless conflict against outside forces hostile to the nation, as in the following phrase from one of the party's political reports:

> We must make the mental and psychological preparation to link up Arab life fully with the exigencies of long term confrontation. Economy, politics and everyday life must all be directed toward leading the Arab struggle towards the battlefields.[3]

---

[3] Quoted in Marion Farouk-Slugglett and Peter Slugglett, "Iraqi Ba'thism: Nationalism, Socialism and National Socialism", in CARDRI, *Saddam's Iraq, Revolution or Reaction?*, London, 1986, p. 94.

Though the Ba'thists have, on occasion, formed alliances with the communists, they generally regarded them with hostility because communism was considered a "foreign" ideology, and because it threatened the harmony and unity of the nation by emphasizing the class struggle. "Socialism", therefore, has little to do with the equitable distribution of wealth. Initially, socialism was described as simply a form of economic nationalism, or, in the words of 'Aflaq, that "the economic wealth of the fatherland belongs to the nation".[4] Later, and in keeping with the times, socialism came to mean the state's leading role in economic development, though again, this has been revised with the recent talk of liberalizing the economy.

The rule of the 'Arif brothers

In 1963, under Ba'thist leadership and the support of several disillusioned army officers, including 'Arif, a coup was staged which overthrew Qasim. While many of the participants were moved by pan-Arabist ideals, the more pressing issue was the elimination of the communists. Lacking a broad social base, the Ba'th quickly organized a paramilitary squad, the National Guard, to carry out a grisly, house-to-house slaughter or arrest of known communists and their sympathizers. Qasim and a handful of his followers were killed in the fighting. True to his nature, Qasim had earlier refused the appeals of crowds for arms to help to defend him. Intense street battles continued for several days with the most stubborn resistance offered in the poor neighborhoods. As most of their leading cadres had already been imprisoned by Qasim, the communists were unable to hold out. Sports grounds and schools were transformed into concentration camps and interrogation centers, the most notorious of which was set up in 'Abdul-Ilah's old villa in Baghdad and renamed *Qasr al-Nihaya* (Palace of the End). Between 3000 and 5000 were killed during the first weeks of the coup with many thousands more detained. Evidence of US and French intelli-

---

[4] *Ibid.*, p. 103.

gence support for the coup cannot be far fetched, given the atmosphere of the Cold War and the fear of communist influence in the region. The ICP never really recovered its past power after this blow, and as it was further weakened by splits it failed to pose a significant threat to the new regime.

The new government was completely dominated by the Ba'th, though, significantly, the president, 'Arif, was not a Ba'thist. Still commanding support within the army, 'Arif was considered indispensable to the coup. Another military officer of lesser acclaim, Ahmad Hasan al-Bakr, a Ba'thist, became Prime Minister. This coalition between 'Arif and his pan-Arabist supporters on the one hand, and the Ba'th on the other, was soon strained to breaking point with the Ba'th's continued expansion of its National Guard forces. These forces received little training, were unruly, prone to criminal activities and behaved more like a collection of gangsters rather than a force for law and order. Popular hatred for the National Guard and deepening divisions within the Ba'th gave 'Arif the opportunity to remove them from government and install direct military rule. The National Guard was dissolved, leading Ba'thists imprisoned and general repression loosened somewhat. Sunni Ba'thists managed to survive with light or no prison terms thanks to their contacts within the army, whose officers (including 'Arif) were still mostly Sunni. This facilitated the ascendency, within the party, of one faction composed largely of members who hailed from the Sunni district of Tikrit. The two men responsible for this reorganization around a Tikriti leadership were Ahmad Hasan al-Bakr and Saddam Husayn. In 1966, al-Bakr assumed formal leadership of the party.

'Arif's military-based regime was even more unstable than Qasim's. Lacking developed civil society institutions, 'Arif tried to form a base by relying on his kinsmen from the Jumayla tribe in the district of Ramadi. One of his earliest acts was to recognize the independence of Kuwait, but the exact border between the two countries remained undetermined. He sought to strengthen the legitimacy of his government by calling for a new union with Egypt and Syria. Several unity meetings were held in 1963 and 1964, but other than the symbolic adoption of a single flag and national anthem, not much else was achieved. Nasir was far more cautious after his UAR debacle, and differences arose over power-sharing measures that eventually ended all serious discussions on this question. Nasirist influence, however, was apparent in the regime's internal policies. In 1964, a series of broad nationalizations was declared. Banks, insurance companies, large industries and much of the country's foreign trade came under the direct control of the state. Essentially, this was an attempt at rapid industrialization by concentrating capital in the hands of the state, which could then reinvest it in chosen projects. As with other underdeveloped countries, this approach soon resulted in capital flight and mismanagement ending with the overall stagnation of the economy. The government retreated from this policy in the following years. The oil industry also received some attention with the establishment of the Iraqi National Oil Company and the signing of agreements with the Soviet Union to help in the development of the southern oilfields. Nevertheless, the regime's instability limited its effectiveness. From 1964 to 1968, the country had eight ministers for industry, seven for public works, six for planning and six for the agrarian reform.

A few months after the Ba'thist coup the Kurdish question, which had contributed to Qasim's downfall, came to haunt the 'Arif regime. In terms of its pan-Arabist bent, the new regime could not have been expected to show much sympathy to Kurdish national aspirations. Yet, ironically, Barazani secretly gave the plotters assurances of support by declaring a cease fire in Kurdistan once they had seized power. In return he expected a more favorable treatment and initially, attempts were made to resolve the differences on the basis of guaranteeing Kurdish national rights in the north. Once again, however, the talks broke down and fighting resumed. The army launched several offensives all of which ended in disastrous defeats. During this conflict, old divisions within the Kurdish camp, partly ideological and partly tribal, became more pronounced with Jalal Talbani emerging as a serious contender to Barazani. Still, the war dragged on, once again contributing to the weakening of the regime. Two other events sealed its fate. In 1966, 'Arif died in a helicopter crash. His energetic, if at times impetuous, personality had kept a shaky coalition going. 'Arif's brother, 'Abdul-Rahman 'Arif, was the only candidate acceptable to all the factions within the army, probably because he was the weakest. The other event was the 1967 Arab–Israeli War. The overwhelming Israeli victory left the Arab world spinning and disgraced Nasir and all who had supported his line. Other than a symbolic military presence and the breaking of diplomatic relations with the USA and Britain, Iraq had not contributed much to the effort. The following year, the reorganized Ba'th Party struck in a largely bloodless coup. Initially, it required the help of some non-Ba'thist commanders, but soon after their seizure of power the Ba'th expelled all others from the coalition and assumed full control of the government.

The Ba'th return to power

The Ba'th Party of Ahmad Hasan al-Bakr and Saddam Husayn still lacked a broad social base but it was more united and tightly organized than it had been in 1963. To prevent the recurrence of internal divisions, Saddam Husayn was entrusted with the establishment of an internal security apparatus, which became his personal power base within the party. Al-Bakr, the General Secretary of the party, assumed the offices of president, Prime Minister, and commander in chief of the armed forces. He was also the chairman of the Revolutionary Command Council (RCC), the highest government authority. Saddam Husayn was the deputy secretary of the party and vice-chairman of the RCC. Though the actual seizure of power was bloodless, the wave of repression that followed was directed primarily against the communists who were beginning to show signs of revival. Taking advantage of the instability, the shah of Iran suddenly announced the abrogation of the 1937 Sa'dabad border treaty. Iranian patrol boats were sent to enforce his demand that the border should run through the mid-point of the river. This aggressive posture by Iran was part of an overall attempt to fill the vacuum in the Persian Gulf left by the withdrawal of Britain. Iraq's relations with its Arab neighbors were also strained. Ba'thist rhetoric continued to condemn the "reactionary" monarchies of Jordan and the Gulf. Iraq's relations with Syria were adversely affected by the 1966 split of the Ba'th Party and the two countries' traditional regional rivalry. Threatened by both internal and external enemies, the Ba'th moved to broaden its support or, at least, win over the acquiescence of the population.

In 1969/1970, a second land reform law was passed which further lowered the limits on land ownership, placed more emphasis on distribution, and called for the establishment of cooperatives and state farms. While this did not greatly aid production, it did complete the process of combating landlessness that was initiated by the 1958 land reform. A far more popular measure was taken in March 1970 when the government announced an agreement with Barazani to finally settle the Kurdish question. The agreement specifically called for the establishment of a Kurdish autonomous region with its own elected parliament. Kurdish and Arabic were recognized as the region's official languages and a Kurd became the country's vice president. However, the euphoria of finally ending this destructive conflict soon wore off. Kurdish fears of Baghdad's authority and Arab nationalist concerns of secession, continued. In 1972, the government signed a Treaty of Friendship and Cooperation with the Soviet Union. This move won the regime important international support and helped to pacify the ICP. In 1974, the ICP and other groups (but not the KDP) agreed to join in a Ba'thist-led National Progressive Front. The communists, were given a seat in the cabinet and allowed to publish a daily paper.

Perhaps the most significant accomplishment of the Ba'thist government during this period was the nationalization of the country's oil industry in 1972. At first only the IPC's concessions were nationalized, but after the 1973 Arab–Israeli War, the remaining foreign assets were also taken. The timing of these measures was fortuitous. Soviet technical assistance was important, but the government benefited more from the phenomenal rise in oil prices after the so-called Arab oil boycott of 1973. The cut-back in production was intended to punish the West's support for Israel. While this measure had little effect on the Arab–Israeli conflict, it did increase the power and profile of the Organization of Petroleum Exporting Countries (OPEC). The cartel followed this up with a series of price hikes throughout the 1970s. Iraq's oil revenues jumped from $600 million in 1972 to $8.5 billion in 1976 and $26.5 billion in 1980. The development of the southern fields and the expansion of production in the north resulted in Iraq becoming the second largest oil producer in the Gulf.

This wealth, however, was a double-edged sword. The government was now able to invest massive amounts in industrial development projects and the overall economic figures do appear impressive. Iraqi officials were even claiming that the country was poised to enter the lower ranks of the industrialized nations by the turn of the century. Most of the industrial development was in the oil-related industries such as petrochemicals, but fertilizers and iron and steel also received investments. Nevertheless, the high oil revenues meant that the country was now largely dependent on a single commodity. By 1980, oil was responsible for 98 per cent of foreign currency earnings and 90 per cent of state revenues. At the same time, it was a vulnerable source because the country still lacked the security of a dependable outlet to the sea. Being almost completely land-locked, exports remained hostage to relations with neighboring countries. To help to remedy this situation, the port facilities in the south were expanded but even this could not solve the underlying problem. This great wealth was now also concentrated in the hands of the state. As a largely self-contained industry that was hardly dependent on other sectors, oil permitted the state to achieve a high degree of autonomy from society.

Toward the establishment of a totalitarian state

On many levels, the achievements of the Ba'th were notable. By the early 1980s electrification had reached 75 per cent of the countryside and the urban–rural balance was reversed. In 1957, 38.8 per cent of the population lived in the main urban areas, and by 1983 it had risen to 75 per cent. Baghdad, alone had 27 per cent of the country's population. Thanks to improved and mostly free health care, infant mortality declined, life expectancy increased and the population doubled from 1958 to 1983 reaching a total of 14 million. In 1979, the United Nations awarded Iraq special recognition for a literacy campaign that was launched with much fanfare. Free education expanded at all levels, with women making up a growing percentage of the student body. The overall standard of living improved with per capita income rising from 96.9 ID in 1968, to 135.5 ID in 1973 and 825.9 ID in 1979. Such accomplishments allowed the state to extend its control over society far beyond the ability of any previous government. The oil revenues also transformed the state into the country's chief employer. In 1974, a law was passed guaranteeing all the right to work. Most of the jobs were in the state sector so that by the end of the decade around 40 per cent of Iraqi households depended directly on the state for their income. Much of the state's investments benefited the private sector which grew significantly during the Ba'thist period. To shore up its power the Ba'th spent freely on the state's repressive apparatus. By 1978, a full 20 per cent of all state employees worked in one of several state security services. The army was also expanded from 50,000 in 1958 to 200,000 by the mid-1970s with military equipment now coming primarily from the Soviet Union and France.

Having secured its stability, the government moved toward a systematic policy of Ba'thization. A number of "Popular Associations", directly under party control, were set up to provide links with the different sectors of society and actively propagate Ba'thist ideology. Among these were associations of professionals, workers, students, youth, women and peasants. Members received various benefits and were given official recognition as leaders in their communities. Parallel associations independent of party control were forbidden. Every neighborhood had a local party council that kept detailed records of each household. Non-Ba'thists were banned from civil service and most university positions. By the end of the 1970s, the distinction between party and government was blurred. Ba'thist indoctrination was applied to the regular army in an effort to create a so-called "Ideological Army". Officers who were not trustworthy were purged and, by 1980, all the officers were Ba'thists. Children received military training in youth brigades and a separate "People's Army" was established in which women were allowed to enroll. The school curriculum was changed to include a strong element of Ba'thist indoctrination emphasizing militancy, a "love for order", suspicion of "foreigners" and, above all else, loyalty to the regime. In the words of Saddam Husayn:

> To prevent the father and the mother dominating the household with backwardness, we must make the small one radiate internally to expel it. Some fathers have slipped away from us for various reasons, but the small boy is still in our hands and we must transform him into an interactive radiating center inside the family ... You must surround adults through their sons, in addition to other means. Teach the student to object to his parents if he hears them discussing state secrets and to alert them that this is not correct. .... You must place in every corner a son of the revolution, with a trustworthy eye and a firm mind that receives its instructions from the responsible center of the revolution.[5]

Multiple security services kept an eye on the population and each other. Most of the commanders of these shadowy services came from the provincial towns in the so-called "Arab Sunni Triangle" covering the region from Baghdad to Mosul and west to the Syrian border. Their strong tribal ethos was the basis for a powerful loyalty to their

---

[5] Quoted in Samir al-Khalil, *Republic of Fear: The Politics of Modern Iraq*, Berkeley, 1989, pp. 77–8.

commanders (often their kin), especially to Saddam who oversaw their development. Their impoverished rural background bred a sense of hunger for the better life. In the words of Isam al-Khafaji: "No brain-washing was needed to turn envy of the lavish lifestyle of 'soft' city dwellers, especially Baghdadis, into a sense of gratitude and devotion towards those who enabled the ... recruits to conquer that alien city."[6] Opposition was ruthlessly dealt with as torture and executions became more frequent. Communal divisions were exasperated through a policy of punishing the entire family or kin of opponents. An atmosphere of fear came to hang over all conversations or transactions. One foreign journalist wrote, in 1984, of "the claustrophobic feeling to which most foreign residents confess."

> Whatever the degree [he continued] of surveillance of aliens, it is far sur-
> passed by the controls that the regime imposes on its own people, accord-
> ing to diplomats and other foreigners working here. "There is a feeling
> that at least three million Iraqis are watching the eleven million others,"
> ... The security services permeate society to a degree that "no one ever
> knows who's who."[7]

These policies had a profound social impact. In place of tribe, or reli-gious community, and with independent civil institutions not allowed to emerge, the individual came to be linked directly to an all-control-ling state. Due to the oil revenues, the state became the largest con-sumer in the country. To satisfy its veracious appetite for various projects an army of entrepreneurs, contractors and brokers was hired to provide the links with foreign companies. By the late 1970s this para-sitic class, which provided little in the form of actual production, grew to become the regime's most important social base. The individuals who formed this class depended mainly on good contacts (usually

---

[6] Isam al-Khafaji, "State Terror and the Degradation of Politics", in Fran Hazelton, *Iraq Since the Gulf War: Prospects for Democracy*, London, 1994, p. 25.

[7] Quoted in *ibid.*, pp. 62–2.

based on kinship or regional affiliation) with the powerful men in government and party. In this manner, the state sought to reward loyalty by granting lucrative contracts. Contracts were handed out for the importation of everything from consumer goods and food to machinery and construction materials. By 1980, construction was ranked above manufacturing and agriculture in its share of GDP. Trade with the Western countries rose dramatically with the increase in oil revenues. This included the United States, even though the two countries did not have formal diplomatic relations.

The development of the totalitarian state was naturally incompatible with the existence of opposition parties. The first victim of the Ba'th was the Kurdish national movement still under the leadership of Barazani's KDP. Not long after signing an agreement granting Iraqi Kurdistan autonomy in 1970, disagreements flared up over the exact borders of this region. The major point of contention was the oil-rich area of Kirkuk. The KDP correctly contended that the government was forcibly removing thousands of Kurdish families from that area in an effort to change its ethnic composition to justify its exclusion from the autonomous region. In 1974, war broke out and it appeared that yet another offensive from Baghdad was heading for stalemate. This time, however, events did not favor the Kurds. For several years, Kurdish resistance had depended on support from the Iranian government which, despite its own repressive policies towards Iranian Kurds, was all too eager to destabilize Iraq. In 1975, Saddam Husayn met with the shah of Iran in Algiers and signed an agreement in which Iraq gave up its claims in the Shatt al-'Arab and recognized the mid-point as the border line. In return, the shah promised to end all support for the Kurdish movement and close the border, thereby preventing weapons transfers and denying Kurdish fighters a safe haven in case of retreat. Kurdish resistance collapsed almost immediately. Barazani fled, eventually reaching the United States where, in 1979, he died. There then followed a vigorous and ruthless policy of ethnic cleansing that was designed to remove all Kurdish villages from the border areas with

Turkey and Iran. By 1978, an estimated 200,000 people were moved and many villages destroyed. Land reform was introduced to destroy the power of the Kurdish aghas and Arab tribes were encouraged to settle in the north. Arabic again became the sole language of government and education. This blow led to the reorganization of the Kurdish national movement with the eventual rise of two main parties. The old KDP was now led by Barazani's two sons, and a new Patriotic Union of Kurdistan formed under the leadership of Jalal Talbani. After the defeat of the Kurds, the ICP came under increasing harassment. By 1979, hounded and with most of its members imprisoned or killed, it withdrew from the National Progressive Front and went underground. Iraq also enjoyed greater influence regionally, particularly after Egypt's isolation as a result of its peace treaty with Israel. Up to that point, Iraq's position on the Arab–Israeli conflict had been so radical that its relations with most Arab countries, including the Palestine Liberation Organization, were extremely strained. In 1978, Iraq played host to an emergency meeting of Arab heads of state to organize an effective opposition bloc against the peace treaty. This provided the country with the opportunity to improve its relations with its neighbors, especially Jordan and the monarchies of the Gulf. Relations with Syria were also improved to the point where the borders were opened and the two governments even announced their intention to form a union. These relations, however, soon faltered over the question of who would lead the proposed union.

The revolution of 1958, carried out by the army, was initially popular because it eliminated the political power of the big landowners and created greater opportunities for broader sectors of the population. It also took a more independent posture with respect to international relations and placed the country on the road to establish complete control over the oil industry. National unity appeared much stronger, particularly the first two years after the revolution. The revolution also gave way to a decade of intense power struggles. Often these struggles represented the personal ambitions of the leading participants to fill the gap left by the fall of the monarchy. But they also involved an ideological struggle over the future nature of the republic, its regional and international position, and the institution best suited to lead this transformation. While focusing on urban power, most of the leading figures involved during the turbulent decade of the 1960s came from rural provincial backgrounds where notions of tribal solidarity were especially strong. In this atmosphere of political instability, national unity began to suffer. After 1968, the Ba'th Party attempted to establish itself, in place of the army, as the central institution of the state. In many ways, Ahmad Hasan al-Bakr, an army officer with links to the old Free Officers Movement and the leader of the Ba'th Party, represented this transitional phase. By the late 1970s, both the army and the party were gradually yielding power to the security services of Saddam Husayn. The security services had come to be regarded as indispensable as a result of the continuing power struggles and fear of plots. Though intimately integrated with the party, the security services tended to downplay ideology and emphasized control and obedience. This last transition occurred in 1979, when al-Bakr resigned for health reasons. In his place, he appointed Saddam Husayn who, true to his role in the security services, eventually commanded unquestioned dictatorial powers with the party's ideology ultimately losing all relevance.

chapter seven

THE DICTATORSHIP OF SADDAM HUSAYN, 1979–2003

Almost immediately after assuming the presidency, Saddam Husayn conducted an extensive purge of the government and party. One after the other party officials, many who had worked with him for decades, were paraded on national television. With Saddam looking on they "confessed" to being party to a Syrian "plot" against Iraq. Once the terrifying show was over 22 were duly executed with others receiving long prison terms. Naturally, the relationship with Syria that had just improved, deteriorated greatly. After the elimination of all his rivals, Saddam arranged for the country's first elections for a National Assembly since the 1958 revolution. The elections were a complete sham with no meaningful opposition permitted. The National Assembly was a powerless body which basically rubber-stamped all the president's decisions. For the next 24 years the dictatorship would put Iraq through several grueling wars, paralyzing international sanctions, and a reign of terror that threatened the country's national unity.

Saddam Husayn's rise to power was accompanied by an unparalleled personality cult. His picture appeared in every newspaper, on every wall, and huge murals of his image covered entire buildings. Iraqis joke that there were enough of his larger-than-life statues to make sure that each citizen had one. Every house was expected to display his picture and his birthday became a nationally celebrated holiday. Everything from towns and neighborhoods to convention halls and scholarships carried his name. Presented as the Harun al-Rashid of modern Iraq, he even emulated the mythical image of the benevolent caliph who would periodically sneak out of his palace to walk among his subjects. He was seen every evening on television in various sections of the country, chatting with peasants, having tea in "impromptu" visits to working-class homes, attending class with secondary school pupils, and discreetly dropping in on hospitals to make sure the public was being served properly. He was considered an authority on all subjects from philosophy and art to marriage and child-rearing. As with most Muslim countries, the televised call for prayer in Iraq is usually followed by quoting a passage from the Qur'an and a statement from the

Prophet. Under Saddam's regime, it was also followed by a long quotation from one of Saddam's many speeches. No singer could hope to have a career without at least one original song glorifying the "Great Leader", the "Mind of the Revolution", the "Knight". Students were instructed to add "may God preserve him" after mentioning his name. History books were hastily rewritten to show that he was at the center of every important event in the country's recent past – the true hero of Iraq and the Arabs. A film was made of his life with the actor strictly forbidden to play any other role in the future. Ironically, this actor was later branded a traitor and put to death.

The opposition

In February 1979, the Middle East was shaken by a massive popular revolution in Iran which overthrew the monarchy. The driving ideology of the revolution was a brand of Islamic militancy that believed the application of Islamic ideals and laws to be the cure for social injustice and foreign domination. Its leader and chief ideologue, Ayatollah Khomeini, wasted little time in attempting to export the revolution to Iraq (with its Shi'i majority) by calling for the overthrow of the "atheist Ba'th" regime. His chief ally in Iraq was the Da'wa (the Call) Party. The Da'wa was organized in 1968 by leading Shi'i religious figures such as Ayatollah Muhammad Baqir al-Sadr. It emerged in response to centuries of Sunni domination and as a reaction to such secular parties as the ICP that were attracting Shi'i support. Emboldened by the Iranian revolution, Da'wa members carried out a series of daring assassinations of top Ba'thists. They also organized several mass demonstrations in the Shi'i centers of the south, their main base of support. The state responded with a severe crackdown. Ayatollah al-Sadr and his sister were arrested; their fate remains unknown, but they were most likely killed. Leading cadres of the party suffered similar fates. To deter the opposition, a new policy was formulated whereby the families of those implicated in anti-government activities would be held responsible and punished accordingly. Membership in any opposition movement became a capital offense. Such repression had its effect on the Da'wa which continues to suffer today from the absence of an acknowledged guiding force similar to that of al-Sadr.

In 1982, the Iranian government, then at war with Iraq, sponsored a meeting of all the Iraqi Islamic parties including the Da'wa. An umbrella organization was formed known as the Supreme Council of the Islamic Revolution in Iraq (SCIRI). Relations between its members, however, were not always congenial, and the Da'wa, in particular, were uncomfortable with Iranian meddling. In 1988, the Da'wa froze its membership in the SCIRI claiming that it was becoming an instrument of Iranian interests. Its relations with the other opposition forces were also problematic. The party's Islamic ideology runs diametrically opposed to that of the communists and has failed to formulate a clear program with respect to the Kurdish question. According to its brand of political Islam, national identities should be downplayed in favor of religious affiliation. Since both Kurds and Arabs are overwhelmingly Muslim, the question of autonomy should not arise. The Da'wa eventually reformulated this outlook, giving more consideration to Kurdish national aspirations but the ideological tension remains. Unlike the majority of the other opposition groups, the Da'wa has also been slow to adopt the slogan of democracy, arguing that this was a Western notion. Lastly, the Da'wa continues to suffer from being a specifically Shi'i organization, thus alienating Sunnis and non-Muslims and failing to convince with respect to the issue of national unity.

Other than the Shi'i opposition, the Kurds were able to regroup after their 1975 setback. In 1979, the KDP held a congress and elected Mas'ud Barazani, Mulla Mustafa's son, as its new leader. He promised a new direction which would rid the KDP of tribal influences. In spite of their joint plight, the KDP's relations with Jalal Talabani's PUK continued to be strained, at times even leading to armed conflict. Talabani's party tended to appeal more to the urban Kurds, especially those of Sulaymaniyya. After 1979, the ICP also set up bases in the north but, in 1988, they were forced to move many of their offices to Syria where their freedom of action was often curtailed. During the 1980s, and especially after the fall of the Soviet Union, the ICP took up a more critical view of its past positions. The communists have now emphasized greater democratization within their party and allowed more diversity in their press. During Iraq's war with Iran, Kurdistan formed a base for the opposition's guerrilla movement. A number of Arab nationalist groups, including dissident Ba'thists (usually allied to Syria) also declared their opposition to Saddam's regime. Organizationally the Arab nationalists are weak but they claim to have significant support within the army and the Ba'th Party. There have been numerous attempts at creating a united front or at least some form of coordinated action, but the ideological differences, old suspicions and the intervention of regional powers such as Syria and Iran, have prevented this from happening. There have also been periodical cracks and crises within the ruling circle of Saddam's relatives who often found it difficult to get along with each other. This was the case, for example, in 1983, after a series of defeats in the war with Iran when Saddam's half brother was sent into semi-exile.

The war with Iran, 1980–1988

Though Iran and Iraq have had a history of border disputes, the war that flared up in 1980 was the direct result of the Iranian revolution and Saddam's tendency to pursue his personal ambitions with reckless abandon. The war lasted for eight years, resulted in over one million casualties (400,000 from Iraq), cost an estimated $128 billion, and was eventually resolved by returning to the pre-war status quo. It was the largest conflict since World War II and often threatened to expand beyond the two countries. Like the Iraqi revolution of 1958 which affected the stability of the monarchic regimes in the region, the Iranian revolution of 1979 sent most of the surrounding countries scrambling for ways to contain it. In its early days the Iranian revolution was extremely popular among the people of the region who celebrated the downfall of the shah. It also caused concern among the regimes who feared that it might prove contagious. These fears were confirmed by Khomeini's statements clearly indicating his desire to export the revolution to other Islamic countries, especially to neighboring Iraq. At the same time the revolution weakened the shah's once mighty army. Purges of top officers, scarcity of spare parts (especially for the air force) due to an embargo by the United States, and the general chaos normally associated with popular upheavals, all left Iranian defenses vulnerable. This, in addition to Iran's international isolation as a result of its worsening relations with both the United States and the Soviet Union, led Saddam to believe that the opportunity was ripe for a quick military strike that would rid him of a major rival. He probably hoped for an alteration in the borders in favor of Iraq, greater control over the oil-rich area of Khuzistan, and the emergence of Iraq as the undisputed power in the Gulf. At most, he might have thought that a quick victory would also result in a favorable regime change in Iran.

On 17 September 1980 Saddam announced the abrogation of the Algiers Treaty, which had defined the border between the two countries since 1975. On 22 September, after a series of border clashes and against the advice of his top commanders, Saddam sent Iraqi tanks pouring across the border into south-western Iran. The city of Khurramshahr fell after brutal house-to-house fighting but, surprisingly, Abadan held out. Instead of a complete collapse, the invasion actually solidified Iranian resolve and rallied the various factions around the pro-Khomeini camp. By November, the Iraqi advance had stalled. Iran had refused all mediation insisting that Iraq must withdraw, admit its guilt in starting the war, and pay reparations. To make matters worse for Saddam, Israel, fearing the development of atomic weapons, launched an air attack that destroyed Iraq's Osirak atomic reactor in 1981. That same year, Iraq's request to join the Gulf Cooperation Council was snubbed. This council, composed of all the Arab countries in the Gulf, was formed to act as a counterweight to both Iranian and Iraqi designs. The following year, Syria, which had sided with Iran, closed its borders to Iraqi oil exports. This last action drove home the economic vulnerability of the country. Of all the leading oil-exporting nations, Iraq is the only one that suffers from its limited access to port facilities. By contrast, Iran continued to export its oil from ports further south, away from the front, thus avoiding the need to borrow heavily in order to finance its war effort.

In 1982, an Iranian counter-offensive achieved great success in driving out most of the Iraqi forces and, for a while, it seemed as if Saddam's hold on power was in doubt. But Iranian announcements about installing an Islamic government in Baghdad rallied Saddam's commanders around his leadership once again. The Iranian offensive lacked air cover or sufficient armor. To make up for this deficiency the Iranians resorted to outmoded tactics of human wave attacks, resulting in extremely high casualties. Nevertheless, they persisted and in 1986 they seized the port of Fao, Iraq's only access to the sea. To many observers, it seemed like only a matter of time before Basra, and with it the whole south, would fall into Iranian hands. Iraq responded by attempting to cripple the Iranian economy. Armed with newly purchased French Exocet missiles, the Iraqi air force targeted Iranian ports, cities, oil facilities and tankers. The Iranians responded by attacking the tankers of nations, like Kuwait, seen as supporting Iraq. The war was on the verge of being dangerously broadened when both the United States and the Soviet Union agreed to escort the oil tankers.

During the war, Iraq began to shift its regional alliances away from the so-called "radical" countries, such as Syria and Libya, toward the "traditional" countries such as the monarchies of the Gulf and Jordan. It also improved its relationship with Egypt despite the latter's peace treaty with Israel. The Gulf countries, especially Kuwait and Saudi Arabia, agreed to provide Iraq with generous financial backing, while Jordan opened its port facilities to Iraqi trade and military imports. New highways were constructed with Turkey, Kuwait and Jordan. Egypt provided Iraq with direct military assistance in the form of experts and, perhaps, some special operation forces. Iraq also made use of imported Egyptian labor to help to run its economy. Turkey was permitted to conduct cross-border raids against its own Kurdish insurgents in return for keeping Iraq's oil lines open. This arrangement has continued to the present. Internationally, Iraq began to look more toward the West, especially the United States with whom it had had a problematic relationship since 1958. Diplomatic relations were restored in 1984, and the United States agreed to provide Iraq with some intelligence reports on Iranian troop movements. Fearing that an Iranian victory might destabilize the oil kingdoms in the Gulf, the United States leaned toward Iraq especially at the end of the war. But overall, the United States seemed eager that both sides should emerge weaker after the war.

The support that Iraq enjoyed finally paid off in 1988 when the tide of the war shifted once again. For several years, Iraq had been employing chemical weapons, including mustard and nerve gas, in the war. In March 1988, the Kurdish town of Halabja near the Iranian border was bombed with the deadly agents. Kurdish insurgents had been receiving support from Iran and Iraq's decision to punish them by targeting the population shocked the world. Photographers' images of parents cuddling infants as they lay motionless in the streets of the town were shown throughout the world. An estimated 5000 civilians died. Despite this setback to its image, Iraq continued to push its advantage and finally succeeded in driving the Iranians out of Fao. This last operation, where chemical weapons were again used, was directly supported by United States forces which attacked several Iranian ships and oil platforms. By July, Iran had announced its readiness to accept a cease fire. Though, in the words of Khomeini, this decision was "more deadly than taking poison", the Iranian leader was forced to acknowledge that his country could no longer hope for complete victory. The news triggered spontaneous celebrations in Iraq, which the regime quickly transformed into "victory" celebrations. In August, the cease fire was formally signed with an agreement to return to the status quo prior to the hostilities. After eight devastating years, the war had failed to resolve any of the outstanding issues. In addition to the old border disputes, new disagreements emerged over the withdrawal of all forces and the exchange of POWs. But the war did demonstrate the strength of the Iraqi regime. As brutal and unpopular as it was, it survived the massive losses. The war also demonstrated how strong Iraqi national unity had become. With the notable exception of many Kurds, Iraq's communities remained loyal. Between 1982 and 1985, for example, a number of Arab Shi'i tribes in the south organized their own resistance to Iranian attacks independently of state direction.

The end of the war gave the regime a chance to settle scores with its internal enemies, particularly the Kurds. Beginning in late 1987, forces were moved north against the insurgents. By August of the following year, the notorious "Anfal"[1] campaign had turned into a broad attack on Kurdish civilians as well as combatants. A large number of Kurdish villages, especially those near the borders or in inaccessible mountain terrain, were destroyed, and their inhabitants were removed to camps near major highways or executed along the way. Villages that were too heavily defended by insurgent forces were bombed with chemical weapons. In a meeting with Ba'thist leaders, the man in charge of this operation, 'Ali Hasan al-Majid, a cousin of Saddam, said:

> As soon as we complete the deportations, we will start attacking them [the Kurdish insurgents] everywhere according to a systematic military plan ... then we will surround them in a small pocket and attack them with chemical weapons. I will not attack them with chemicals just one day, but I will continue to attack them with chemicals for fifteen days.[2]

---

[1] The word is the title of the eighth chapter of the Qur'an, which deals with the spoils of war.

[2] Human Rights Watch, *Genocide in Iraq, the Anfal Campaign Against the Kurds*, New York, 1993, p. 349.

The campaign, which continued unabated into the following year, resulted in the destruction of 90 per cent of Kurdish villages and at least 20 small towns. An estimated 15 million land mines were placed throughout the evacuated areas. Hundreds of thousands of Kurds were relocated to camps, some of which were in the southern part of the country. An estimated 100,000 refugees poured into Turkey.

Economic and social developments

During the war, the Iraqi regime promoted both nationalist and religious symbols designed to show the justice of its case. For the first time, Iraq took the initiative in sponsoring various Islamic conferences; Saddam was often shown praying or visiting religious sites, and the state-directed media began to discuss the possibility of applying Islamic laws. To the Arab countries, Iraq was presented as the "Guardian of the Eastern Gate", while the war was officially called the "Second Qadisiyya" or "Saddam's Qadisiyya", in reference to the seventh-century battle between the Arab Muslims and the Sassanid Persians. Internally, more emphasis was laid on the Arab nature of Iraqi nationality, which naturally called into question the loyalty of non-Arabs, particularly Kurds and Iraqis of Persian origin. Even before the war had started, the regime ordered the deportation of around 250,000 Iraqis of Iranian descent, confiscating their properties which were then distributed to selected supporters. A broad campaign was launched against all things Persian. In 1982, a law was passed offering financial rewards to men who divorced their Iranian wives. History books were rewritten to portray the Persians as the historic enemies of the Arabs, and a negative and corruptive influence on Islamic civilization. Among these books was a "study" by Saddam's uncle in which he declares that Persians are "animals God created in the shape of humans".[3] Language, traditions and habits had to be purged of Persian influence. At the same time, Saddam Husayn was presented as the great Arab warrior, the worthy heir of Sa'd

---

[3] Quoted in Samir al-Khalil, *Republic of Fear: The Politics of Modern Iraq*, Berkeley, 1989, p. 17.

ibn Abi Waqqas or even the Caliph 'Umar himself. Even before the end of the war a colossal monument was erected to commemorate the victory. The "Hands of Victory" monument was built at the entrance to a new parade ground. Two Arab swords with 24 ton blades made from the metal of rifles of Iraq soldiers killed in battle, were held by two huge hands. The hands, sculpted to resemble those of Saddam, emerge from two piles of 5000 Iranian helmets collected from the front.

By 1988, there were 950,000 men in the army and 250,000 in the People's Army constituting over one-half of the adult male population – a massive drain on the labor and resources of the country. The infrastructure of Iraq did not suffer as much damage as that of Iran. Its oilfields in Kirkuk, for example, were hardly touched by the war. Nevertheless, its port facilities were almost completely destroyed and extensive damage was done to the oil refineries at Basra. Before the war, Iraq had a healthy foreign exchange reserve of around $35 billion; by the end of the war its foreign debt was anywhere between $100 and $120 billion. Overall, the estimated cost of reconstruction stood at around $452.6 billion – a heavy burden for any economy. To make matters worse, international oil prices had declined steeply since 1986. The state responded by broadening the practice of confiscating the properties of anyone deemed undesirable. Those who benefited most from the re-distribution of these properties were usually supporters of the regime from the Arab Sunni provincial regions such as the Tikritis, Kubaysis and Jubur. Grateful for the state's largesse, these newly enriched elements replaced the old urban elites as the country's dominant political and economic class. In 1987, the regime adopted a policy of rapid privatization by selling off all state farms and industries except those deemed necessary for national security such as oil, defense and steel. This was accompanied by a deregulation of the labor market by abolishing the full employment law, cutting subsidies, and removing price ceilings. Other than benefiting a few families who took advantage of the new opportunities, these policies led to a decline in production, greater foreign economic dependency and a sharp rise in inflation and unemployment. The hardest hit were the salaried middle classes whose wages took a severe blow as a result of inflation. A sure sign of the troubled economy was the increasing number of people making their living from informal activities or very small businesses. Fearing the demobilization of the army in such a depressed economy, the import of cheap Egyptian labor continued, helping to keep wages low and further reducing the overall purchasing power of the population.

Two years of tenuous peace

In spite of these massive problems hopes for recovery were still high. Iraq's estimated 100 billion barrels of oil reserves continued to be a valuable asset and international creditors were not wanting. In 1989, Saddam even showed some hints of easing his grip on power by announcing new elections for the National Assembly, the legalization of some opposition parties, and a general amnesty. A committee was established to complete the draft of a permanent constitution, something the country had lacked since the 1958 Revolution. Within the ruling circle, however, the regime became even more dependent on elements drawn from Saddam's tribe, the Bayjat. In addition to their monopoly on power, it is rumored that Saddam's family demanded kickbacks of 7 per cent on all major business transactions. His two sons, 'Uday and Qusay, were put in charge of sensitive areas while his half-brothers, cousins and other relatives also received important posts transforming the regime into a form of family rule under republican garb. During this time the media started to pave the way for the succession of Saddam by one of his sons. For example, Saddam's personal poet, 'Abdul-Razzaq 'Abdul-Wahid, wrote of 'Uday:

> What we could not perceive of your great secret
> We see now, oh Great Lord
> In the eyes of your Great Son.[4]

---

[4] Quoted in Fatima Mohsen, "Cultural Totalitarianism", in Fran Hazelton, *Iraq Since the Gulf War: Prospects for Democracy*, London, 1994, p. 17.

After the war, Iraq emerged as the strongest military power in the Gulf. Saddam sought to make the most of this advantage in dealing with his neighbors. Military aid was given to select Palestinian and anti-Syrian Lebanese groups who acted as vehicles for the projection of Iraq's regional influence. Israel, Syria, Iran and even Turkey were publicly threatened on different occasions and demands were made of Kuwait to cede its off-shore Island of Bubyan. Heavy investment in enhancing the country's military capabilities continued by aggressively acquiring or developing advanced weapons of various sorts. The collapse of the Soviet Union offered more possibilities to purchase internationally banned chemical and biological weapons. Bogus companies were set up to acquire the components needed for the manufacture of nuclear weapons. These activities, plus the regime's dismal human rights record, invited growing criticism from the West. Such non-productive investments also acted as an additional drain on the country's exhausted economy.

By 1990, the country was in crisis. Over 500,000 men were still under arms with little prospects of being released from active service into an economy incapable of absorbing them. Restlessness was apparent among the soldiers who had suffered much during the war with little to show for it. There were increasing reports of isolated uprisings by angry soldiers and frequent purges and transfers of officers. Saddam's hopes that Kuwait and Saudi Arabia might write off Iraq's debt or even offer funds for reconstruction were not realized. During that year, oil prices dropped from $20 a barrel to $13.70, resulting in an annual revenue loss to Iraq of around $7 billion. By the summer of 1990, Saddam publicly accused Kuwait and the United Arab Emirates of deliberately keeping oil prices down by exceeding their OPEC export quotas. This, he declared, was nothing short of economic warfare which the country would not tolerate. He later accused Kuwait of illegally pumping oil from the Iraqi oil wells adjacent to the border. The crisis grew worse with Iraqi military maneuvers appearing more threatening and a number of Arab and international efforts to mediate the dispute reaching a dead end.

The disaster of Kuwait

On 2 August 1990, Iraqi troops invaded Kuwait in response, it was claimed, to a call by Kuwaiti officers who had seized power earlier that day. Saddam, encouraged by statements of non-involvement by the US ambassador, had gambled on international inactivity. Shortly after the occupation was completed, he made peace with Iran by basically reaffirming the 1975 Algiers Agreement. The invasion was so massive (over 300,000 soldiers) that many expected another invasion of Saudi Arabia, but it did not take place. A few days after the invasion Iraq announced "the return of the branch to the stem" by annexing Kuwait. International response was swift. The United Nations condemned the act and, under Resolution 661, imposed strict sanctions effectively establishing a complete blockade of Iraq. Britain and the USA followed this action by forming a military coalition of 34 countries with the stated goal of liberating Kuwait. The coalition included a number of Arab countries such as Egypt, Syria and Saudi Arabia, but US troops accounted for over 75 per cent of the forces. Saddam tried to win some support by linking Iraqi withdrawal to Israeli withdrawal from occupied Palestinian lands and a Syrian withdrawal from Lebanon. Jordan and the Palestine Liberation Organization reacted positively to this move and their media strongly sided with Iraq. Many in the Arab world also voiced support for Iraq on the grounds that it was facing a new imperialist invasion of the Middle East.

The developing hostility between Saddam's regime and the USA went well beyond Iraq's invasion and annexation of Kuwait. American interests in the region revolved around three key issues: opposition to Soviet influence, the strategic commitment to Israeli military superiority, and oil. During the 1980s, relations had warmed somewhat as Saddam suppressed the communists, condemned the Soviet invasion of Afghanistan, and established Iraq as the first line of defense against Iranian expansion. By the end of the decade, however, several factors had changed. The decline and later collapse of the Soviet Union reduced the need for the USA to support anti-communist regimes such as that of Saddam Husayn. At the same time, Iraq's development of an ambitious program for the production of various weapons of mass destruction, and the capability to deliver them across the region, raised concerns over the balance of power with Israel. Iraq's rising military capabilities also raised fears over the possibility of a single power eventually dominating the oil-rich Gulf area. The goal of the USA at this point, therefore, was to cripple Iraq's military so that it would no longer be able to project its power regionally. At no point did the question of human rights seriously figure in these considerations.

After a flurry of diplomatic activity reached a deadlock, coalition forces struck on 16 January with a massive air bombardment. Iraq offered little resistance but tried to win support within the Arab world by firing a number of modified Scud missiles into Israel. After one full month of unrelenting air strikes by the coalition forces (over 116,000 sorties), which destroyed almost the entire infrastructure of the country and killed scores of soldiers and civilians, a ground offensive was ordered. As coalition forces advanced quickly into Kuwait and southern Iraq, the retreating Iraqi troops set fire to most of Kuwait's oil wells, which continued to burn several weeks after the cessation of hostilities causing a great environmental disaster. As about 60,000 Iraqi soldiers surrendered without a fight, it seemed to most observers that the regime's days were numbered. The USA, however, ordered its troops to stop short of Baghdad, giving Saddam valuable time to regroup his forces. While the regular conscript army was decimated, the regime's elite Republican Guard units were held back and suffered little damage. The final figures show that the "Mother of All Battles", as Saddam called it, was truly a one-sided affair. Other than the destruction of Iraq's infrastructure, the country suffered anywhere between 94,000 and 281,000 killed during the war and in the subsequent uprisings. Coalition casualties did not exceed several hundred.

During the campaign, US President George Bush called on the Iraqi people to rise up against Saddam's dictatorship. In March 1991, an uprising did take place initiated by the retreating troops near Basra. It later spread north where Kurdish groups seized the opportunity to capture the entire region of Kurdistan. The uprising, which lasted over two weeks, soon engulfed the entire country leaving only Baghdad and the area just north of the capital in government hands. The collapse of state control allowed masses of people to seek revenge against Ba'thists, state security personnel, or practically any symbol or institution representing the dictatorship. But the opposition being so divided and the refusal of the USA to support the insurgents, allowed the regime to launch a brutal counter-attack which re-established control. Saddam's forces attempted to transform the uprising, which began as a spontaneous movement for the overthrow of the dictatorship, into a sectarian conflict. Tanks were painted with anti-Shi'i slogans, newspapers carried articles attacking Shi'ism, and the sanctuary of Shi'i shrines in Najaf and Karbala was not respected. After securing the south, government forces turned against the Kurds. Fearing another wave of chemical attacks thousands fled, once again to Turkey, and by April the resistance had collapsed. Overall, around two million people were displaced during these turbulent months. The leaders of the Kurdish opposition, Barazani and Talabani, both gave up on international support and went to Baghdad to try to reach some kind of agreement with Saddam. Unlike the south, where the atrocities of the regime remained mostly hidden from public view, the plight of the Kurds received broad coverage with television providing images of streams of refugees and individual stories of suffering. The coverage contributed to European calls for the creation of a protected "Kurdish enclave" and eventually US and British troops escorted most of the refugees back. The UN later declared the area north of the 36th parallel a "no fly" zone for the Iraqi air force causing Baghdad to relinquish its control of the area. This Kurdish "safe haven" was later extended to include Sulaymaniyya and Halabja. A no-fly zone was also eventually established to the south of the 32nd parallel, but no UN troops were introduced into the area. As a result, the government was free to act. It diverted valuable resources to drain most of the marshes where many of the insurgents had hidden. By 2000, large areas that had been teeming with wildlife, similar to the Everglades of the USA, were transformed into barren desert. Once again, the country lay devastated, and once again Saddam claimed victory. For Saddam, his survival as ruler of the country was the most important achievement. Not only did he weather the assault from the world's most powerful military, but the Iraqi army, which had posed a threat to his regime, was now in tatters.

Iraq under international sanctions

The hardships caused by the physical and human destruction were multiplied many times over by the severe penalties imposed on Iraq by the United Nations. The border was altered in favor of Kuwait, 30 per cent of Iraqi oil exports were set aside for war reparations (estimated at well over $100 billion), and the strictest, most comprehensive sanctions in history were to remain in place until Iraq fulfilled several conditions. These conditions include the elimination of its weapons of mass destruction, monitored by a UN Special Committee (UNSCOM), the release of Kuwaiti prisoners, and the regular payment of compensation. Compensation was controlled by a special fund handled by the UN. In effect, those restrictions mortgaged Iraq's oil for the foreseeable future, and took most of the financial controls away from the Iraqi government. UNSCOM's work revealed a massive nuclear, biological and chemical weapons program. Workers dismantled 40 nuclear research centers and destroyed 38,000 chemical munitions and 625 tons of chemical agents, including those that go into making deadly VX and mustard gas. Records uncovered show that, before the Gulf War, Iraq had stockpiled up to 8400 liters of anthrax and 19,000 liters of botulinum. One gram of anthrax spores could conceivably have killed 100 million people.

The sanctions, which initially included 90 per cent of regular imports and 97 per cent of exports, were gradually eased. Such conditions, plus the already heavy debt incurred during the war with Iran, triggered hyperinflation which practically eliminated the Iraqi middle classes.

The Iraqi dinar (ID), which exchanged at around $3, fell to the rate of $1 = 20,000 ID. As a result, food prices increased over 50 times and GNP per capita fell from $2840 in 1989 to only $200 in 1997. There is growing concern that the rising cancer rates, especially in the south, are a direct result of the 300–800 tons of depleted uranium that went into the making of the bombs dropped on Iraq. The scarcity of medicines, the decline in access to clean water and adequate nutrition, resulted in a steep climb in the under-5 mortality rate from 56 per 1000 live births between 1984 and 1989, to 91.5 in 1989–1994, and to 130.6 between 1994 and 1999. Malnutrition among children under 5 rose by one-third. UNICEF estimated that over half a million children died as a direct result of the sanctions.

Such figures were sure to lead to increasing international criticism of the wisdom and the morality of the sanctions. Statements by US officials that the sanctions "target the regime and not the people" failed to hold up, particularly when considering that the regime was actually quite successful at stabilizing its rule and adapting well to the conditions of scarcity. In 1995, the sanctions were modified slightly to allow Iraq to sell part of its oil for the purchase of food and medicine. The so-called "oil-for-food program" came into effect in 1997 but was still criticized for falling well short of the humanitarian needs. In 1998, the UN Assistant Secretary General Denis Halliday condemned the sanctions as "genocidal" and promptly resigned his post. Just over a year later, his successor also resigned in protest. On the UN Security Council, France, China and Russia all called for a significant easing of the sanctions if not outrightly removing them. By the late 1990s, there was increasing talk of applying "smart sanctions" which would only target Iraq's military capability. Nothing, however, came of this idea as US policy changed to include a demand for the removal of Saddam from power as a condition for lifting the sanctions giving the regime no incentive to comply. In 1998, Iraq stopped cooperating with the UN and UNSCOM was ordered out of the country, resulting in renewed air strikes.

The effect of the sanctions on Iraqi society has been great. After 10 years, over 16 million Iraqis were still directly dependent on some form of assistance. The regime survived and even strengthened its hold on power by distributing the scarce revenues to its most loyal supporters. It also benefited from the development of a parallel economy of smuggling in which connections were even more important. Arab Sunnis from provincial backgrounds continued to be favored, but the regime also won the support of a very small number of Shi'is, Kurds and Christians who benefited from the state's largesse. While rationing and subsidized food were instituted, the state withdrew most of its previously plentiful support for broad sectors of the population. The rate of privatization accelerated rapidly bringing huge profits to those few with the right connections, but resulted in unemployment or underemployment for most. Hardest hit were the salaried professionals. Stories abound in Baghdad of university professors forced to drive taxi cabs to survive. Schools suffered from a lack of resources and high student absenteeism. As a result, literacy among the adult population declined from 80 per cent in 1987 to 58 per cent in 1995. In the absence of many state services people resurrected old social institutions, such as tribes or communal networks, for support. Sectarianism and tribalism received encouragement from the state, especially after the 1991 uprising. The state gave official recognition to a number of tribal shaykhs by establishing an Assembly of Tribes, a practice not seen since the days of the monarchy. Not long after the 1991 March uprising, delegations of tribal shaykhs, each carrying its distinctive tribal banners, were received by Saddam. At that meeting, Saddam made a public apology for the harm done to the shaykhs by the land reform laws and promised compensation. Tribal authority was recognized over some judicial and revenue-collecting sectors, and practices, long thought extinct, such as the payment of blood money, received government consent. The state dealt with tribes through an informal hierarchical arrangement based on the extent of tribal loyalty to Saddam. Saddam's Bayjat tribe were naturally regarded as the elite. But these "new" tribes showed some important differences with their earlier counterparts.

They were more tightly linked to the state, had no clearly demarcated territories, and their leaders were based in the cities. While tribal identity continued to be based on the myth of shared kinship, the new tribes lacked the material foundations for a lasting community. In the highly urbanized society of modern Iraq, tribal members did not work and live together as a separate group. Still, they were more autonomous than the normal state agencies, and, at times, demonstrated the willingness to challenge the police or even the security services.

The regime's favoritism (especially in times of acute scarcity) in dealing with various groups contributed to an atmosphere of cut-throat competition between sects and tribes. The parallel economy also gave rise to crime and turf wars between rival gangs who very often included senior government officials. One such example was the rather bizarre case of the defection, return and murder of Saddam's two sons-in-law in 1995. In 1994, the state responded with a number of draconian laws including branding, amputation and death of even minor criminals. They were, however, applied selectively and yielded no tangible results. This atmosphere left a deep psychological scar on the people and affected social values where, for example, bribes, once unheard of in Iraq, became commonplace. To counter this sense of moral decline and find some peace during hard times, overall religious observance appeared to be on the rise. As with other parts of the Islamic world, more women were wearing the veil, mosques showed higher attendance, and more people were fasting during the month of Ramadan. Among Iraqis there was much cynicism toward the rest of the world. Many believed that Saddam was deliberately kept in power for so long by the USA to further its interests in the region, or that the USA's goal was the complete annihilation of Iraq simply out of spite. Today, out of a total population of 25.5 million, there are between 3 to 5 million Iraqi refugees abroad.

The Kurdish haven in the north, protected by UN guarantees, escaped much, but not all, of the hardships caused by the sanctions. The relative safety created the basis for a more stable economy, but its uncertain future, fear of Turkish intentions, and the continuous rivalry between the KDP and PUK also gave rise to smuggling and profiteering, with the two Kurdish parties making the most of this parallel economy. In 1992, under international supervision, elections were held for a Kurdish parliament based in Irbil. During the elections disputes arose between the competing parties, but eventually the KDP, which controlled Irbil, and PUK, based in Sulaymaniyya, shared the seats almost evenly. The new Kurdish government called for federation (rather than autonomy) with Arab Iraq, implying a greater degree of Kurdish independence short of outright secession. The declaration raised grave concerns in Iran, Turkey and Syria, all with substantial Kurdish minorities of their own. Between 1994 and 1998, there were serious clashes between the KDP and PUK which called into question the viability of a Kurdish state and threatened to unleash another wave of refugees. Baghdad, Tehran and Ankara exacerbated the differences by playing one against the other. In 1998, the USA successfully brokered a peace deal whereby administrative functions were divided territorially between the two parties. While this arrangement continued to hold, a new threat emerged with the so-called Partisans of Islam (*Ansar al-Islam*) group. Taking advantage of widespread disillusionment, and aid from radical Islamic groups abroad, this new Islamic party began to stake a claim to some representation.

The Iraqi opposition failed miserably to take advantage of opportunities, especially during the March 1991 uprising. As the uprising was developing, a meeting was held in Beirut where, for the first time, all the major opposition groups and figures participated. It was not long, however, before their old differences dominated the meetings. Islamists objected to a statement about the equality of the sexes, Arab nationalists questioned the notion of Kurdish autonomy, and communists raised the alarm over growing US influence. A joint declaration did come out of the Beirut conference calling for the establishment of a democratic Iraq, but no lasting organizational institutions emerged.

In 1992, an Iraqi National Congress was formed in Vienna. It claimed to be an umbrella organization of various groups but suspicions of US influence kept many of the most active parties away. Exhausted by wars, repression and sanctions, the Iraqi population is unlikely to wage another mass uprising in the foreseeable future. Some argued that the most likely source of change would come from within the regime itself. But Saddam was so insulated that at least six coup attempts have failed to dislodge him. In addition, Saddam's reign of terror continued to dissuade many would-be conspirators, as was evident in the following testimony of an army officer captured during the Gulf War of 1991:

> We are very afraid of this man. Even now that I am talking to you, an American, you will notice that by habit, I will lower my voice when I want to say his name. He has spies everywhere. If he knows that I say bad things about him to you he will kill my wife, my children, and my parents in Iraq. If my division commander every (sic) ordered me to turn my guns against Saddam Hussein, I will do it. But who will be the officer to give this order? I will never give this order.[5]

The question of succession between his two sons was settled in favor of the younger, more sober yet quite ruthless, Qusay. Apparently, 'Uday's wayward manners, long a source of terror among Iraqis, even offended his father. In 1988, he killed one of his father's loyal bodyguards causing Saddam to imprison him for several months. In 1996, his stature was further reduced after an assassination attempt left him partially paralyzed.

While scarce resources were wasted in rebuilding Saddam's numerous grand palaces, statues and murals, Iraq, to the surprise of many observers, adapted well to the sanctions. In Baghdad and the Arab

---

[5] Quoted in Ahmed Hashim, "Saddam Husayn and Civil-Military Relations in Iraq: The Quest for Legitimacy and Power," in *Middle East Journal*, vol. 57, no.1, winter 2003, p. 27.

Sunni region to its north, roads, bridges, power generators and many factories were rebuilt. Embargo-busting planes started flying regularly from Jordan, Syria and Lebanon. Scarcity, at least in Baghdad, seemed less acute, where hospitals received better access to medicines, and shops appeared well stocked. The currency showed signs of stability, though not recovery, and incomes actually started to increase again. Food imports continued to be high, but agricultural development received a boost through the encouragement of private farms in the Jazira region. While the south continued to deteriorate, these gains, especially in the all-important city of Baghdad, should not be dismissed. Internationally, Iraq's image changed from one of an aggressor state to a victim of US and British imperialism. Sympathy with Iraq's suffering children was particularly strong in the Arab world. In the Arab summit held in March 2002, Iraq restored its relations with Saudi Arabia and went some way toward mending its relations with Kuwait. Saddam has also attempted to use the ongoing Palestinian uprising as a means of breaking out of his isolation by offering cash to families of killed militants. To demonstrate the country's defiance and to further add to Saddam's image as a victorious leader, the government announced the construction of one of the world's largest mosques in Baghdad. Dubbed the Mother of All Battles Mosque, its minarets are shaped like Iraq's Scud missiles used in the 1991 war.

The crisis with the USA

The ability of the regime to withstand a decade of sanctions, loss of sovereignty over the north, and periodic air raids convinced policy-makers in the USA and Britain that "active containment" had failed to remove the danger that Saddam posed to regional stability. International and regional developments also encouraged the USA to act more decisively. The fall of the Soviet Union gave the USA a free hand in dealing with the Middle East, and the Kuwait war allowed it to establish a powerful military presence in the Gulf. The suicide bombing of the World Trade Center in New York and the Pentagon by the Islamist al-Qa'ida group on 11 September 2002 was the straw that broke the camel's back. Policy-makers became convinced that the USA needed to play a far more direct and aggressive role globally to prevent such attacks and further its strategic interests. In this respect, President Bush Jr took the initiative in raising the rhetoric against Iraq by labeling it as part of an "axis of evil" (along with Iran and North Korea), and openly called for a "regime change" in the country. The success of the US-led invasion of Afghanistan further encouraged similar action in Iraq. An attack against Iraq, it was hoped, would be a demonstration of American strength and a deterrent to those who might challenge it. "By defeating this threat [Bush stated in early 2003] we will show other dictators that the path of aggression will lead to their own ruin."[6]

Outside the United States and Britain the call for military action in Iraq received almost no support. Russia, China, France and Germany criticized such proposals, and Iraq's neighbors trembled at the thought of what might happen to the region in the aftermath of any US action. Few doubted that the removal of Saddam Husayn could only take place through violence and much bloodshed. Years of dictatorship and war had deepened communal divisions so that the collapse of central authority was likely to engender civil war, refugees and years of regional instability. Largely as a result of its continuing support for Israel and the legacy of Western imperialism in the region, the United States is not viewed with particular affection in most parts of the Middle East. Countries with strong ties to the United States, such as Saudi Arabia, Jordan, Egypt and even Turkey, feared an angry popular backlash in the wake of strong action against Iraq. The collapse of central authority in Iraq might also encourage separatist movements among the Kurds, which Turkey vehemently opposed, or the extension of Iranian influence in the south, which the Gulf countries fear would undermine their stability.

---

[6] Quoted in *The Washington Post*, 21 February 2003, p. A20.

Such objections, however, did not deter the United States and Britain from moving against Iraq. Diplomatically, they accused Saddam of reactivating his weapons of mass destruction programs and forming unspecified links with the al-Qa'ida group. On 8 November 2002 the United Nations Security Council passed Resolution 1441 which afforded Iraq "a final opportunity to comply with its disarmament obligations under relevant resolutions of the Council".[7] These obligations required the country to fully reveal and destroy all chemical, biological and atomic weapons and the means to deliver them; and to dismantle all weapons of mass destruction programs. The resolution also called for the return of international inspectors through a special United Nations Monitoring, Verification and Inspection Commission (UNMOVIC), and the International Atomic Energy Agency (IAEA). The inspectors were given widespread rights including,

> ... immediate, unimpeded, unconditional, and unrestricted access to any and all, including underground, areas, facilities, buildings, equipment, records, and means of transport which they wish to inspect, as well as immediate, unimpeded, unrestricted, and private access to all officials and other persons whom UNMOVIC or the IAEA wish to interview ... inside or outside of Iraq ... without the presence of observers from the Iraqi Government.[8]

At the same time, a massive military build-up was continuing so that by early March, 2003, there were around 250,000 mostly American soldiers in the Middle East. As these preparations were being finalized, the US Secretary of State Colin Powell raised the stakes once more. In a speech to the United Nations Security Council on 5 February, he accused Iraq of having violated Resolution 1441 by impeding the inspectors' work, ignoring the ban on the development of weapons of mass destruction, and by directly supporting the al-Qa'ida group.

---

[7] Quoted in *The Washington Post*, 9 November 2002.
[8] *Ibid.*

Though war appeared more likely, the United States still failed to build a broad coalition similar to the one that defeated Iraq in 1991. France and Germany, backed by Russia, China and the Arab countries (except Kuwait), stood firmly against war. An international anti-war campaign grew more effective and played a significant role in limiting support for the United States. The Iraq crisis caused serious fissures to appear within the United Nations, NATO, the European Union and the Arab League. In addition to the fear of an aggressive American neo-imperialism, there is little doubt that oil played an important part in determining international posturing over Iraq. Russia was Iraq's leading trading partner, and Russian oil companies have secured lucrative deals that were to take effect after the removal of the sanctions. French exports to Iraq have steadily climbed from $330 million in 2000 to $661 million in 2001 and over one billion in 2002. The French oil giant, Total Fina Elf, also signed agreements with the Iraqi government to exploit the Majnun oilfields which alone contain enough oil to satisfy France's needs for the next 30 years. On the other hand, American companies, like Exxon-Mobil and Chevron-Texaco, that control Kuwait's oil industry, are eager to expand their operations across the border. Rather than risk its interests by adopting the American program of "regime change", France argued that it was possible to push Saddam into gradually reforming his rule without necessarily going to war.

Within Iraq the mood was one of great anticipation that the end of the dictatorship might be near, mixed with deep apprehension as to what may befall the country after Saddam's removal. Fears of communal bloodshed were initially raised by some Turkoman leaders (backed by Turkey) who called for international protection from possible Kurdish attacks. On more than one occasion, US officials cautioned neighboring countries from stoking the fires of communalism. Referring to the possible post-war situation, one official said:

> We don't want a weak government that plays into the hands of regional

powers. . . . We don't want the Iranians to be paying the Shiites, the Turks the Turkmen and the Saudis the Sunnis."[9]

After several years of division and inactivity the Kurdish Parliament met in November 2002. Despite specifically rejecting secession, the meeting greatly alarmed Turkey which saw in it a first step toward the formation of an independent Kurdish state. A month later, a broad meeting of Iraqi opposition groups finally took place in London. Several prominent individuals and groups, such as the Communist Party and the Da'wa, boycotted the meeting claiming unfair representation and concern over the "hegemonic" role of United States' representatives. Significantly, the pro-Iranian Supreme Council of the Islamic Revolution in Iraq played an active role in ensuring its success. The conference called for a "democratic, parliamentarian, federal, pluralistic" Iraq with a strong commitment to the unity of the country and the equality of all its communities. It refused foreign military rule but welcomed any assistance by the "international community", specifically the USA and Iran, to overthrow the dictatorship. Within the region, Arab diplomacy focused on trying to convince Saddam to leave the country. Ironically, the strongest support for Iraq came from Syria which, after decades of hostility, opened its borders for trade and travel.

During this flurry of diplomatic posturing and war preparations, US officials gradually unveiled their plans for a post-Saddam Iraq. In a nutshell, these plans appear ominously similar to those of the British Mandate nearly 90 years earlier. As with Genral Maude in 1917, President Bush claimed that the United States would liberate, not conquer, Iraq. Like the British Mandate, the United States hoped to transform the country into a model of democracy and prosperity; a glorious example of American generosity. Bush boldly stated that "a free Iraq can be a source of hope for all the Middle East. . . . Instead of threatening its neighbors and harboring terrorists, Iraq can be an

---

[9] Quoted in *The Washington Post*, 21 February 2003, p. A1.

example of progress and prosperity in a region that needs both."[10] In order to achieve this miracle and avoid years of chaos and regional instability the United States plans to maintain direct military control of the country followed by the establishment of an American interim administration. This administration would direct efforts at securing law and order, post-war reconstruction and the establishment of a new "representative" government. The latter would require a policy of "de-Ba'thification" of the existing administrative structures without large scale purges. US companies would enjoy something of a bonanza since they would receive the lion's share of the reconstruction contracts. In the end, a strong, peace-loving, post-Saddam Iraq would become a solid ally allowing the USA unrivaled influence in the region.

Such plans, however, assume that the people of Iraq will remain passive participants when history clearly shows that this is unlikely. Even many of the United States' allies within the Iraqi opposition, such as Kanan Makiyya and Ahmed al-Chalabi, have criticized these plans as "catastrophic" and "imperialistic". It is worth remembering that Arnold Wilson's vision for post-World War I Iraq lay in tatters after the 1920 Revolt, and that the British-backed monarchy remained bitterly unpopular to the end. The extent of anti-British feelings were again expressed during the 1958 Revolution. It is true that, this time, Iraqis had experienced terrible tragedies at the hands of a "national" government and, thus, might be more agreeable to foreign assistance in shaping the future of their country. But it is also true that the United States enters the Middle East with considerable political baggage. The view that it is driven only by its oil interests, its partisan support for Israel and its backing of Saddam Husayn up to 1991, are liabilities that will surely impede the smooth functioning of future US–Iraqi relations. It remains to be seen whether the United States will be willing to invest the considerable energy and funds needed to overcome the possible obstacles.

---

[10] Quoted in *The Washington Post*, 21 February 2003, p. A1.

Nearly two and a half decades of dictatorship have not been good for Iraq. Repression, wars, uprisings, a suffocating international embargo, and the eventual loss of national sovereignty are the main legacies of Saddam Husayn's rule. All have contributed to great loss of life, economic devastation and a bleak future. As with other authoritarian governments, Saddam Husayn's regime seemed to thrive on keeping the country constantly preoccupied with real or imagined crises. But perhaps the most destructive legacy of Saddam's rule has been the damage done to national integration. Not since the early days of the British Mandate has national unity appeared so brittle, leading many to question whether the country might be on the verge of dismemberment. Having crushed any semblance of civil society, the regime responded to opposition by brandishing the weapon of sectarianism. This was evident during the Iran–Iraq War and the 1991 uprising. During the past decade, as the sanctions limited the state's largesse, tribes were resurrected and encouraged to compete for the limited sources. Even within the dominant Sunni Arab community the established pecking order was based on tribal and regional affiliation. It is not clear how deepseated these divisions have become. Tribes have objectively lost their old practical function as a means of social organization suited for nomadic or isolated rural life. Yet, even among the opposition, tribal, regional and ethnic divisions appear stronger, working to thwart the numerous attempts at forming some type of united front. Essentially, Saddam's rule marks the complete failure of the Arab nationalist dream which swept the region in the 1960s. In place of pan-Arab integration, Iraq became a regional pariah, and internal divisions deepened. As national sovereignty becomes more threatened with the crisis with the United States, some Iraqis appear ready to applaud even Western colonialism if only it would rid them of the dictatorship.

In light of these developments, many observers are now quite pessimistic about the ability of the Iraqi people to create a stable, representative, alternative to the dictatorship in the near future. While such pessimism is certainly justified, it is also true that political culture can, and often does, change radically in the course of life-and-death struggles. Not a single leader of note, even among the Kurds, has openly advocated the dismemberment of the country. Most of the Kurdish and Arab tribal leaders, despite their parochial veneer, represent modern cosmopolitan interests with strong ties to Baghdad and the rest of the country. Iraq's neighbors also fear the instability that dismemberment will surely cause within the region and the United States has vowed to support the building of a strong unified country once Saddam is overthrown. The threat of a US occupation has had the effect of galvanizing sectors of the opposition, and has encouraged the closing of ranks in the hope of acting as a force for the building of a new democratic Iraq.

CONCLUSION

Throughout the past 14 centuries the people of Iraq have been divided along five major lines: urban–rural, Sunni–Shi'i, Kurd-Arab, regional and tribal. The struggle of Iraq's different communities for harmonious coexistence went through numerous phases. In the mid-seventh century, a level of social harmony was established under the rule of an Arab Muslim warrior caste which tended to respect the autonomy of each community. By 750, tribal divisions among the Arab elite and the demands of non-Arab Muslims for equality undermined stability and gave way to a revolutionary transformation of Iraq's social relations. Under the 'Abbasid Caliphate, Sunni Muslim equality became the corner stone of a sophisticated cosmopolitan empire in which great urban centers like Baghdad, Wasit, Basra and Mosul dominated the countryside. Baghdad, in particular, rose to become the center which tied the different regions of Iraq together. By 950, class divisions, weakened central authority and Turkic migrations strained communal relations, intensified tribalism and deepened the Sunni-Shi'i divide. With the Mongol invasion of 1258, central authority virtually collapsed giving free reign to tribal power at the expense of the cities, further exacerbating Iraq's social fragmentation. For the next three centuries, the country suffered from repeated invasions and a sharp economic, demographic and cultural decline. In spite of this, Baghdad, though much diminished in power, continued to act as a regional center. The rule of the Ottoman Turks went some way toward reversing this decline by checking the power of the tribes and bringing about limited stability. Communal relations generally improved but animosity with Shi'i Persia gave the Sunni-Shi'i conflict a dangerous political dimension. The last century of Ottoman rule saw the development of an embryonic national unity in the main urban centers based on the concept of citizenship. This was also the first time that opposition to Ottoman rule was expressed in terms of a more inclusive Arab nationalism rather than Shi'i sectarianism or tribal parochialism.

In 1920, Iraqi national unity showed signs of further development through an initially collaborative effort to resist the newly established rule of Britain. Throughout the Mandate and Monarchy periods, national integration gradually proceeded, receiving encouragement from both the centralizing state and the opposition. The people who showed the greatest resistance to national integration were the Kurds. Long isolated in their mountainous homeland, Kurdish leaders also felt alienated by the ideology of Arab nationalism which influenced much of the political dialogue of the time. Another major obstacle to national integration was the persistence of highly oppressive semi-feudal and tribal relations in the countryside. Among the opposition, socialism found a receptive ear through its appeal for social justice, independence from foreign domination, emphasis on class solidarity and its rejection of sectarian or ethnic divisions. The revolution of 1958, which swept away the old landowning elites and ushered in a republican form of government, was accompanied by a great deal of optimism. National unity appeared to be much stronger, with progressive legislation aimed at fostering social justice, eliminating tribal and religious laws and encouraging greater fraternity between Arabs and Kurds. The republic, however, soon fell victim to a series of leadership struggles over the direction of the new state. As these political struggles intensified, communal divisions made themselves felt once again in the nature of the competing blocs. In addition, the emphasis, by later republican regimes, on Arab nationalism encouraged the growth of an opposing Kurdish nationalism which continues to form a significant obstacle to national unity.

The continuing difficulties have not completely derailed the overall progress toward national integration. By the 1970s, the state, assisted by rising oil revenues and a growing repressive apparatus, was able to extend its control to the most remote corners of the country. Structural transformations, such as the land reforms and the encouragement of the industrial sector, gradually destroyed the economic autonomy of communities, while rural electrification and the development of modern roads tied the country more firmly together. The totalitarian nature of the state, however, did not allow national integration to proceed smoothly. The elimination of all semblances of civil society helped to keep old communal ties alive as the only alternative to the suffocating control of the state. Under the dictatorship of Saddam Husayn, sectarian and communal divisions sharpened from the strain of wars, sanctions and brutal repression. In times of weakness, the state actively fostered such divisions to avoid the emergence of a national alternative to Saddam's regime. The opposition, though aware that no progress can be made without a platform of national unity based on a respect for diversity, is itself not immune from communal divisions.

Relations between the country's various communities were tested once again in March 2003 when the crisis with the United States led to yet another war. Saddam's last stand proved to be quite weak. By April, United States and British forces had practically occupied the entire country, forcing the Ba'thist leadership into hiding. While many Iraqis rejoiced at the end of the dictatorship, they remained wary of foreign occupation. The immediate post-Saddam period seemed to confirm these fears. During the first three months, the occupying powers failed miserably in providing law and order or in initiating a clear program of reconstruction.

While the threat of communal divisions is bound to remain real for many decades after the end of Saddam's rule, such speculation should not detract from the historic unifying role that the two rivers and the centrality of Baghdad had on the various peoples of Iraq. The fact that the country has held together despite the devastation of recent wars, sanctions, internal repression and foreign occupation, is testimony to the extent of national unity. Should the country be allowed a modicum of external peace and stability, the setbacks of the dictatorship might yet be overcome.

SELECT
BIBLIOGRAPHY

Abdullah, Thabit, *Merchants, Mamluks and Murder: The Political Economy of Trade in Eighteenth-Century Basra*, Albany, N.Y., 2001.

'Ali, 'Ali Shakir, *Ta'rikh al-'Iraq fi al-'Ahd al-'Uthmani, 1638–1750: Dirasa fi Ahwalihi al-Siyasiyya*, Naynawa, Iraq, 1984.

Arnove, Anthony (ed.), *Iraq Under Siege: The Deadly Impact of Sanctions and War*, London, 2000.

Ashtor, E., *A Social and Economic History of the Near East in the Middle Ages*, London, 1976.

Al-'Azawi, 'Abbas, *Ta'rikh al-'Iraq Bayn Ihtilalayn*, vols 3–4, Qumm, Iran, 1939.

Batatu, Hanna, *The Old Social Classes and Revolutionary Movements of Iraq: A Study of Iraq's Old Landed and Commercial Classes and of its Communists, Ba'thists, and Free Officers*, Princeton, 1978.

Cole, Juan and Momen, Moojan, "Mafia, Mob and Shiism in Iraq: The Rebellion of Ottoman Karbala 1824–1843", in *Past & Present*, no. 112, August 1986, pp. 112–43.

Dann, Uriel, *Iraq Under Qassem: A Political History, 1958–1963*, New York, 1969.

Deyoung, Terri, *Placing the Poet: Badr Shakir al-Sayyab and Postcolonial Iraq*, Albany, NY, 1988.

Farouk-Sluglett, Marion and Sluglett, Peter, *Iraq Since 1958: From Revolution to Dictatorship*, London, 1987.

Farouk-Sluglett, Marion and Sluglett, Peter, "The Transformation of Land Tenure and Rural Social Structure in Central and Southern Iraq c.1870–1958", in *International Journal of Middle East Studies*, 15 (1983), pp. 491–505.

Farouk-Sluglett, Marion and Sluglett, Peter, "Iraqi Ba'thism: Nationalism, Socialism and National Socialism", in CARDRI, *Saddam's Iraq, Revolution or Reaction?*, London, 1986, pp. 89–107.

Fattah, Hala, "Representations of Self and the Other in Two Iraqi Travelogues of the Ottoman Period", in *International Journal of Middle East Studies*, vol. 30, no. 1, Feb. 1998, pp. 51–76.

Garfield, Richard, "The Public Health Impact of Sanctions:

Contrasting Responses of Iraq and Cuba", in *Middle East Report*, no. 215, summer 2000, pp. 16–19.

Ghanima, Yusuf Rizq-Allah, *Nuzhat al-Mushtaq fi Ta'rikh Yahud al-'Iraq*, second edition, London, 1997.

Graham-Brown, Sarah, "Sanctioning Iraq: A Failed Policy", in *Middle East Report*, no. 215, summer 2000, pp. 8–35.

Graham-Brown, Sarah, *Economic Sanctions and the Future of Iraq*, London, 2000.

Guest, John, *The Euphrates Expedition*, London, 1992.

Hadarat al-'Iraq, vol. 10, Baghdad, 1985.

Haj, Samir, *The Making of Modern Iraq, 1900–1963*, Albany, NY, 1997.

Hashim, Ahmed, "Saddam Husayn and Civil-Military Relations in Iraq: The Quest for Legitimacy and Power," in *Middle East Journal*, vol. 57, no. 1, winter 2003, pp. 9–41.

Hitti, Philip K., *History of the Arabs*, New York, 1970.

Holt, P.M., *Egypt and the Fertile Crescent, 1516–1922: A Political History*, Ithaca, 1996.

Hourani, Albert, *A History of the Arab Peoples*, New York, 1991.

Human Rights Watch, *Genocide in Iraq, the Anfal Campaign Against the Kurds*, New York, 1993.

al-'Iraq fi al-Ta'rikh, Baghdad, 1983.

Ismael, Tareq, *Iran and Iraq: Roots of Conflict*, Syracuse, 1982.

Issawi, Charles (ed.), *The Fertile Crescent, 1800–1914: A Documentary History*, Oxford, 1988.

Jabbar, Faleh A., "Shaykhs and Ideologues: Detribalization and Retribalization in Iraq, 1968–1998", in *Middle East Report*, no. 215, summer 2000, pp. 28–48.

Jayyusi, Salma Khadra (ed.), *Modern Arabic Poetry: An Anthology*, New York, 1987.

Jwaideh, Albertine, "Midhat Pasha and the Land System of Lower Iraq", in *St. Anthony's Papers*, no. 16, London, 1963, pp. 106–36.

Jwaideh, Albertine, "Aspects of Land Tenure and Social Change in

Lower Iraq During Later Ottoman Times", in Tarif Khalidi (ed.), *Land Tenure and Social Transformation in the Middle East*, Beirut, 1984.

al-Khafaji, 'Isam, "The Parasitic Base of the Ba'thist Regime", in CARDRI, *Saddam's Iraq, Revolution or Reaction?*, London, 1986, pp. 73–88.

al-Khafaji, 'Isam, "State Terror and the Degradation of Politics", in Fran Hazelton, *Iraq Since the Gulf War: Prospects for Democracy*, London, 1994, pp. 20–31.

al-Khalil, Samir, *Republic of Fear: The Politics of Modern Iraq*, Berkeley, 1989.

Khoury, Dina, *State and Provincial Society in the Ottoman Empire: Mosul, 1540–1834*, Cambridge, 1997.

Lewis, Bernard, *Islam: From the Prophet Muhammad to the Capture of Constantinople*, vols 1 and 2, New York, 1974.

Longrigg, Stephen Hemsley, *Four Centuries of Modern Iraq*, Oxford, 1925.

Makiya, Kanan, *The Monument: Art, Vulgarity, and Responsibility in Iraq*, Berkeley, 1991.

Marr, Phebe, *The Modern History of Iraq*, Boulder, 1985.

McCarthy, Justin, *The Ottoman Peoples and the End of Empire*, London, 2001.

Mohsen, Fatima, "Cultural Totalitarianism", in Fran Hazelton, *Iraq Since the Gulf War: Prospects for Democracy*, London, 1994, pp. 7–19.

Momen, Moojan, *An Introduction to Shi'i Islam*, New Haven, 1985.

Nieuwenhuis, Tom, *Politics and Society in Early Modern Iraq: Mamluk Pashas, Tribal Shaykhs and Local Rule Between 1802 and 1831*, The Hague, 1981.

Owen, Roger, *The Middle East and the World Economy, 1800–1914*, London, 1981.

Owen, Roger and Pamuk, Sevket, *A History of Middle East Economies in the Twentieth Century*, Cambridge, MA, 1999.

Ra'uf, 'Imad 'Abdul-Salam, *'Adila Khatun: Safha min Ta'rikh al-'Iraq*, Baghdad, 1997.

Rejwan, Nissim, *The Jews of Iraq: 3000 Years of History and Culture*, Boulder, 1985.

Sanctions on Iraq: Background, Consequences, Strategies, Cambridge, 2000.

Savory, Roger, *Iran Under the Safavids*, Cambridge, 1980.

Sbahi, 'Aziz, *'Uqud min Ta'rikh al-Hizb al-Shuyu'i al-'Iraqi*, vol. 1, Damascus, Syria, 2002.

Shaw, Stanford, and Shaw, Ezel Kural, *History of the Ottoman Empire and Modern Turkey*, vols 1 and 2, Cambridge, 1977.

Spuler, Bertold, *History of the Mongols, Based on Eastern and Western Accounts of the Thirteenth and Fourteenth Centuries*, New York, 1972.

Stripling, George William Frederick, "The Ottoman Turks and the Arabs, 1511–1574", in *Illinois Studies in the Social Sciences*, vol. 26, no. 4, Urbana, 1942.

Al-Suwaydi, 'Abdul-Rahman bin 'Abdullah, *Ta'rikh Hawadith Baghdad wa al-Basra min 1186 ila 1192 AH/1772–1778 AD*, Baghdad, Iraq, 1978.

Tarbush, Mohammed, *The Role of the Military in Politics: A Case Study of Iraq to 1941*, London, 1982.

Tripp, Charles, *A History of Iraq*, Cambridge, 2002.

Yapp, M.E., *The Making of the Modern Near East, 1792–1923*, London, 1987.

Yapp, M.E., *The Near East Since the First World War: A History to 1995*, London, 1996.

In addition, the relevant articles in:

The *Encyclopedia of Islam, New Edition*, Leiden, The Netherlands.

Al-Hayat, Arabic language newspaper, published in London,

Al-Sharq al-Awsat, Arabic language newspaper, published in London.

The New York Times, published in New York.

The Washington Post, published in Washington, DC.

INDEX